Cultural Norms, War and the Environment

sipri

Stockholm International Peace Research Institute

SIPRI is an independent international institute for research into problems of peace and conflict, especially those of arms control and disarmament. It was established in 1966 to commemorate Sweden's 150 years of unbroken peace.

The Institute is financed mainly by the Swedish Parliament. The staff, the Governing Board and the Scientific Council are international.

The Governing Board and Scientific Council are not responsible for the views expressed in the publications of the Institute.

sipri

Stockholm International Peace Research Institute
Pipers väg 28, S-171 73 Solna, Sweden
Cable: PEACERESEARCH STOCKHOLM
Telefax: 46 8/55 97 33
Telephone: 46 8/55 97 00

Cultural Norms, War and the Environment

Edited by
Arthur H. Westing

sipri

Stockholm International Peace Research Institute

United Nations Environment Programme

OXFORD UNIVERSITY PRESS

1988

Oxford University Press, Walton Street, Oxford OX2 6DP
Oxford New York Toronto
Delhi Bombay Calcutta Madras Karachi
Petaling Jaya Singapore Hong Kong Tokyo
Nairobi Dar es Salaam Cape Town
Melbourne Auckland
and associated companies in
Berlin Ibadan

Oxford is a trade mark of Oxford University Press

Published in the United States
by Oxford University Press, New York

British Library Cataloguing in Publication Data
Cultural norms, war and the environment.
1. War—Sociological perspectives
I. Westing, Arthur H. II. Stockholm International Peace Research Institute
III. United Nations Environment Programme
303.6'6
ISBN 0–19–829125–6

Library of Congress Cataloging in Publication Data
Cultural norms, war and the environment / edited by Arthur H. Westing.
p. cm.
On t.p.: Sipri, Stockholm International Peace Research Institute; UNEP, United Nations Environment Programme.
Includes index.
1. War and society. 2. War—Environmental aspects. 3. Pacific settlement of international disputes. 4. Nuclear weapons—Environmental aspects. I. Westing, Arthur H. II. Stockholm International Peace Research Institute. III. United Nations Environment Programme.
HM36.5.C85 1988
303.6'6—dc19 88–10002
ISBN 0–19–829125–6

Set by Wyvern Typesetting, Bristol
Printed and bound in
Great Britain by Biddles Ltd.,
Guildford and King's Lynn

Cultural Norms, War and the Environment has been prepared by SIPRI as a project within the SIPRI/UNEP programme on 'Military activities and the human environment'. The present volume is an outgrowth of a select symposium convened by the Stockholm International Peace Research Institute (SIPRI) in co-operation with the United Nations Environment Programme (UNEP) in Stockholm, 15–18 March 1987.

This book represents the fifth and last in a series that has been produced under the SIPRI/UNEP programme. The prior four titles are:

1. *Herbicides in War: the Long-term Ecological and Human Consequences* (edited by A. H. Westing; Taylor & Francis, London, 210 pp., 1984);

2. *Environmental Warfare: a Technical, Legal and Policy Appraisal* (edited by A. H. Westing; Taylor & Francis, London, 107 pp., 1984), in co-operation with UNIDIR;

3. *Explosive Remnants of War: Mitigating the Environmental Effects* (edited by A. H. Westing; Taylor & Francis, London, 141 pp., 1985); and

4. *Global Resources and International Conflict: Environmental Factors in Strategic Policy and Action* (edited by A. H. Westing; Oxford University Press, Oxford, 280 pp., 1986).

Preface

This book is the fifth and final in a series on military activities and the human environment resulting from a research programme jointly financed by SIPRI and the United Nations Environment Programme (UNEP).

The study *Cultural Norms, War and the Environment* sets out to cover a wide range of complex, important and also controversial issues, such as population growth, education problems and non-violent conflict resolution. None of these problems lends itself to easy solutions. And in a world as culturally, politically and economically diverse as ours, there is reason to caution against blueprint-proposals for global solutions. In fact, it can be argued that to wait for global solutions will amount to nothing but failure to cope with the solvable questions on a national or regional level.

Any findings, opinions, conclusions or recommendations expressed in this book are those of the editor and authors and do not necessarily reflect the views of either SIPRI or UNEP. Contributors to this volume would, of course, accept no other responsibility than their own for the analysis provided and views expressed.

Dr Walther Stützle
Director
SIPRI

Dr Mostafa K. Tolba
Executive Director
UNEP

March 1988

Acknowledgements

The editor is pleased to acknowledge the very able research assistance of Carol Barta, editorial assistance of Jetta Gilligan Borg and secretarial assistance of Cynthia Loo.

December 1987

Contents

Conventions, glossary and units of measure

I. Conventions and glossary

Bible	Biblical references are to the 'revised standard version' (May & Metzger, 1977).
ICRC	International Committee of the Red Cross (Geneva); established in 1863.
IUCN	International Union for Conservation of Nature and Natural Resources (Gland, Switzerland); established in 1948.
Koran	Koranic references are to the translation by Dawood (1974).
PRIO	International Peace Research Institute, Oslo; established in 1959.
SIPRI	Stockholm International Peace Research Institute (Solna, Sweden); established in 1966.
Tao Te Ching	Taoist references are to the translation by Lau (1963).
UNEP	United Nations Environment Programme (Nairobi); established in 1972.
UNESCO	United Nations Educational, Scientific and Cultural Organization (Paris); established in 1945.
UNIDIR	United Nations Institute for Disarmament Research (Geneva); established in 1980.

II. Units of Measure

The units of measure and prefixes (and the abbreviations) employed in the text are in accordance with the international system (SI) of units (Goldman & Bell, 1981). Standard conversion factors are used (Weast & Astle, 1979–80, pp. F307–29).

gram (g) = 10^{-3} kilogram = 2.204 62 × 10^{-3} pound

kilo- (k-) = $10^{3}\times$

kilogram (kg) = 2.204 62 pounds

kilometre (km) = 10^{3} metres = 0.621 371 statute mile = 0.539 957 nautical mile

kilometre, square (km^2) = 10^{6} square metres = 100 hectares = 247.105 acres = 0.386 102 square statute mile

litre (L) = 10^{-3} m^3 = 0.264 172 US gallon = 0.219 969 British gallon

metre (m) = 3.280 84 feet

milli- (m-) = $10^{-3}\times$

millimetre (mm) = 10^{-3} metre = 0.039 370 1 inch

second (s) = unit of time (see Goldman & Bell, 1981, p. 3)

tonne (t) = 10^3 kilograms = 1.102 31 US (short) tons = 0.984 207 British (long) ton

References

Dawood, N. J. (ed.). 1974. *Koran* [translated from the Arabic by N. J. Dawood]. 4th edn. Harmondsworth, UK: Penguin Books, 447 pp.

Goldman, D. T. & Bell, R. J. (eds). 1981. *International system of units (SI)*. Washington: US National Bureau of Standards, Special Publication No. 330, 48 pp.

Lau, D. C. (ed.). 1963. *Lao Tzu: tao te ching* [translated from the Chinese by D. C. Lau]. Harmondsworth, UK: Penguin Books, 192 pp.

May, H. G. & Metzger, B. M. (eds). 1977. *New Oxford annotated bible with the apocrypha: revised standard version.* New York: Oxford University Press, 1564+340 pp. + 14 maps.

Weast, R. C. & Astle, M. J. (eds). 1979–80. *CRC handbook of chemistry and physics.* 60th edn. Boca Raton, Florida: CRC Press, [2447] pp.

Introduction

This project explores cultural norms regarding militarism and war on the one hand and nature and the environment on the other. This is being done in order to define existing societal constraints on military disruption of the biosphere and possibilities for strengthening such constraints.

The principle that 'the right of belligerents to adopt means of injuring the enemy is not unlimited' (from the Hague Conventions of 1899) has long been established in international law. A rather more recent elaboration of this principle has legally established that 'it is prohibited to employ methods or means of warfare which are intended, or may be expected, to cause widespread, long-term and severe damage to the natural environment' (from the 1977 additions to the Geneva Conventions of 1949). Thus, the present project in essence examines what is actually meant by these concepts, what the cultural foundations are which underlie them, what cultural norms might be in conflict with constraints on the use of military force and a respect for nature, how malleable all such underlying norms are, and the extent of any links between a respect for nature and a disdain for militarism.

In short, the objective of the project is to examine the role of cultural norms, past and present, in inhibiting the preparation for and conduct of war as these relate to the environment; and to suggest how such norms could be strengthened and developed.

This multi-authored volume begins with a conceptual overview of the constraints on military disruption of the biosphere (chapter 1). That survey is followed by in-depth analyses of the historical evolution of cultural norms relating to war and the environment, both global (chapter 2) and with special emphasis on the USSR (chapter 3). Examined next is the influence of gender (chapter 4) on the cultural norms in question. Then singled out are cultural norms relating to nuclearism (i.e., in relation to the nuclear arms race, nuclear proliferation and nuclear war) as the special challenge of our time (chapter 5).

The volume continues with analyses of a series of societal institutions or forces both as portrayers (reflectors) and as shapers (moulders) of cultural norms relating to war and the environment: the law, both international and domestic (chapter 6); formal education especially at the primary and secondary levels (chapter 7); the mass media (chapter 8); and the arts, especially fiction and poetry (chapter 9). The book concludes with a synthesis and policy recommendations that aim towards non-violent conflict resolution within the context of environmental protection (chapter 10).

The text of the volume is complemented by a selection of apropos background references (appendix 1) as well as excerpts from relevant multilateral treaties (appendix 2), international declarations or charters (appendix 3) and professional codes of conduct (appendix 4).

The present volume is an outgrowth of a select symposium convened by SIPRI in co-operation with UNEP in Stockholm, 15–18 March 1987. The authors of this book are:

Dr *Geoffrey Best* (Department of International Relations; London School of Economics & Political Science; London, WC2A 2AE; United Kingdom), an authority on military and legal history;

Prof. *Birgit Brock-Utne* (Institute for Educational Research; University of Oslo; N–0317 Oslo; Norway; temporarily at the University of Dar es Salaam, Tanzania), an authority on peace education;

Prof. *Richard A. Falk* (Department of Politics; Princeton University; Princeton, NJ 08544; USA), an authority on international law and world order;

Prof. *Virginia Held* (Department of Philosophy; City University of New York; New York, NY 10036; USA), an authority on ethics and political philosophy;

Prof. *Grigori S. Khozin* (Scientific Council for Philosophical & Social Problems of Science & Technology; Moscow, 119 842; USSR), an authority on the politics of the environment;

Dr *Rosalind J. Marsh* (Department of Russian; University of Exeter; Exeter, EX4 4QJ; United Kingdom), an authority on Soviet culture;

Prof. *David M. Rubin* (Center for War, Peace, & the News Media; New York University; New York, NY 10003; USA), an authority on journalism;

Prof. *Christopher D. Stone* (Law Center; University of Southern California; Los Angeles, CA 90089; USA), an authority on environmental law; and

Prof. *Arthur H. Westing* (International Peace Research Institute, Oslo; N–0260 Oslo 2; Norway; previously at SIPRI, during the course of this project), an authority on environmental impact of military activities.

The authors are pleased to acknowledge valuable advice from Mr Frank T. Blackaby (London), Mr Haroldo M. de Lemos (UNEP), Dr Kenton R. Miller (IUCN) and Prof. Alfred E. Opubor (University of Lagos) at a planning workshop (Stockholm, 30 April–2 May 1986); and thoughtful suggestions from Prof. Christian Bay (University of Toronto), Mr Johan Galtung (Oslo), Mr Naigzy Gebremedhin (UNEP), Mr Jozef Goldblat (SIPRI) and Mr Frank von Hippel (Dartmouth College) during the symposium.

1. Constraints on military disruption of the biosphere: an overview

ARTHUR H. WESTING
Stockholm International Peace Research Institute

I. Introduction

1945 ushered in the most momentous period in all human history for two basic reasons. The first of these—the dawn of the atomic age—was impressed upon the world by a brief series of cataclysmic events: the explosions at Alamogordo, Hiroshima and Nagasaki. The second of these was an occurrence of more subtle and diffuse, though equally grave, nature: an increase in human numbers that for the first time went beyond the global carrying capacity.

Both the nuclear problem and the environmental problem have become progressively worse over the four decades since 1945 despite a slowly growing public awareness of their vital importance. As a result, today the two most immediate threats to humankind are military devastation on the one hand and environmental exhaustion on the other, both on a world-wide scale. Moreover, each of these two threats is reinforced by the other.

The growing dimensions and interlocking nature of these awesome environmental and military dilemmas are suggested below; touched upon next are the social forces that have permitted this human flirtation with self-destruction. Not only is the urgent necessity for reversals of the nuclear arms race and of the over-exploitation of nature pointed out, but evidence is also presented that the evolution of cultural norms that will be required to bring about these reversals is at least feasible. Noted next is the connection between the public and its governments and the role of international organizations. Looked at then are the functions of a number of societal institutions in bringing about the changes in human attitude and behaviour that will be necessary in order to avoid environmental and thus human disaster, whether by military or civil means. Examined especially are the roles in influencing public opinion of mass media and formal education, of international law, of religion and of individuals and citizen groups. Actions necessary for achieving non-violent conflict resolution within the context of a sustained balance between humans and nature are considered elsewhere (chapter 10). Sources of general background information for this chapter are also provided elsewhere (see appendix 1).

II. The environmental threat

The human species, *Homo sapiens,* has inhabited the earth for perhaps 300 thousand years. Total human numbers at any one time remained below 1000 million until about 1850, and have been increasing dramatically ever since then (Westing, 1981a). Indeed, between 1850 and 1945, the end of World War II, the global human population more than doubled, reaching the then unprecedented total of about 2300 million.

Even though some 50 million people were killed during the six years of World War II—the largest number of fatalities of any war in human history—population growth had become so rapid by the mid-twentieth century that the world was, in fact, confronted by 150 million more individuals in 1945 than had existed in 1939 (Westing, 1982). Given even the technology of today, the world can benignly support no more than perhaps 2500 million people at a standard of living to which the peoples of the world rightly aspire, in other words, at a standard comparable to that of the two dozen or so developed nations (Westing, 1981d; 1988).

Between the end of World War II and today the human population has fully doubled once again, to about 5000 million. And despite all of the scientific and technological advances of these past four decades, more people by far than ever before in the history of the human species are today undernourished; more by far than ever before are inadequately housed; and more by far than ever before are without access to clean water. The three major renewable natural resources—forests, grasslands and fisheries—are, on a world-wide basis, now being utilized faster than their rate of natural replenishment (Brown *et al.*, 1987; Holdgate *et al.*, 1982; Mathews *et al.*, 1986). This disastrous process of over-exploitation continues relentlessly (Brown & Jacobson, 1986). Nevertheless, the human species permits its global population to continue to increase by 230 thousand people per day, that is to say, to add in numbers the equivalent of one Sweden every 37 days.

In considering the magnitude of the over-population of the human species, one must not lose sight of the relentless inroads, both quantitatively and qualitatively, that this one species makes on the other species with which it shares the earth. In 1850, humans plus their livestock accounted for about 5 per cent of all terrestrial (non-marine) animal life on earth, when measured in terms of biomass, in a terrestrial habitat that was fully occupied (Westing, 1981c; 1981d). By 1945, humans plus their livestock had grown sufficiently in numbers to take over about 10 per cent of the world's terrestrial habitat. This process of replacement has continued, and thus today humans plus their livestock have substituted for more than 20 per cent of all terrestrial wildlife. Within another extraordinarily brief period of four decades or so the human numbers will have inexorably doubled once again, and (given past trends) the same will have occurred with the livestock numbers. Thus, in less than four decades from now, humans plus their entourage of domestic animals will have replaced fully 40 per cent of all terrestrial wildlife on earth—with the inevitably concomitant and tragic extinction of numerous species of wild plants and animals.

To recapitulate, the human species is dependent for its well-being and very survival on a continuing exploitation of the natural resources of the earth. First, its food and various other necessities of life must be harvested on a renewable basis; and second, its multifarious waste products must be disposed of—that is, discharged into the environment—in a safe fashion. Humans are unfailingly dependent upon freshwater, soil and mineral resources, all of them limited (scarce) resources which are distributed most unevenly throughout the world. During past times, human demands have often outstripped the *local* availability of such crucial natural resources. And for the past several decades—and despite great advances in technology—human demands have finally outstripped even the *global* availability of some of them. In yet another self-defeating action, human use of the atmosphere for the disposal of ever increasing amounts of municipal and industrial waste products (air pollutants) is now also occurring at a rate faster than decomposition and dissipation can accommodate such discharges.

III. The military threat

There are several obvious connections between war and the environment. Given the highly uneven distribution among nations of various natural resources of vital importance, and the increasing world-wide shortfalls of some of them, it should come as no surprise that wars of plunder or aggrandizement have frequently been, and continue to be, fought (Westing, 1986). As a second connection between war and the environment, it is clear that natural resources are consumed in large quantities in the preparation and pursuit of wars. (It must also be noted here at least in passing that intellectual resources are in huge measure devoted to preparation for war, and it is readily arguable that if these were devoted at least in part to coping with environmental and other human necessities, the felt need for many wars would be diminished [Westing, 1984].) It is not only clear that warfare is destructive of resources, but it is additionally demonstrable that such environmental disruption is in this century becoming an ever more prominent aspect of warfare (Westing, 1980, chap. 1; 1981b). Moreover, not only does nuclear-weapon testing exert an adverse effect on the human environment, but nuclear war might be so environmentally disruptive as to actually threaten human civilization as a whole (Pittock *et al.*, 1985–86), the import of which is dealt with below.

The link between humanity (i.e., humanness or the quality of being human) and war is an intimate one. For many millennia now, and perhaps from very earliest times, humans have functioned in discrete groups. These groups are formed and held together by ties of kinship, language, religion, forceful leadership and various accidents of geography and history. These functional groups into which the human species is divided have waged wars against each other for at least the past 9000 years, that is, at least since the Neolithic Age

(Ferrill, 1985, p. 20; Roper, 1975). More than a dozen wars are in progress at this very moment, a state of human affairs certainly comparable to any moment in time during this century (Westing, 1982) and probably comparable to any moment in time since at least the Bronze Age.

The many tens of thousands of wars have been initiated by one human group or another with a complete awareness of the inevitably associated killings and other deaths, maimings, property destruction, population displacements and miscellaneous suffering, and of the frequently associated rural devastation. Whereas the desirability of avoiding or alleviating such calamities *within* a group has long been accepted (and fairly generally adhered to), human practice to date has demonstrated no true commitment by a group to extending such acceptance to the species as a whole, and only rarely with any consistency to one or more other groups.

IV. The acceptability of war

Much has been written about the ultimate causes of war and of the extent to which human aggressiveness and its translation into societal bellicosity (the propensity to wage war) are learned characteristics as opposed to innate ones. To the extent that bellicosity is a learned attitude *cum* behaviour, or one imposed upon society by how humans live, there remains the possibility that this trait can be counteracted through education, perhaps in conjunction with a change in life-style or social system.

The suggestion has been put forth that bellicosity is largely a product of civilization. Thus, it appears that the more primitive a society is, the less the likelihood for it to be bellicose (Broch & Galtung, 1966; Eckhardt, 1975). Moreover, it seems that the rise of the state might not have occurred without a combination of natural-resource limitations and the acceptance of war as an appropriate means for achieving societal aims (Carneiro, 1970; Cohen, 1984). A trend of increasing bellicosity has been discerned through time; and a similar, presumably related, trend of increasing bellicosity has been discerned with reference to societal structure, from nomadic hunter-gatherer societies to sedentary agricultural societies and further to urbanized societies (Eckhardt, 1982).

It is clear that over the past nine millennia or more war has been widely recognized as a successful societal strategy in the acquisition of needed or desired natural resources as well as of status and power. This has led to the suggestion that martial attributes and bellicosity might well have been selected for in the human species, and thus reinforced during this time.

Even if individuals within a group are not themselves aggressive or bellicose by nature or nurture, their leaders might well be. Indeed, these very traits might help propel people into positions of leadership. Such leaders can then depend upon thoroughly widespread tendencies towards group loyalty (often to the point of chauvinism) and towards other-group distrust (often to the point of xenophobia) to overcome any individual feelings within the group that are antithetical to war. They can especially depend upon the strong human urge to group conformity (Eckhardt, 1982).

Most of the numerous civilizations and societies about which we know—past and present, primitive and advanced—have, on the one hand, been consistently bellicose in action and, on the other, primarily patriarchal or patricentric in structure. This congruence has led to the suggestion that masculine traits are the cause of war (Brock-Utne, 1985; Divale & Harris, 1976; Easlea, 1983; Eisler & Loye, 1983; 1986; García, 1981; Reardon, 1985). The masculine traits or ethos referred to include especially aggressiveness, competitiveness, toughness and chivalry. And, indeed, the few apparently matriarchal or matricentric societies that have been described are said to have displayed a tendency to shy away from bellicosity (Fromm, 1973, pp. 167–68). Thus, it may well be that gender structure is the single most relevant feature of society to be revised in order to achieve a less bellicose way of life, a subject persuasively argued by Held (see chapter 4). She suggests that men's aggressive and non-caring tendencies would be mitigated if mothering activities were more equally shared between the sexes. She further suggests that international relations would become more nearly pacifistic if women were to become more centrally involved in the affairs of state, this improvement owing to their more holistic approach to problem-solving and their more non-violent approach to conflict resolution.

A certain amount of rhetoric to the contrary, it is overwhelmingly clear from human actions that war has long been, and continues to be, an accepted and routine human endeavour for the resolution of inter-group conflicts. The concepts and mechanisms for non-violent conflict resolution have been eloquently presented, described in scholarly detail and are widely known; nonetheless, they are just as widely ignored or even denigrated.

As noted earlier, warfare has caused much grief and suffering over past centuries; and also much environmental disruption, especially in recent decades. However, the human species *per se* was never until this century in danger of extermination. That former condition of safety—which had lasted and been taken for granted for so many millennia—began to disintegrate four decades ago and has perhaps by now disappeared. Albert Einstein captured the human predicament with uncanny precision within less than a year of Alamogordo when he stated that 'The unleashed power of the atom has changed everything save our modes of thinking and we thus drift toward unparalleled catastrophe' (Times, 1946).

In summary, some combination of inborn and externally imposed factors, the latter including the structure of society and the huge mismatch between human population numbers and availability of natural resources, will unfortunately continue to provide the support and impetus for the acceptability of war. Nevertheless, it has now become imperative that the human instinct for self-preservation be aroused into action against the ever growing threat to human civilization of nuclear annihilation, whether directly or via environmental disruption. The difficulties in achieving such arousal are cogently presented by Falk (see chapter 5). He suggests that to overcome the existing state of nuclearism will require a strengthening of the currently incomplete legal condemnations of nuclear war and nuclear weapons. But—as Falk goes on to explain—it becomes crucial that such strengthened legal norms rest on a foundation of appropriate cultural norms. Some signs do exist that these latter norms are emerging, but such tendencies must be diligently nurtured because, in fact, they can be seen to go counter to the prevailing pro-nuclear norms.

V. The acceptability of environmental degradation

It has long been widely accepted—and essentially without question—that humans have supreme authority over the earth and all of its other living things, both plant and animal. This concept of dominion is deeply ingrained in Western civilization (Callicott, 1982; Passmore, 1980; Toynbee, 1972; White, 1967), and is, at least now, also widely accepted by all of the other major civilizations (Passmore, 1980, chap. 1; Zaidi, 1981). Thus, the earth and the fauna and flora it supports are simply treated by society as human property. The state owns and jealously guards all of the natural resources within its limits of jurisdiction, at present collectively amounting to somewhat less than half of the global surface. The state in turn establishes the extent of individual (and corporate) property rights regarding the natural resources under its control.

As property, the natural resources, both non-living and living, are extracted, harvested or otherwise used as the owner (whether governmental or, secondarily, individual) sees fit. Few cultural norms have restricted such use other than those that serve to prevent immediate overt harm or danger to fellow citizens. Thus, the use by an owner of his or her natural resources to their exhaustion or other detriment has, by and large, been a socially acceptable and legally permissible activity.

When needed natural resources were or became unavailable to individuals or states, these entities have traditionally coped with this dilemma—and still do—in one or more of the following ways: (*a*) by obtaining them from areas beyond any national jurisdiction; (*b*) by purchasing them from other individuals or states; (*c*) by plundering them from another state; or (*d*) by forcibly annexing another state or portion thereof.

Any incentive which might exist for preventing or minimizing the degradation of privately or nationally owned natural resources has been based far less (if at all) on ethical principles or other cultural norms related to the rights of non-human living things than on short-term human self-interest (often to the point of greed). Moreover, when it comes to commonly owned (shared) resources—and especially when it comes to those resources beyond any national jurisdiction—strong and in practice largely unchallenged cultural pressures actually exist for their exhaustion (Hardin, 1968). Again, it has now become imperative that the human instinct for self-preservation be aroused into action against the ever-growing threat to the human species of environmental exhaustion. It is here that Western civilization can perhaps benefit from the more egalitarian perspective attributed to women (Merchant, 1980; Zimmerman, 1987); from the more nearly usufructuary traditional native North American attitudes towards nature (Callicott, 1982; Cronon, 1983, chap. 4; Rogers, 1975); and, with special reference to warfare, perhaps even from those of the early Israelites (see appendix 4.I).

VI. The mechanism for change

To recapitulate, a point in human history has finally been reached at which the well-being, and perhaps even survival, of the human species itself is threatened by both civil means—that is, rampant over-population—and military means—that is, nuclear holocaust. The question before humankind, then, is whether nine millennia or more of complacency towards, if not active acceptance of, warfare and environmental abuse can be overcome in time. Are human inner drives or culturally imposed norms sufficiently flexible to be changed into ones that will permit, not to say ensure, patterns of social behaviour of sufficient benignity and common sense to prevent disaster?

First, one must accept the conclusion of various scholars that the bellicosity of the human species is largely a product of social rather than genetic circumstances (Dunbar, 1985; Eckhardt, 1982; Kemp, 1987); and, moreover, that human abuse of the environment is largely a product of misguided anthropocentrism and ignorance (Catton, 1980; Ehrenfeld, 1978; Ehrlich & Ehrlich, 1981; Leopold, 1949; Marsh, 1864).

Second, the cultural norms that underlie the prevailing martial and anti-environmental behaviours of the human species, although modest in their breadth, do have a long cross-cultural history, a theme thoroughly developed by Best (see chapter 2). He points out, moreover, that the codes of martial behaviour that would prevent damage to the human environment appear to rest largely upon a variety of self-serving foundations rather than upon altruistic, religious or ecological ones. Nonetheless, Best concludes that the traditional norms provide an adequate basis from which could emerge the codes of restraint necessitated by the exigencies of today. Indeed, it is clear that such norms are not immutable, but, in fact, display societal differences (Galtung, 1981; Levine, 1975; Toynbee, 1972); and, moreover, have evolved considerably over the years (Boulding, 1983; Glacken, 1967; Stone, 1972; Thomas, 1983). The USSR provides an example of a society that has undergone major social transformations during this century, among them a growing respect for nature, the details of which are developed by Khozin (see chapter 3). He emphasizes the Soviet awareness of the needs for a reversal of the arms race and for international co-operation in environmental protection in order to establish a sound basis for the betterment of the human lot.

Third, public opinion—and thereby presumably, in time, cultural norms—is subject to change through the vehicle of such societal institutions or forces as the mass media, schools, the arts, citizen groups, both professional and lay, and even individuals. Moreover, changes in public opinion in both East and West translate into changes in government policy, the latter a *sine qua non* for human survival. The revised cultural norms will then provide a stable basis for the formalities of international law necessary for non-violent and environmentally sound intra-national and international relations (Ferencz, 1985; Schachter, 1977).

Governments and international organizations

It is a now widely accepted principle that national governments should act not only in the best interests of their citizenry, but actually on behalf of their citizenry; and, therefore, that concomitant legal mechanisms should exist for transmuting public will into governmental policy and action. And, indeed, the major powers of today do function in more or less close conformity with that ideal.

On the other hand, a variety of social forces in both East and West prevents a full realization of the concept of a government acting in conformity with the will of its citizenry. Thus, there always exists at least some level of adversarial relationship between a people and its leadership. Moreover, even though a government may function in conformity with the public will, one cannot overlook the fact that it has a certain ability to mould that will through the control it exerts (in both East and West) over the domestic mass media, schools, and other societal institutions and forces. And, of course, it must be stressed that many governmental decisions are simply stupid (Janis, 1982; Tuchman, 1984).

There is no denying that the best interests of a government—that is, of its leaders and bureaucrats—may differ in various respects from those of its citizenry. However, countering the advantages a government has in the relationship with its citizenry are such more or less subtle factors as the innate intelligence, reasoning ability, spunk and mettle of the human species; and the information that reaches a people of one country through its various interactions with the peoples of other countries. But the most encouraging factor by far in this apparent dilemma is that when it comes to the abolition of nuclear war there should be no doubt for anyone at any level that the interests of government and people coincide fully and with equal urgency. Although such interests coincide just as fully when it comes to global over-population, at least in the long run, this might well not be so obvious from the standpoint of the relatively privileged leadership of a country, making an amelioration of this problem a more formidable educational challenge.

In considering the role of international organizations in the shaping of cultural norms, a distinction must be drawn between intergovernmental agencies (e.g., the United Nations Environment Programme; Food and Agriculture Organization of the United Nations) and non-governmental organizations (e.g., the International Committee of the Red Cross; Greenpeace). Intergovernmental agencies, of which there exist a few hundred, are for all practical purposes limited in their actions to the desires of their sovereign member states and by the bureaucratic lethargy of their secretariats (Bennett, 1984; Goldblat, 1986). These agencies can rise above their co-ordinating and meeting-ground functions only to the extent that a skilful and dedicated secretariat tactfully nurtures aspirations that have been enunciated by the world community. Non-governmental organizations, of which there exist a few thousand, are to a greater or lesser extent independent of the influence of governments. These organizations often attempt, more or less subtly and more or less successfully, to assume the role of a societal conscience.

Mass media and formal education

Public opinion against nuclear war must be reinforced through the mass media (newspapers, magazines, radio, television) (MacBride, 1980; Manoff, 1984) as well as through the schools (elementary, secondary and higher) (Brock-Utne, 1980; Eckhardt, 1987; Markusen & Harris, 1984), so that the citizens and leaders of both today and tomorrow fully recognize the vital importance to the human species of categorically rejecting the use of nuclear weapons and thus even their possession. A recognition of the absolute inadmissibility of nuclear war—and thus also of the absolute inadmissibility of the nuclear weapons themselves—must be reinforced in as many ways as possible so that such attitudes simply become part and parcel of the human ethos.

The press and other news media would seem to be in a good position to keep the public informed on such vital issues as national security and environmental protection; and, thereby, to play a role in shaping public opinion in these matters, often presumably in a more or less adversarial relationship with the government. However, it is difficult for the news media of a nation to challenge their government, whether libertarian or authoritarian, as is made amply clear by Rubin (see chapter 8). He demonstrates that the mass media are, for various reasons, remarkably pro-government in the USA, the USSR, and elsewhere in the world. He concludes that it might well require some catastrophe to shake them out of their conformity.

It seems clear that formal education often fosters competitive, hierarchical, non-questioning and anthropocentric attitudes, a matter that Brock-Utne develops at some length (see chapter 7). She recommends curricular restructuring in ways that will counter such learning, thereby laying the foundation for an egalitarian, non-militaristic and pro-environmental society.

The establishment of a pervasive cultural norm against nuclear weapons and war should not be as difficult as it may at first appear because the immensely anti-social and anti-ecological nature of nuclear weapons is already widely perceived among both the peoples and governments of the world. Public opinion polls in both nuclear-weapon and non-nuclear-weapon countries have consistently revealed a widespread, and by some measures growing, antipathy towards their use (Capitanchik & Eichenberg, 1983; Kramer *et al.*, 1983; Oudsten, 1985; Yankelovich & Doble, 1984–85). In the intergovernmental arena, 133 or more non-nuclear-weapon governments (81 per cent of them), including a considerable number that could readily produce nuclear weapons, have to date formally renounced such weapons through joining the 1968 Nuclear-weapon Non-proliferation Treaty (see appendix 2.VII) and in other ways. And 113 nations have declared as a guiding principle that the human environment must be spared the effects of nuclear weapons (see appendix 3.I). At the non-governmental level, all Soviet physicians now swear to work for the prevention of nuclear war (see appendix 4.II) and some 7000 US scientists and engineers (and a considerable number of Japanese and British ones as well) have to date pledged to not work on weapon programmes they judge likely to trigger a nuclear war (see appendix 4.IV).

The mass media (Friedman, 1983; Schoenfeld, 1980; Sellers & Jones, 1973) and schools (Emmelin, 1977) have an equally important, although considerably more difficult, task in bringing home the crucial importance of protecting the human environment from degradation. But here again the situation is less than hopeless because public concern is both widespread and in places growing (Dunlap, 1987; Harcourt *et al.*, 1986; Leonard & Morell, 1981; Mitchell, 1980; 1984).

International law

Various multilateral treaties are in force today that serve to constrain military disruption of the human environment. An indication of the strength and pervasiveness of the underlying environmental norms can be gleaned from: (*a*) the number of such treaties the central focus of which is environmental (rather than human) protection; (*b*) the severity of their strictures; and (*c*) the levels to which they are supported.

To a certain extent such treaties also have the effect of reinforcing these norms, a subject explored by Stone (see chapter 6). He stresses the potential value of such feedback not only in strengthening and clarifying the norms in question for the parties involved, but also as an aid to attracting new parties into the fold. Stone goes on to explain the several normative foundations upon which environmental protection treaties and other such legislation can rest.

Thus, at least 95 nations of the world, or 56 per cent of them, have to date agreed not to take any deliberate measures which might harm certain natural areas of outstanding universal value (see appendix 2.X). And 67 or more nations, or 39 per cent, have to date agreed not to employ means of warfare that would cause widespread, long-term and severe damage to the natural environment (see appendix 2.XII). A number of other treaties serve to constrain military disruption of the environment through restrictions on certain weapons, targets or theatres or in other ways (see appendix 2), but their central focus is human rather than natural.

Finally, some importance must be attached to such intergovernmental pronouncements as the 1972 Declaration on the Human Environment (see appendix 3.I) or the 1982 World Charter for Nature (see appendix 3.II).

Religion

The question arises of the extent to which the religious norms of a people influence their cultural norms relating to war and the environment. It is concluded here that the answer in either domain may well be hardly at all. Indeed, it appears that the influence flows largely in the opposite direction.

As to martial norms, by way of example, the Shinto religion of Japan and the Islamic religion of the Muslims are clearly militaristic in their origins and essence and, indeed, the associated societies have a history replete with warfare (Ferguson, 1977). On the other hand, the Christian religion of Western civilization and the Buddhist religion of central and east Asian civilizations are strongly pacifist in their origins and essence. Indeed, one of the central tenets of Christianity is that 'Blessed are the peacemakers, for they shall be called sons of God' (Matthew 5:9). And the very first of the five precepts of Buddhism teaches that 'I undertake to observe the rule to abstain from taking life' (Conze, 1959, p. 70). Nonetheless, the associated societies have records of military activity unsurpassed in magnitude and ferocity.

As to environmental norms, it has been suggested that the callous and increasingly detrimental approach to nature which has been a hallmark of Western civilization through the centuries finds its roots in Christianity (White, 1967). Presumably taken as an unquestioned article of faith in this regard is that humans shall 'be fruitful and multiply, and fill the earth and subdue it; and have dominion over the fish of the sea and over the birds of the air and over every living thing that moves upon the earth' (Genesis 1:28).[1] On the other hand, it has been suggested as well that the roots of the despotic approach to nature in Western civilization can be traced with equal cogency to its Greek heritage (Passmore, 1980).

The Islamic religion also teaches that humans have dominion over the environment (Zaidi, 1981). According to the Muslim 'Recital' (*Koran* 14:32): 'It was Allah who made the heavens and the earth. He sends down water from the sky with which He brings forth fruits for your sustenance. He drives the ships which by His leave sail the ocean in your service. He has created rivers for your benefit, and the sun and the moon, which steadfastly pursue their courses. And He has subdued to you the night and the day. . . .'

In the Far East, the traditional Chinese Taoist philosophy is one of harmony with nature (*Tao Te Ching* 1:34):

> The way [Tao] is broad, reaching left as well as right.
> The myriad creatures depend on it for life yet it claims no authority.
> It accomplishes its task yet lays claim to no merit.
> It clothes and feeds the myriad creatures yet lays no claim to being their master. . . .

[1] It is interesting to note that the governing body of Massachusetts in the seventeenth century specifically cited this biblical passage (Genesis 1:28), supported by two comparable passages elsewhere (Genesis 9:1 and Psalms 115:16), as the legal basis for land ownership in the colony (Cronon, 1983, p. 63).

However, this harmonious philosophy has not prevented environmental abuse in China on a grand scale (Tuan, 1968). Moreover, Japanese civilization has permitted a despoliation of nature in the East surpassing that in the West despite its intimate relationship with Shintoism, a religion clearly noted for its nature worship (Huddle & Reich, 1975; Kelley *et al.*, 1976).

Thus it seems clear that both the interpretations of religious dogma and the actual religious practices which are associated with the major societies on earth essentially reflect the cultural norms of those societies rather than shaping them. On the other hand, the nuclear threat has begun to elicit a revived interest in the pacifist tenets inherent in some of the major religions, for example, in certain groups or denominations of Roman Catholics (Kim, 1985; National Conference, 1983; Russett, 1984), Buddhists (Ikeda, 1985) and Protestants (White *et al.*, 1986).

Individuals and citizen groups

The potential importance of the mass media and schools in shaping and reinforcing anti-nuclear and pro-environmental norms has been emphasized above. Perhaps equally important in these matters are such other shapers of public opinion—and presumably thereby of cultural norms—as the arts (essays, fiction, poetry, theatre, painting, etc.), and religious, professional, scientific and other citizen groups.

Although 'popular culture' has generally upheld the militaristic sentiments prevalent in society as a whole, 'high culture' has, especially during this century, had a strongly anti-militaristic and pro-environmental bias, a matter thoroughly examined by Marsh (see chapter 9). She demonstrates that the arts—particularly literature, poetry and painting—have a distinct contribution to make in relation to war and the environment. This is so because they engage not only the intellect, but the imagination and emotions as well. Indeed, poets and other writers act to a substantial extent as the conscience of their nations, a phenomenon (as Marsh shows) especially widely accepted in the USSR.

Professional norms, as reflected by professional codes of conduct such as the 1983 Soviet physicians' oath (see appendix 4.II) or the 1984 scientists' code (see appendix 4.III), are also of greater or lesser importance in contributing to societal attitudes.

Perhaps the extent of the power of individuals and citizen groups can best be appreciated simply by recalling the more or less influential nature of such items, events, and actions in recent history as: (*a*) Pablo Picasso's 1937 *Guernica* (Bruckner *et al.*, 1984, pp. 88–89; Keegan & Darracott, 1981, pp. 200–201; Silva *et al.*, 1963, pp. 63–64); (*b*) Rachel Carson's 1962 *Silent Spring* (Carson, 1962; Lutts, 1985); (*c*) Stanley Kubrick's 1964 *Dr. Strangelove* (Kubrick, 1964; Suid, 1985–86); (*d*) the US Catholic bishops' pastoral letter in 1983 on war and peace (Kim, 1985; National Conference, 1983; Russett, 1984); (*e*) the work since 1981 of the International Physicians for the Prevention of Nuclear War (Humphrey, 1985; UNESCO, 1985); (*f*) the work of peace groups, especially in the West (Kaltefleiter & Pfaltzgraff, 1985; Salomon, 1986; Wittner, 1984); (*g*) the development of the feminist movement (McAllister, 1982; Zimmerman, 1987); and (*h*) the progress of various unofficial exchanges across ideological barriers (Cracraft, 1986).

VII. Conclusion

In closing, it is hoped and expected that the people—and, through the people, the handful of nuclear-armed governments—will renounce the use of nuclear weapons for any purpose whatsoever, including deterrence or retaliation—and thereby obviate even a perceived need for their possession. This *must* be done owing to the profoundly disruptive nature of nuclear war; it *can* be done owing to the ever-growing awareness at all levels that nuclear war threatens the very existence of human civilization. Moreover, the potential for disaster is so grave that even unilateral renunciations are called for. There is the further hope and expectation that, given such an immensely civilizing act as nuclear disarmament, humans will then be able to come to grips with the similarly serious predicament of having exceeded the global carrying capacity for their species. And with these two giant steps behind them, the people might then in due course even be able to learn to resolve all of their international conflicts through non-violent and equitable means (see chapter 10).

References

Bennett, A. L. 1984. *International organizations: principles and issues.* 3rd edn. Englewood Cliffs, New Jersey: Prentice-Hall, 498 pp.

Boulding, K. 1983. Conditions and prospects of global demilitarization: reflections on values, science, war and peace: what signs of hope? *Bulletin of Peace Proposals*, Oslo, 14:351–354.

Broch, T. & Galtung, J. 1966. Belligerence among the primitives: a re-analysis of Quincy Wright's data. *Journal of Peace Research*, Oslo, 3:33–45.

Brock-Utne, B. 1980. Disarmament education in Norway: an action-oriented case study. *Bulletin of Peace Proposals*, Oslo, 11:288–295.

Brock-Utne, B. 1985. *Educating for peace: a feminist perspective.* New York: Pergamon Press, 175 pp.

Brown, L. R. & Jacobson, J. L. 1986. *Our demographically divided world.* Washington: Worldwatch Institute Paper No. 74, 54 pp.

Brown, L. R. *et al.* 1987. *State of the world 1987: a Worldwatch Institute report on progress toward a sustainable society*. New York: W. W. Norton, 268 pp.

Bruckner, D. J. R., Chwast, S. & Heller, S. 1984. *Art against war: 400 years of protest in art.* New York: Abbeville Press, 128 pp.

Callicott, J. B. 1982. Traditional American Indian and Western European attitudes toward nature: an overview. *Environmental Ethics*, Athens, Georgia, 4:293–318.

Capitanchik, D. & Eichenberg, R. C. 1983. *Defence and public opinion*. London: Royal Institute of International Affairs, Chatham House Paper No. 20, 98 pp.

Carneiro, R. L. 1970. Theory of the origin of the state. *Science,* Washington, 169:733–738.

Carson, R. 1962. *Silent spring*. Boston: Houghton Mifflin, 304 pp.

Catton, W. R., Jr. 1980. *Overshoot: the ecological basis of revolutionary change.* Urbana: University of Illinois Press, 298 pp.

Cohen, R. 1984. Warfare and state formation: wars make states and states make wars. In: Ferguson, R. B. (ed.). *Warfare, culture, and environment.* Orlando, Florida: Academic Press, 417 pp.: pp. 329–358.

Conze, E. (ed.). 1959. *Buddhist scriptures* [translated from the Sanskrit & Pali by E. Conze]. Harmondsworth, UK: Penguin, 250 pp.

Cracraft, J. 1986. Unofficial thaw in the cold war. *Bulletin of the Atomic Scientists,* Chicago, 42(5):20–22.

Cronon, W. 1983. *Changes in the land: Indians, colonists, and the ecology of New England.* New York: Hill & Wang, 241 pp.

Divale, W. T. & Harris, M. 1976. Population, warfare, and the male supremacist complex. *American Anthropologist*, Washington, 78:521–538. [Cf. *ibid.* 80:110–118, 379–386, 665–673; 81:349–351.]

Dunbar, R. 1985. Sociobiology of war. *Medicine & War*, London, 1:201–208.

Dunlap, R. E. 1987. Polls, pollution, and politics revisited: public opinion on the environment in the Reagan era. *Environment,* Washington, 29(6):6–11, 32–37.

Easlea, B. 1983. *Fathering the unthinkable: masculinity, scientists and the nuclear arms race*. London: Pluto Press, 230 pp.

Eckhardt, W. 1975. Primitive militarism. *Journal of Peace Research*, Oslo, 12:55–62.

Eckhardt, W. 1982. Atrocities, civilizations, and savages: ways to avoid a nuclear holocaust. *Bulletin of Peace Proposals*, Oslo, 13:343–349.

Eckhardt, W. 1987. Task of peace education: a value theory of peace education. *Bulletin of Peace Proposals*, Oslo, 18:63–71.

Ehrenfeld, D. 1978. *Arrogance of humanism*. New York: Oxford University Press, 286 pp.

Ehrlich, P. & Ehrlich, A. 1981. *Extinction: the causes and consequences of the disappearance of species.* New York: Random House, 306 pp.

Eisler, R. & Loye, D. 1983. 'Failure' of liberalism: a reassessment of ideology from a new feminine-masculine perspective. *Political Psychology,* New Brunswick, New Jersey, 4:375–391.

Eisler, R. & Loye, D. 1986. Peace and feminist theory: new directions. *Bulletin of Peace Proposals*, Oslo, 17:95–99.

Emmelin, L. 1977. Environmental education at university level. *Ambio*, Stockholm, 6:201–209.

Ferencz, B. B. 1985. *Common sense guide to world peace.* London: Oceana Publications, 112 pp.

Ferguson, J. 1977. *War and peace in the world's religions.* London: Sheldon Press, 166 pp.

Ferrill, A. 1985. *Origins of war: from the Stone Age to Alexander the Great.* New York: Thames & Hudson, 240 pp.

Friedman, S. M. 1983. Environmental reporting: problem child of the media. *Environment,* Washington, 25(10):24–29.

Fromm, E. 1973. *Anatomy of human destructiveness.* New York: Holt, Rinehart & Winston, 521 pp.

Galtung, J. 1981. Social cosmology and the concept of peace. *Journal of Peace Research*, Oslo, 18:183–199.

García, C. 1981. Androgyny and peace education. *Bulletin of Peace Proposals*, Oslo, 12:163–171.

Glacken, C. J. 1967. *Traces on the Rhodian shore: nature and culture in Western thought from ancient times to the end of the eighteenth century*. Berkeley: University of California Press, 763 pp.

Goldblat, J. 1986. Role of the United Nations in arms control: an assessment. *Arms Control*, London, 7:115–132.

Harcourt, A. H., Pennington, H. & Weber, A. W. 1986. Public attitudes to wildlife and conservation in the Third World. *Oryx*, London, 20:152–154.

Hardin, G. 1968. Tragedy of the commons. *Science*, Washington, 162:1243–1248.

Holdgate, M. W., Kassas, M. & White, G. F. (eds). 1982. *World environment 1972–1982: a report by the United Nations Environment Programme*. Dublin: Tycooly International, 637 pp.

Huddle, N. & Reich, M. 1975. *Island of dreams: environmental crisis in Japan*. New York: Autumn Press, 351 pp.

Humphrey, J. 1985. Development of the physicians' peace movements. *Medicine & War,* London, 1:87–99.

Ikeda, D. 1985. New waves of peace toward the 21st century: Buddhist approaches to peace. *Bulletin of Peace Proposals*, Oslo, 16:185–195.

Janis, I. L. 1982. *Groupthink: psychological studies of policy decisions and fiascoes*. 2nd edn. Boston: Houghton Mifflin, 351 pp.

Kaltefleiter, W. & Pfaltzgraff, R. L. (eds). 1985. *Peace movements in Europe & the United States*. London: Croom Helm, 211 pp.

Keegan, J. & Darracott, J. 1981. *Nature of war*. New York: Holt, Rinehart & Winston, 276 pp.

Kelley, D. R., Stunkel, K. R. & Wescott, R. R. 1976. *Economic superpowers and the environment: the United States, the Soviet Union, and Japan*. San Francisco: W. H. Freeman, 335 pp.

Kemp, G. 1987. Biology of non-violence. *Medicine & War*, London, 3:181–190.

Kim, S. S. 1985. US Catholic bishops and the nuclear crisis. *Journal of Peace Research*, Oslo, 22:321–333.

Kramer, B. M., Kalick, S. M. & Milburn, M. A. 1983. Attitudes toward nuclear weapons and nuclear war: 1945–1982. *Journal of Social Issues,* New York, 39(1):7–24.

Kubrick, S. 1964. *Dr. Strangelove: or, how I learned to stop worrying and love the bomb*. Hollywood, Calif.: Columbia, 35 mm B&W film, 93 min.

Leonard, H. J. & Morell, D. 1981. Emergence of environmental concern in developing countries: a political perspective. *Stanford Journal of International Law*, Stanford, Calif., 17:281–313.

Leopold, A. 1949. *Sand county almanac: and sketches here and there*. New York: Oxford University Press, 226 pp.

Levine, L. D. (ed.). 1975. *Man in nature: historical perspectives on man in his environment*. Toronto: Royal Ontario Museum, 133 pp.

Lutts, R. H. 1985. Chemical fallout: Rachel Carson's *Silent Spring,* radioactive fallout, and the environmental movement. *Environmental Review,* Denver, 9:210–225.

MacBride, S. 1980. Mass media's role in the search for disarmament. *Bulletin of Peace Proposals*, Oslo, 11:229–233.

Manoff, R. K. 1984. The media: nuclear secrecy vs. democracy. *Bulletin of the Atomic Scientists*, Chicago, 40(1):26–29.

Markusen, E. & Harris, J. B. 1984. Role of education in preventing nuclear war. *Harvard Educational Review,* Cambridge, Mass., 54:282–303.

Marsh, G. P. 1864. *Man and nature: or, physical geography as modified by human action.* Cambridge, Mass.: Harvard University Press, 472 pp., 1965.

Mathews, J. T. *et al.* 1986. *World resources 1986: a report by the World Resources Institute and the International Institute for Environment and Development.* New York: Basic Books, 353 pp.

McAllister, P. (ed.). 1982. *Reweaving the web of life: feminism and nonviolence.* Philadelphia: New Society Publishers, 440 pp.

Merchant, C. 1980. *Death of nature: women, ecology, and the scientific revolution.* San Francisco: Harper & Row, 348 pp.

Mitchell, R. C. 1980. *Public opinion on environmental issues: results of a national public opinion survey.* Washington: US Council on Environmental Quality, 49 pp.

Mitchell, R. C. 1984. Public opinion and environmental politics in the 1970s and 1980s. In: Vig, N. J. & Kraft, M. E. (eds). *Environmental policy in the 1980s: Reagan's new agenda.* Washington: CQ Press, 377 pp.: pp. 51–74.

National Conference of Catholic Bishops. 1983. *Challenge of peace: God's promise and our response.* Washington: US Catholic Conference, Publication No. 863, 103 pp.

Oudsten, E. den. 1985. Public opinion. *SIPRI Yearbook,* London, 1985:31–38.

Passmore, J. 1980. *Man's responsibility for nature: ecological problems and Western traditions.* 2nd edn. London: Duckworth, 227 pp.

Pittock, A. B. *et al.* 1985–86. *Environmental consequences of nuclear war. I. Physical and atmospheric effects. II. Ecological and agricultural effects.* Chichester, UK: John Wiley & Sons, 2 vols (359+523 pp.).

Reardon, B. A. 1985. *Sexism and the war system.* New York: Teachers College Press, 111 pp.

Rogers, E. S. 1975. The Indian and the European: two views of the land. In: Levine, L. D. (ed.). *Man in nature: historical perspectives on man in his environment.* Toronto: Royal Ontario Museum, 133 pp.: pp. 90–109.

Roper, M. K. 1975. Evidence of warfare in the Near East from 10,000–4,300 B.C. In: Nettleship, M. A. *et al.* (eds). *War, its causes and correlates.* Hague: Mouton, 813 pp.: pp. 299–343.

Russett, B. 1984. Statement of the American Catholic bishops: a moral-theological critique of nuclear deterrence. *Bulletin of Peace Proposals*, Oslo, 15:197–204.

Salomon, K. 1986. The peace movement: an anti-establishment movement. *Journal of Peace Research*, Oslo, 23:115–127.

Schachter, O. 1977. *Sharing the world's resources.* New York: Columbia University Press, 172 pp.

Schoenfeld, A. C. 1980. Newspersons and the environment today. *Journalism Quarterly,* Athens, Ohio, 57:456–462.

Sellers, L. & Jones, D. W., Jr. 1973. Environment and the mass media. *Journal of Environmental Education,* Washington, 5(1):51–57.

Silva, A. de, Simson, O. v. & Hinks, R. 1963. *Man through his art. I. War and peace.* London: Educational Productions, 64 pp. + 20 pl.

Stone, C. D. 1972. Should trees have standing?: toward legal rights for natural objects. *Southern California Law Review*, Los Angeles, 45:450–510. Also: Los Altos, Calif.: William Kaufmann, 103 pp., 1974.

Suid, L. H. 1985–86. Hollywood and the bomb. *Air University Review*, Maxwell Air Force Base, Alabama, 37(2):103–109.

Thomas, K. 1983. *Man and the natural world: changing attitudes in England 1500–1800.* London: Allen Lane, 425 pp.

Times, N.Y. 1946. Atomic education urged by Einstein. *New York Times* 1946 (25 May): 13.

Toynbee, A. 1972. Religious background of the present environmental crisis: a viewpoint. *International Journal of Environmental Studies,* London, 3:141–146;4:157–158.

Tuan, Y.-F. 1968. Discrepancies between environmental attitude and behaviour: examples from Europe and China. *Canadian Geographer,* Montreal, 12:176–191.

Tuchman, B. W. 1984. *March of folly: from Troy to Vietnam.* New York: Alfred A. Knopf, 447 pp. + 24 pl.

UNESCO. 1985. *UNESCO prize 1984 for peace education.* Paris: UNESCO, 60 pp.

Westing, A. H. 1980. *Warfare in a fragile world: military impact on the human environment.* London: Taylor & Francis, 249 pp. [a SIPRI book]

Westing, A. H. 1981a. A note on how many humans that have ever lived. *BioScience,* Washington, 31:523–524;32:6.

Westing, A. H. 1981b. Environmental impact of conventional warfare. In: Barnaby, W. (ed.). *War and environment.* Stockholm: Royal Ministry of Agriculture, Environmental Advisory Council, 154 pp.: pp. 58–72.

Westing, A. H. 1981c. How much of this land is our land? *Environment,* Washington, 23(6):5,44–45.

Westing, A. H. 1981d. World in balance. *Environmental Conservation,* Geneva, 8:177–183.

Westing, A. H. 1982. War as a human endeavor: the high-fatality wars of the twentieth century. *Journal of Peace Research,* Oslo, 19:261–270.

Westing, A. H. 1984. The arms race versus environmental and human welfare. In: *Ponències.* Sant Cugat del Vallès, Spain: Universitat Internacional de la Pau, 248 pp.: pp. 173–177.

Westing, A. H. (ed.). 1986. *Global resources and international conflict: environmental factors in strategic policy and action.* Oxford: Oxford University Press, 280 pp. [a SIPRI book]

Westing, A. H. 1988. Our place in nature: reflections on the carrying capacity for humans. *International Conference on Environmental Future,* Edinburgh, 3: forthcoming.

White, C. D. *et al.* (United Methodist Council of Bishops). 1986. *In defense of creation: the nuclear crisis and a just peace.* Nashville, Tennessee: Graded Press, 96 pp.

White, L., Jr. 1967. Historical roots of our ecologic crisis. *Science,* Washington, 155:1203–1207.

Wittner, L. S. 1984. *Rebels against war: the American peace movement, 1933–1983.* 2nd edn. Philadelphia: Temple University Press, 364 pp.

Yankelovich, D. & Doble, J. 1984–85. Public mood: nuclear weapons and the U.S.S.R. *Foreign Affairs,* New York, 63:33–46.

Zaidi, I. H. 1981. On the ethics of man's interaction with the environment: an Islamic approach. *Environmental Ethics,* Athens, Georgia, 3:35–47.

Zimmerman, M. E. 1987. Feminism, deep ecology, and environmental ethics. *Environmental Ethics,* Athens, Georgia, 9:21–44.

2. The historical evolution of cultural norms relating to war and the environment

GEOFFREY BEST
London School of Economics & Political Science

I. Introduction

The capacity of war to cause 'widespread, long-term and severe damage' to the natural environment constitutes a menace that is historically novel. Methods and means of warfare did not really place the doing of such damage to the natural environment within the reach of belligerents until World War II. What was however within their reach from earliest recorded times was the ability to damage or destroy parts of the anthropogenic environment. The history of civilization, past and present, scanned with a view to ascertaining what kinds and degrees of concern may have been shown about belligerents' religious, ethical or legal responsibilities in this respect, discloses: (*a*) a small but consistent canon of laws and customs aiming to control the impact of hostilities on the anthropogenic environment; and (*b*) some lessons as to the value of those laws and customs and the value of the whole body of norms relating to warfare of which they form a part.

This chapter reviews the range and quality of sources available for identification of the cultural concerns most commonly shown about the environmental effects of war. It also evaluates the actual operation of those laws and customs which expressly embody such concerns. Some relevant background information is provided elsewhere (Best, 1980; Spaight, 1911).

II. Historical contexts and conditions of cultural norms concerning restraint on warfare

It is understandable that a generation anxiously concerned to establish effective norms for the control of the impact of warfare on the environment should look over its shoulder to see what may be learned from the past. The reasonableness of such inquiry is all the greater because contemporary norms regarding the conduct of war—norms expressed in and diffused throughout, for example, the 1907 Hague Conventions on Land Warfare, the 1949 Geneva Conventions and the 1977 Protocols Additional to them (see appendix 2)—have roots going far back in historical time and cultural space (Roberts & Guelff, 1982; Schindler & Toman, 1981). Current international law of armed conflict is not as Eurocentric as the titles of those treaties might suggest. Such law has proved largely acceptable the whole world over precisely because all of its main general principles and many of its particular rules coincide with principles and rules long familiar in every continent and culture to the theoreticians, planners and directors of interstate wars.

Moreover, upon this common cultural basis rests the viability of that part of the law of armed conflict that seeks most directly to protect the victims of such conflicts. Commonly known as international humanitarian law, it depends for its efficacy on its appeal beyond cultural, political and military élites to their armed forces and, indeed, to their entire civilian populations. Its prime philosopher, Jean Pictet, has recognized that 'human nature is the same everywhere . . ., that humanitarian principles are common to all nations and that they are deeply rooted in all lands'; thus international humanitarian law may justly be regarded as 'the quintessence, the heritage of humanity', a body of law embodying ideas 'which, because they are completely in accord with human nature, are acceptable to [people] of all races, cultures and opinions' (Bello, 1980, p. vii).

Such sturdy universalism presents difficulties that cynics and sceptics, relativists and so-called realists are not slow to point out. Much may be disputed about the definition of 'human nature'. Cause for disquiet may be found time and again in the facility with which in armed conflicts humanitarian law and principles appear to be honoured more in the breach than in the observance. And yet it remains true that, within the mixed principles and inconsistent practices of every world religion and recorded civilization, there is enough of respect for human dignity and right to life, of good will towards neighbours and of disapproval of wanton cruelty and destructiveness for these reasonably to be regarded as universal humanitarian principles. The principal props of humanitarian law, and of the general law of armed conflict to which it must relate, are a certain recognition of the essential sanctity of human life and the likely value of human productions and properties, drawn both of them from the religions and cultures that have found it good to propose norms of distinction between what may be permitted and what may not be permitted in the way of killing and injuring, of expropriating and destroying.

Therefore, it might be supposed that codes of military conduct, which characteristically aim to impose restraints and prohibitions for the sake of human beings and their products and properties, should show concern also for the natural environment in relation to which the major religions somehow or other place humankind and from which the material achievements of humankind are wrought. Such a supposition is understandable, but upon inquiry is found to be mistaken. The reason appears to be no more than this, that from the first syllable of recorded time until 1945, the making of war—even the most total and deadly of wars—included no serious capability of permanently damaging the natural environment.

The considerable damage done throughout the ages to the natural environment (soil erosion, deforestation, species extermination, land exhaustion and so on) has for the most part been done in the long course of economic and cultural use and misuse, not by war (Hughes, 1975). Damage to the natural environment by warfare was not the problem. Damage by war to what humans had wrought from the natural environment—that is, the anthropogenic environment—has been another matter. This is a matter about which the law of armed conflict from its earliest obscure origins has had much to say. It is a matter relevant to the present inquiry and brings with it much religious and ethical force. But at no point except perhaps one (water sources) has the natural environment ever been truly at risk from belligerent actions. The will was no doubt there, but the capacity was not, until twentieth-century science and technology at last provided it. The evolution that matters most here is as much the evolution of technological capabilities as it is of the evolution of cultural norms. From their fruitful interplay has come a variety of laws and customs relating to the conduct of war that apply to this exclusively twentieth-century problem, by way of analogy or logical extension.

The most obvious and applicable norm is that of restraint and discrimination. Indeed, this is the corner-stone, the *sine qua non*, of every known code or law of war, from the most ancient and undeveloped to the most recent and elaborate. In one way or another it suggests and supports all the main elements of the law of war: (*a*) restraint in the manner of attacking enemy combatants (which can almost equate with the basic military principle of 'economy of force'); (*b*) restraint in the handling of enemy property (as anything, whether natural or otherwise, on enemy soil has always been regarded); (*c*) restraint in the treatment of prisoners and non-combatants; and (*d*) restraint with regard to the wounded and sick plus all those tending to their needs. War being by definition no mere anarchic violence, but rather a regulated and normative activity, its practice is scarcely separable from the proclamation of rules to keep it within its designed bounds; and those rules have normally included what, in given circumstances, may or may not be done to an enemy (Bull, 1977, chap. 8). Such rules still fill the pages of international military law where their fundamental grounding and justification has, since 1899, been stated in these terms: 'The right of belligerents to adopt means of injuring the enemy is not unlimited' (see appendix 2.I). Post-1945 extensions of that principle from its traditional application to enemy persons and properties to the natural environment are no more than logical, given the novel and awful circumstances that have suggested them.

Such extension is all the more easily and naturally done, because the same religious and philosophical writings that direct human attention to the need for restraint in war can also direct humankind to admire and respect the environment. Contemporary theologians and religiously minded environmentalists have no difficulty in finding, in the great books of all the major religions, texts that express delight in the beauties and benefits of the divinely created environment as well as in the inhabited environment, and that at least suggest respect and restraint in human approaches to it. Some religions go much further in this direction than others, and comparative analysis of them has produced and popularized a distinction between those religious faiths that embody an 'exploitative' or 'dominionist' approach to nature and those that are more 'respectful' or 'conservationist', the latter capable of observing absolute prohibitions and restraint in ways unpersuasive or even unintelligible by the lights of the others (Aho, 1981). However, it must be added that there is no real agreement among authorities as to the classification of religions in this respect.

The matter of religious influence is obviously of great interest and, in so far as it may relate to the problem in question, of potential value. However, there are two layers of difficulty in bringing it to bear on the subject at hand. The first layer has to do with the very understanding and description of cultures and their religions. The social scientist cannot recognize in them the unitary bodies of people and principles that their own theorists and expositors like to present. Going behind identifiable religions and what might be identified as cultures to the 'civilizations' englobing them, Wright (1965, p. 108) has suggested that 'Each civilization is distinguished by a unique complex of fundamental values in which its members believe and which to some extent guides their choices. Usually this belief is manifested by the general acceptance of a religion, but sometimes the forms of the same religion conceal fundamental differences in the substance of the values it supports in different areas of its realm'.

More recently, Tuan (1970) has brought the same point home to the environmental question in suggesting that the publicized ethos of a culture about its environment seldom covers more than a small fraction of the total range of its relevant attitudes and practices; and, moreover, that aesthetic and religious ideals rarely play a major role in this regard. Tuan goes on to point out that neither the Taoist nor the Buddhist supposedly conservationist traditions has had any corresponding effect on their natural environments, which have been subjected to the same erosions and destructions that have elsewhere accompanied supposedly more exploitative religions. Every religion has its gentle and generous aspects, of which much may encouragingly be made, but the full truth about each is only known when its harder and self-regarding aspects are taken into view as well, and the whole subjected to the temptations and tests of economics, politics and war.

The second layer of difficulty is encountered when, moving from contemplation of the question of religion and the environment to scrutiny of the particular question of war and the environment, an attempt is made to give equal value to the military and the environmental sides of that equation. When this is done, it becomes clear that the prescriptions of religion and the behavioural norms inferable from them are, on their own, of no more than limited significance. They have to be evaluated in connection with norms rooted in war, rooted in the nature of war itself, and related inescapably to the characters of particular wars. All talk of norms in connection with war is rendered futile unless it is remembered: (*a*) that the observance of such rules of restraint in some sorts of so-called wars is easier and likelier than in others; and (*b*) that their religious and ethical contents, which can seem so important, are inextricably bound up with large measures of self-interest.

To deal with the first point first: observance of restraining norms in war depends not only on the characters of the participants' religious beliefs and cultural norms, but also—and some would say, rather more—on the character of the war in which they find themselves engaged. War as a peculiar and distinct social activity has its constants as well as its variables; and, of the behavioural moral constants, none is more unyielding than the one that denies to belligerents the right to conduct war exactly in the manner they would wish. Much turns on the severity of the conflict and the weight and texture of its causes. What are for convenience called wars can vary enormously in their severity in the eyes of an objective outsider. For instance, a squabble over a dowry or an alleged personal insult will not seem to a disinterested outsider as momentous a matter as would life-or-death access to water; a disputed bit of territory with nothing profitable associated with it can hardly seem as serious a *casus belli* as one containing oil; but there appears to be no limit to the seriousness which human beings who are deeply *engagés* or *enragés* can invest in even the most (as an outsider might judge them) trivial quarrels, with sometimes terrible consequences. The severity of wars does, in fact, often vary in proportion to the weight of interests objectively at issue, as it may do with the civilizational or cultural distance between the combatants. The history of warfare shows that, unless hostilities are restricted to well-disciplined regular soldiers, wars between peoples without any fellow-feeling for each other easily become total and atrocious.

A tendency is sometimes discernible in writings about the cultural and social relations of the history of war by those with expertise forged in other areas of scholarship, to fail to take adequate note of the very great variety of conflicts popularly subsumed under the title of 'war', and to miss the importance of distinguishing between their differing levels of intensity. It has been the case throughout history, as it is the case still, that the circumstances and characters of some armed conflicts are more conducive to their limitation than the characters and circumstances of others. The religion-rooted ritualized fights between closely-related tribes or between sub-groups within them (from which anthropological examples of mutual understanding and restraint are typically drawn) are at the antipodes of actuality from the wholly unrestrained and savage sort of war that can occur when peoples are in conflict whose cultural patterns have little in common. Restraint may still be shown and it will be rationally explicable, but it will be as unanticipated in this case as it will be anticipated in the other.

The other feature of the laws and customs of war that needs to be borne in mind whenever its religious or ethical contents are under scrutiny, is that the norms by which the military man purports to conduct himself include sizeable elements of self-interest. Moralists and theologians will differ as to whether this in any way diminishes the ethical respectability of those norms. After all, utilitarianism has its ethical dimension like every school of philosophy. It is not Christianity alone that salutes prudence as a virtue; what is right or good to do need not absolutely lack advantage for the doer. Mixed motives and unconscious motivations are taken for granted by modern-minded and psychologically-instructed moralists.

The mismatches between law and justice—*a fortiori*, between law and virtue—are commonplace wherever jurisprudence, ethics and church-state relations are seriously studied. No need, therefore, for surprise that even the more altruistic-seeming rules of war can usually be found to have some measure of self-interest in them, difficult though it may be to disentangle their knots of mixed purposes, and impossible though it may be to analyse their compositions. Two examples can be given. First is the practice of giving quarter to enemy combatants seeking to surrender and of treating prisoners of war decently. These could be largely explained because they encourage other enemy combatants to surrender, thereby sapping the enemy's strength; but such are not normally the explanations given by those quoting religious texts about mercy, generosity or siblinghood. Second is the rule commonly encountered in codes of military conduct from many cultures and since earliest times that forbids the spoiling of springs and wells. At first sight the protection of drinking water looks as good to the environmentalist as it does to the moral absolutist, but the explanation is, at least in part, the self-interest of the military forces that might themselves soon need that water. The many occasions on which the spoiling of water-sources is nevertheless heard of in the history of warfare may be set down to decisions that there was military advantage in doing so, and that the use of such sources could be done without. What proportions of self-interest and altruism might go into the formulation of such rules—and into their subsequent observance—is anyone's guess. However, there may be more matter for satisfaction than for indignation in acknowledging that it is precisely this self-interested element that can best secure the observance of those rules. This should certainly encourage the environmentalist, whose claim to be heard by military planners and legislators can rest on no firmer platform than demonstration to potential despoilers of the environment of the self-damaging consequences of what they might have in mind.

III. Historic norms of martial conduct relating to the environment

A brief analysis of the historical evolution of cultural norms relating to war and the environment may appropriately consider the specific points at which these norms have entered into the codes of martial behaviour with which civilizations have girded themselves. These points can hardly be considered numerous or ambitious, but the regularity with which they appear, from the earliest recorded occurrences of war to the present, reflects the constant uneasiness of thoughtful war-makers about what they have had it in their power to do to the environment, at least in its state as developed by humans. Hugo Grotius (1625), Emmerich de Vattel (1758), Henry Wheaton (1836), August Heffter (1844) and Johann Bluntschli (1868)—to name just five of the most formative writers in international law—called on substantially the same body of examples in the few pages they found it necessary to devote to this side of martial law, and drew them as readily from the past (even from the remote past) as from the time of their writing.

The listing of these recurrent points of prohibition or restraint must be prefaced by the recapitulation of two cautions concerning their instructional usefulness. First, the early authors to whom reference is made (as well as most commentaries on them) generally neglect the crucial distinctions among different types and violence-levels of wars; the citation of injunctions to restraint cannot be taken to mean that restraint was or could be observed even in the limited and ritualistic wars to which reference is often made, let alone in wars of more unlimited and desperate character. Second, it is impossible wholly to explain the sources and motivations of these few, but relatively constant, points of concern about environmental damage. Each is in some degree capable of explanation in prudential as well as in altruistic terms. In the present primitive states of research and reflection on these matters, there is no means of clearly distinguishing one component from another or of weighing the respective components relative to one another. The analyst can do little more than indicate possibilities, and offer what seem to be sensible speculations in explanation of them.

Flora and fauna

One of the two most common sets of norms is the one concerned with preventing the destruction or damage of 'forests', 'orchards', 'fruit trees' or 'vines'. These items are referred to in the earliest texts of every continent (see, e.g., appendix 4.I). However, their interpretation demands caution. Problems of translation compound the difficulty of knowing exactly what is being referred to and the extent to which the environment is natural and the extent to which it is anthropogenic. Vineyards must by common sense fall into the anthropogenic category, but orchards or fruit trees could perhaps fall into either of them. Forests could include what are sometimes expressly described as sacred groves. Some element of normally religious respect for the natural environment *per se* cannot be doubted, but (to repeat the all-important rule) its evaluation as a norm of actual armed conflict would inevitably follow the character of the particular armed conflict in question.

'Herds' are mentioned in the early texts as often as are orchards, but belong more unambiguously to the anthropogenic category of the environment; as do the 'beehives' that make an occasional showing.

In limited conflicts between closely related people sharing a common culture—for use within which these norms must mainly have evolved—such floral and faunal prohibitions could be expected to be observed, as also in successfully managed limited wars of enrichment or territorial aggrandizement. Neither the historical record nor any principle of military science offers a suggestion that they could affect the conduct of total wars or of wars between the culturally unrelated. The destruction of such objects would be undertaken as a matter of course by either side for the clearance of lines of sight, the denial of cover and camouflage and the improvement of fighting positions. Above all, such destruction would be undertaken for the sapping of an enemy's economic strength, not to speak of such baser motives as punitive actions or vindictive vandalism. Indeed, the history of war from its earliest times is replete with devastations, sometimes of the most complete and total description. The worst of these devastations (e.g., what the Thirty Years' War of 1618–48 did to Bohemia or what the Tai Ping Rebellion of 1850–64 did to China) must be considered among the most substantial environmental damages done by war before the twentieth century; their scars long continued to disfigure the face of the land. However, it may not be quite proper to classify them as precursors of the environment-damaging military operations of the present inasmuch as these latter ones can make their dreadful, long-lasting marks irrespective of demographic effects; in the case of most of the earlier ones, the long-term effects must have to varying extents resulted from the death and displacement of population.

Water

Not surprisingly, water is the subject of the other most common set of norms. The destruction, and especially the poisoning, of what is translated as 'wells', 'springs', 'sources' and 'rivers' regularly appears among the martial acts most to be avoided. An evaluation of the force of these prohibitions would follow the same lines as those regarding flora and fauna, with the additional complication of the 'poison' factor.

No prohibition is more often encountered among martial norms of all periods and places than that of poison, whether administered secretly to individuals (as by assassins) or used as anti-personnel weapons or employed to spoil an enemy's most indispensable and basic means of survival. The covert use of poison as well as its shocking, surprising effects—whether introduced through the agency of food, drink or sharp weapon—brings to mind the general horror in which the use of poison gas became held during and after World War I. In the absence of any means of rationally demonstrating that gas is a more painful injurer or killer than many other weapons, the suggestion is inescapable that what is being dealt with here is the persistent presence of some singular element of superstition or taboo.

To the perhaps unusual taboo against poison must be added that the religions of settled pre-industrial peoples, unless they lived in reliably drought-free milieus, were quicker to locate a divine presence in springs and rivers than anywhere else. That much admitted, it was as true of water resources as of other natural resources, that observance of norms protecting them would turn on the already-mentioned military characteristics and circumstances. No device ever worked better to reduce an enemy's fortification than the stoppage of its water-supplies; 'poisoning', when not actually impracticable, would often be more laborious or unreliable than obstruction or diversion, which was regularly undertaken whenever in the less limited sorts of wars it was a practical possibility.

The destruction of irrigation systems, which features so largely in the histories of the decline of some of the earlier civilizations, is a somewhat different and less relevant matter here. That even the most elaborate irrigation systems could be rendered useless by war, is not doubted. But it should be noted that there is no agreement among experts regarding the extent to which the Mongols—who figure in various accounts as the prime malefactors from that point of view—carried out such destruction deliberately and the extent to which such collapse was merely the inevitable consequence of the socio-economic dislocation brought by war or deposited in its wake (Morgan, 1986, pp. 80–83). Not much neglect of channels, sluices and the like would be needed to cause a whole system to break down; no long stoppage would be needed to bring a whole system to ruin, and to return its associated fields to their original dust.

Peasants

The inclusion of norms regarding human beings is to stretch the definition of environment towards the limits of credibility. However, this may be justified here on the grounds, first, that this category often appeared among martial norms as a sort of casual extension of the environment; and second, that it has relevance to our inquiry, at least by way of analogy and suggestion. Injunctions regarding the sparing of what is translated as 'peasants', 'husbandmen' and 'farm workers' are often found among the martial norms of settled civilizations with solid bases in the land and its exploitation. The humanitarian element in this norm need not be taken too seriously. War for the acquisition of potentially profitable territory would be self-defeating to the extent that it destroyed either its natural or its human resources; a peasant whom war bypassed might well only be exchanging one form of slavery or serfdom for another. Nevertheless, the fact that the norm is articulated at all, and not just in Europe's golden age of limited dynastic warfare, from the mid-seventeenth to the late eighteenth century, suggests something about the stretch of moral imagination of which military theorists and legislators have been capable.

Cultural monuments

Cultural monuments constitute yet another stretch of the concept of the environment. A norm of respect for sacred places and buildings is often met with in the same texts from which more obviously environmental norms are drawn. In modern times, and *pari passu* with the historical processes loosely called 'secularization' and (however self-flatteringly by those most given to use it) 'the spread of civilization', that originally religious interest has been enlarged so as to refer in general terms to 'cultural property'; an enormously enlarged concept, of which 'religious property' now forms only a small part.

What is at least obliquely relevant here is the philosophy supporting the norm. It is expressed thus in the 1954 Hague Convention on Cultural Property: '. . . damage to cultural property belonging to any people whatsoever means damage to the cultural heritage of all [humankind] . . .; . . . preservation of the cultural heritage is of great importance for all peoples of the world and . . . it is important that this heritage should receive international protection . . .' (Schindler & Toman, 1981, p. 663).

IV. Conclusion

Concern about the impact of war on the environment can be discerned within all the major civilizations and religions of the world. Such concern has found expression in the codes of martial conduct that have in a practical sense testified to that side of their always ambivalent thoughts about war; the side that has aimed to use, control and limit such martial conduct rather than to let it become unlimited and uncontrolled.

The rules of those codes with specific relevance to the environment are much less relevant to the novel problem of this century than the principles that have prompted them. The rules of martial law evolve and change according to circumstance and need. That the making of war before 1945 did not find the effects of war on the natural environment to constitute an urgent problem need not deter from current recognition of the seriousness and urgency of the problem. Unchanged—and, in fact, unchangeable—remain the fundamental principles that have guided the formulation of rules of restraint in martial law towards the anthropogenic environment—in the context, it is always important to remember, of rules of restraint towards much else, hitherto found to be of more pressing concern.

The world history of the principles of restraint in war, and of the rules derived from them, brings a mixed message to our age. Their story certainly has its discouraging and cautionary aspects. At some vital points, the very facts of the matter are difficult to interpret and evaluate. The record of observance is patchy, and is held by many sound judges to be worse in this century than in the last, if only because the means available for the conduct of total war have suddenly become so much more powerful than ever before. However, it would be a mistake to conclude pessimistically that norms for the conduct of war are useless. Every prisoner who returns home more or less intact from wartime captivity is living proof that they are not useless. Hiroshima was obliterated, but Kyoto was not. Slaughter of civilians is not something of which belligerent parties like to be accused. The laws and customs of war have worked from time to time and from place to place, as they still do. The important thing is to discover why.

The best prospects for norms of restraint in war have always been when the principles of cultural community and of prudence have supported them. The former is the more altruistic, the latter the more self-interested; but their operation is not mutually exclusive, and history shows them supporting one another. Neither is capable of withstanding the grosser gusts of aggressive passion and malevolence. And even prudence is put at risk by the extreme nationalist doctrine that a people in some desperate last resort is entitled to destroy itself—and anything else—rather than to surrender. But, that sinister imponderable apart, it is not unreasonably optimistic to believe that the way ahead lies in enlargement beyond its normal national and racial bounds of that saving sense of cultural community, and the enhancement of that sense of prudence so as to bring home to potential belligerents the extent to which their assaults on the natural environment can recoil.

References

Aho, J. 1981. *Religious mythology and the art of war: comparative religious symbolisms of military violence*. London: Aldwych Press, 264 pp.

Bello, E. G. 1980. *African customary humanitarian law*. Geneva: Oyez, 157 pp.

Best, G. 1980. *Humanity in warfare: the modern history of the international law of armed conflicts*. London: Weidenfeld & Nicolson, 400 pp.

Bluntschli, J. C. 1868. *Moderne Völkerrecht der civilisirten Staaten als Rechtsbuch dargestellt [Modern international law of civilized states presented as a book of law]*. Nördlingen, Germany: C. Beck, 520 pp.

Bull, H. 1977. *Anarchical society: a study of order in world politics*. London: Macmillan, 335 pp.

Grotius, H. 1625. *De jure belli ac pacis libri tres [On the law of war and peace in three books]* [with translation from the Latin by F. W. Kelsey *et al*.]. Oxford: Clarendon Press, 2 vols (663+946 pp.), 1913–25.

Heffter, A. W. 1844. *Europäische Völkerrecht der Gegenwart [European international law of the present time]*. Berlin: E. H. Schroeder, 412 pp.

Hughes, J. D. 1975. *Ecology in ancient civilizations*. Albuquerque: University of New Mexico Press, 181 pp.

Morgan, D. 1986. *Mongols*. Oxford: Blackwells, 238 pp.

Roberts, A. & Guelff, R. (eds). 1982. *Documents on the laws of war*. Oxford: Clarendon Press, 498 pp.

Schindler, D. & Toman, J. (eds). 1981. *Laws of armed conflicts: a collection of conventions, resolutions and other documents*. 2nd edn. Alphen aan den Rijn, Netherlands: Sijthoff & Noordhoff, 933 pp.

Spaight, J. M. 1911. *War rights on land*. London: Macmillan, 520 pp.

Tuan, Y.-F. 1970. Our treatment of the environment in ideal and actuality. *American Scientist*, New Haven, 58:244–249.

Vattel, E. de. 1758. *Law of nations: or, the principles of natural law applied to the conduct and to the affairs of nations and of sovereigns* [translated from the French by C. G. Fenwick]. Washington: Carnegie Institution, 3 vols (541+375+398 pp.), 1916.

Wheaton, H. 1836. *Elements of international law: with a sketch of the history of the science*. Philadelphia: Carey, Lea & Blanchard, 375 pp.

Wright, Q. 1965. *Study of war: with a commentary on war since 1942*. 2nd edn. Chicago: University of Chicago Press, 1637 pp. + tbls.

3. Cultural norms in the USSR relating to war and the environment

GRIGORI S. KHOZIN
Scientific Council for Philosophical & Social Problems of Science & Technology, Moscow

I. Introduction

The implementation of ethical aspects relating to the environment as an important component of cultural norms will radically reduce the immediate destructive impacts on the natural environment during the course of military hostilities. Their implementation will also limit considerably the sphere of activity of militarism as a multifaceted socio-political and economic phenomenon. The cultural norms which form the basis of the human relationship with nature vary in their origin and essence. They also reflect the diversity of cultures of different countries and peoples in their ascent from primitive to contemporary forms of social organization. These cultural norms are integral components of social consciousness, within which at present we witness the emergence of postulates of a new universal outlook. This new outlook rejects as irrational the efforts of some conservative political and miltary-industrial groups to rely on military force as an effective means of solving disputes between states. It has become rather well accepted that the search for unilateral military advantage leads to further deterioration of the global ecological situation. Such a search also creates precursors to global nuclear conflict, which could lead to 'nuclear winter' and even to the elimination of the very foundations of life on earth.

The present chapter traces the evolution of ethical principles and their cultural foundations inherited from previous generations of the peoples, large and small, which are now united in the multinational and coequal community—the USSR. It describes as well the most vividly expressed traditions of stewardship in relation to nature that have originated in the customs, habits, outlooks and religious values of the peoples inhabiting this Union. Major attention is paid to the cultural norms that are incorporated into contemporary philosophical and political concepts in relation to the ecological consequences of war and of any manner of military preparations.

The rejection of destructive impact on the environment derives from a person's interconnected biological and social origins. Nature provides humans not only with their physical environment, but also one in which they can express their creative abilities. Accordingly, the contemporary relation of humans to nature reflects the variety of cultural norms and spiritual and emotional aspects of human experience. Indeed, the rich cultural heritage of humankind has incorporated many mythological, artistic, religious and philosophical images and symbols.

This chapter is based on work by Russian and Soviet natural scientists, philosophers, sociologists and political scientists exploring the interaction of society and nature, as well as the search for means of solving contemporary global problems. Such problems include: (*a*) safeguarding peace and curbing the arms race; (*b*) environmental protection; (*c*) rational use of fuel and non-fuel mineral resources; (*d*) eradication of hunger and malnutrition; (*e*) peaceful exploration of space and of the world ocean; and (*f*) bridging the gap between the developed and the developing countries.

II. Global environmental problems

The relation to nature may be considered one of the most important components of humankind's cultural heritage, which integrates the most rational ethical principles of the past with the contemporary requirements of protection and regeneration of natural resources. Despite the specificity of the cultures of different peoples—determined as they are by national traditions, moral values and political doctrines corresponding to different periods in the history of humankind—their ecological norms have very much in common. Original features of specific cultures cannot suppress the trends to the development of a universal, primarily humanistic, relation to nature.

Cultural aspects of the relation to nature are one component of a generalized system of notions about the world at large. These begin at the point where humans start to explain the essence of the universe and the values governing their lives. Thus, cultural aspects may be considered a combination of the socio-political, scientific, theoretical, philosophical, religious, moral and aesthetic orientations of an individual. One of the most important components of these aspects is the comprehension by the individual of the correlation of natural, socio-political, class and human, national and planetary, economic, ideological, moral, ethical and other factors, which transform all of humankind on the threshold of the third millennium into an integral whole.

All of these cultural aspects of a world-view are included in the concept of global problems as delineated by Soviet political and social scientists. This concept is a synthesis of the findings within the natural, technical, social and political sciences, all of which interact on an equal basis in seeking the most adequate picture of the developments in society and nature that form the global trends of transformation of humankind into an integral community. This is different from the scientific revolutions of the past, when qualitative changes were achieved as a result of 'breakthroughs' in some single basic science (e.g., physics, chemistry, biology). The scientific picture of the global problems of today, to say nothing of means to ameliorate them, can be elucidated only through wide-ranging and co-operative approaches involving many sciences and through radical changes in political outlook. The necessary revolution of today can be achieved only through a fundamental rethinking of the cultural traditions of states and peoples, which would single out primarily their common elements. The fact that current global problems have an integral structure is explained in many respects by the circumstance that the recent decades of the twentieth century have been marked by a steady growth of universal humanistic principles and norms. Indeed, the norms and principles that are growing are precisely those which find irrational the destructive interference of humans with nature and the ruinous political courses of governments capable of initiating military conflict.

Protection of the environment is ranked among the global problems as having the highest degree of complexity of external and internal interactions. Aggravation of the global environmental problem has served as an impetus for both interdisciplinary and applied research. The subject of such research has been, on the one hand, all living matter and, on the other, the progress of human society in all of its different forms of organization. The variety of forms of societal organization is responsible for the choice by various states of technical projects having opposite functions (for instance, tools and equipment designed to foster social progress as opposed to new weapon systems). There are ample grounds to consider protection of the environment the central, interconnecting link within the entire system of global problems.

It is the complexity of the global environmental problem that predetermines one of the essential peculiarities of its analysis and ultimate solution. Success in establishing harmonious relations between technology and nature will depend upon taking into proper account a much wider range than before of natural, technological, socio-economic, political, cultural and philosophical factors. All of those factors must be studied carefully, both separately and in the full complexity of their mutual connections. Both the complex internal structure and the high proportion of social and cultural aspects of the problem make the mission of environmental protection understandable and acceptable to the majority of the peoples of the world. Thus, the ecological imperative of modern times is closely linked with the imperative of safeguarding peace and limiting armaments.

Environmental protection, as well as other global problems alluded to above, has several typological characteristics. These exist on a transnational, and sometimes even planetary, scale. The need for environmental protection is acute by various criteria, all of which indicate the complexity of the problem and its danger to humanity or to the global biosphere. The need for environmental protection is universal in essence and touches upon the vital interests of humankind.

The global environmental problem has three dimensions, which embrace all the major areas of its formation and development, both in the past and in the foreseeable future. The first dimension finds its origin in the social development of contemporary civilization, divided as it is into antithetical socio-political systems. Competition and rivalry between states with different social systems not only impede the harmonization of the relation of society to nature and prevent the taking of adequate measures for protection of the environment, but also stimulate the arms race, which produces ever more elaborate and harmful means of destruction and military manipulation of the environment. The second dimension comprises the entire system of relations between humans and nature, which has already been touched upon above. The third dimension rests on the development of the humane individual, as to personality and outlook and as to the adoption of cultural values and traditions. It is the irreversible ecologization of that outlook and the steady growth of environmental consciousness of the public at large in many countries that have made the struggle for protection of the environment a focus of unity within political parties, public organizations and religious, alternative and other movements. Despite all the differences in the causes of deterioration of the global ecological situation, and the variety of practical recommendations aimed at its improvement, the watchwords in defence of the biosphere are nevertheless shared in all states by political parties, trade unions, youth organizations, alternative movements and other associations. Calls for the formulation of new ecological ethics for the protection and rational use of the natural resources of the planet have become a powerful stimulus for establishing strict governmental controls over material production and services with the aim of reducing harmful impacts on the biosphere. As far as military manipulations and intentional destructive impacts on the environment are concerned, these are ever more unequivocally recognized as inadmissible, not only in terms of cultural and ethical principles, but also within the realm of realistic politics.

Cultural approaches to the global environmental problem aimed at safeguarding the natural foundations of civilization become powerful incentives for joint action by states with different social systems. These cultural aspects also form a solid basis for bringing together the universal spiritual heritage of humankind that rejects the rationality of war as a means of solving interstate disputes. At the same time, they contribute to further strengthening constructive co-operation among states, which are not as yet members of a socially homogeneous international community even though they gravitate towards integral and united humanity in many areas of their activity.

III. The formation of ecological consciousness in the USSR

One of the essential specific features which has determined the main content and evolution of Soviet ethical principles and cultural norms in relation to nature—shared by the majority of the peoples and national minorities comprising the USSR—is severe natural conditions, far from favourable either for economic activity or for meeting the vital needs of the people, especially during the early stages of societal development. It was this circumstance, in combination with low density of population and great availability of undeveloped territories, that contributed to the choice by many peoples and national minorities of a rather restrained, 'co-existent' position in relation to nature. It is for this reason that the ecological damage that had been inflicted during previous stages in the history of the territory that now comprises the USSR is not as serious as for many other areas of the planet. Indeed, neither in the distant nor immediate past is it possible to identify an ecological disaster in the USSR resulting from natural-resource exploitation that is comparable in magnitude to catastrophes of such origin that have in the past undermined the natural foundations of society in such regions as Mesopotamia, Greece, Asia Minor or Western Europe. It was also such human action that brought about the collapse of the Mayan civilization (Deevey *et al.*, 1979) and that eliminated the bison (*Bison bison*) and caused substantial erosion on the Great Plains of the USA. The greatest damage that has been inflicted on the environment of Russia or the USSR since the sixteenth century has been the result of invasion by other states. The ecological damage experienced by the USSR during the course of World Wars I and II was far greater than that experienced by any other country on the planet.

Until the beginning of the seventeenth century the tsarist government of Russia set practically no limitation on the use of domestic natural resources. Before Peter I assumed actual control in 1689 there existed limitations only on hunting. Peter I enacted the first laws protecting wildlife. Although these legislative documents reflected the outlook of the monarchical circles that ruled Russia during that period, the legislation nevertheless was in conformity with the moral and ethical inclinations towards nature of the majority of the people, which were in accord with the cultural and religious traditions of the past, venerating nature and endowing it with supernatural qualities.

The ecological outlook embodied in the creative works of Russian philosophers, writers and artists may be considered a cultural and ethical foundation not only of an attitude of care towards nature, but also of the instigation of the first public actions in defence of natural resources. The works of Alexander Pushkin, Alexander Herzen, Feodor Dostoyevsky, Leo Tolstoy and Anton Chekhov organically combine a love of nature with a compassion for human beings. The emotional discourses upon the beauty of nature by the outstanding representatives of Russian society of the eighteenth to the beginning of the twentieth centuries are inseparable from calls for cautious treatment of natural resources, for the liberation of the popular masses and for the establishment of favourable conditions for realizing their creative abilities. Progressive scientists and cultural figures thought of the democratization of Russian society as a realistic means for the advancement of civilization, which at one and the same time requires a businesslike relation to the biosphere and the rational utilization and regeneration of its resources.

As far back as the nineteenth century, the Moscow Society of Explorers of Nature, the Petersburg and Riga Societies of Naturalists, the Russian Society for Advancement of Natural Science, Anthropology and Ethnography and the Russian Geographic Society, among others, took educational and other actions in defence of nature and pointed to the necessity of establishing natural reserves. The beginning of the twentieth century in Russia was marked by the establishment of specialized environmental protection societies which carried out education of the population in the spirit of a conservative attitude towards the natural environment. Moreover, considerable contributions to the development of cultural and aesthetic principles in relation to nature were made by such Russian composers of the past as Mikhail Glinka, Modest Moussorgsky, Peter Tchaikovsky, Nicolai Rimsky-Korsakov and Anatoly Lyadov. No less was the service to the cause of nature protection by such Russian painters as Ivan Shishkin, Arkhip Kuinji, Vasily Polenov, Ilya Repin, Vasily Surikov, Victor Vasnetsov and Isaac Levitan (Lebedev, 1977).

Development of industry in Russia, especially of mining and metallurgy, was accompanied by damage to nature in the areas of industrial concentration, although the scale of such damage was not threatening. As industrial production in Russia grew in complexity and scale, utilitarian and predatory relations towards the riches of nature did not dominate the majority of the population and never became a visible component of national philosophy or practical orientation for the major part of Russian society. In this respect the efforts of some Western researchers (e.g., Goldman, 1972) to characterize the environmental situation in the USSR as identical to that in the industrially developed capitalist countries cannot be considered as well-argued or convincing. Cultural norms in relation to the environment that exist now in the USSR have their own characteristic features, both in their origin and in their historic development. They were taken as a basis for the formulation of environmental legislation in the USSR as well as for the planning of environmental training and education. It has been because of a great attention to cultural and ethical aspects of the interaction of society and nature that the official concept of social progress in the USSR was supplemented by a fundamental thesis that the protection and rational use of natural resources are effective means of improving the natural basis of material production as well as the conditions of life for all of the Soviet people and the harmonious development of every individual.

IV. The Soviet concept of natural resource utilization

Humanistic and constructive principles in relation to nature as a bountiful source of material welfare and aesthetic values are vividly reflected in the political and philosophical doctrines of the USSR. The fundamentals of these doctrines were formulated in the classical works of Lenin. They have subsequently been developed further in the documents of the Soviet Communist Party and of the Soviet government as well as in theoretical writings of Soviet researchers. For an adequate understanding of the anti-militaristic, creative and humanistic essence of the Soviet concept of natural resource utilization it is necessary to pay special attention to the specific socio-political conditions under which the foundations of the concept were laid, as well as to make clear its connections with the principles of Soviet domestic and foreign policy.

From the viewpoint of establishing new cultural norms in relation to the environment, considerable significance must be attached to the circumstance that the first legislative action dealing with foreign policy taken by the newly established Soviet republic was the Decree of Peace, which called upon all the parties to the ongoing hostilities to sign a treaty of peace and thereby put an end to human casualties, to destruction of cultural values and to military damage to the environment. That action was followed directly by the Decree of Land, which put forward new principles of natural resource utilization: that all of the land—including its underground riches, water resources, forests and other endowments of nature—were to be declared national property and taken under the control of the state on behalf of all the people. Both of these decrees reflect not only the general principle of the unity of domestic and foreign policies, but also suggest the incompatibility of arms races and wars with the ideals of social progress; at the same time they reject as inadmissible destructive interferences with nature. Contrary to the notion espoused by some Western researchers (e.g., Hardin, 1972) that public ownership of land and other elements of the environment is ecologically irrational, the Soviet concept of nationalized natural resource utilization proves itself to meet the vital interests of humankind.

Soviet society considers the utilization of natural resources a special kind of socio-economic activity, one that is designed to meet the material and spiritual needs of all members of society, to protect and regenerate the resources of nature and to ensure as well the harmonious balance among economic development, biological stability and the aesthetic integrity of the environment. The utilization of natural resources is concentrated in the following three directions: (*a*) the production of goods and services; (*b*) international co-operation; and (*c*) education and raising of the cultural level of all members of society.

The Soviet concept of natural resource utilization contains a number of basic theses formulated and developed by Lenin, the founder of the Communist Party and the Soviet state. It was as a result of Lenin's initiative and personal participation that more than 90 laws, decrees and other normative legislative documents aimed at the protection of nature and the cautious handling of natural resources were adopted in the first years of the USSR. Lenin's broad philosophical approach to the problems of resource utilization, along with his deep respect for the traditions of the past, made it possible to ensure continuity of the principle of a cautious attitude towards nature, which had been a cultural heritage of the peoples of Russia. In this fashion, a respectful relation to nature and scientifically grounded principles of rational utilization of biospheric resources were directly linked not only with building the material foundation of a new society, but also with the ideals of a world without war and of equal and mutually beneficial relations with all other states in an integrated world economy. The protection and regeneration of the earth's natural resources are by this token recognized as common problems of all humankind. Indeed, their solution will be possible only under conditions of constructive interstate co-operation in political, socio-economic, humanitarian, cultural and other areas—all in the name of safeguarding peace as the primary prerequisite for the further progress of civilization.

Within the Soviet concept of nature utilization the following basic components can be singled out:

1. A state-wide approach to the land and all its riches, reflecting the vital interests of all the peoples and providing for the elimination of private land ownership.
2. A relation to nature as the eternal source of human welfare, with the utilization of natural resources on the basis of comprehensive scientific research into the laws of nature.
3. Compulsory planning and realization, in the course of resource utilization, of measures of protection and regeneration of natural resources for the benefit of both present and future generations.
4. Observance in relation to natural resources of the principle of continuous optimization of nature utilization, taking forceful measures to reduce anthropogenic impacts on the environment and to establish harmonious relations among society, technology and nature.
5. A 'systems' approach to natural resource utilization, taking into account the complex requirements of all aspects of the production of goods and services as well as of the interests of society concerning public health and the interests of every individual concerning comprehensive personal development.
6. Continuous environmental education and training of all members of society, taking into account cultural traditions as well as the latest scientific achievements.
7. A long-term goal of transforming the technospheric component of the biosphere of today into a noöspheric component—into a sphere of reason and common sense, which excludes non-harmonious relations with the natural environment.

The attitude of the Soviet peoples towards nature excludes support for large-scale interventions into nature. At the same time this attitude by the Soviet peoples does not accept a Rousseauistic ban on the exploitation of natural resources. The rapid and contradictory processes of the scientific and technical revolutions of today, are treated by the Soviet peoples as a basis for the rational use of natural resources and as a stimulus for comprehensive development of the peoples' culture and of their creative enthusiasm—a stimulus driven by the most humanistic ideals of harmonious interaction between humans and nature.

The Soviet system is in principle against war and military preparations. It declares disarmament as the most important condition for socio-economic progress and as a motive force for the development of equal and mutually beneficial co-operation among all states for the benefit of present and future generations. It recognizes that the military employment of science and technology, cannot be qualified as productive. The primary consequences of such activity appear to be grave damage to the vital interests of all the peoples on earth and diminution of the prospects for biospheric development.

The creative and cultural heritages of the Soviet peoples reveal a number of points of principle regarding the relations among humans, technology and nature. Technology *per se* is considered to be neutral and may be employed by any society. Major trends in technological development are heavily influenced by class interests and the structure of society. The function of technology is to serve as a connecting link between humankind and nature; but while advancing technology on the basis of the latest scientific discoveries it is always necessary to take due account of the laws of nature. By adjusting the available technology to the laws of nature, humankind contributes to the progress of civilization in harmony with the biosphere.

Change in technology is a phenomenon that is progressive in essence, one that is capable of providing human society with new instruments for the constructive transformation of nature. The Soviet concept of nature utilization follows the most progressive cultural traditions of humankind in its rejection of the necessity to perfect armaments or to perfect the means of military intervention into the natural environment. For this reason Soviet scholars oppose the thesis put forward by a number of Western philosophers and historians of science and technology that revolutionary transformations in military technology are primary determinants in the development of scientific and technological revolutions. Such conclusions lose sight of the fact that it is political decisions which give priority to the interests of military corporations and distort the implications of scientific and technological advances. Negative socio-economic consequences of activities on behalf of the arms race include damage to the biosphere; they adversely affect humankind as a whole.

In full conformity with the cultural norms of the past and present, the Soviet concept of nature utilization orients not only the peoples of the USSR, but all of humankind, towards excluding any kind of military activity from the national interests of nations and their governments. Such a concept need not clash with views regarding relations of society and nature which might be held by other states or peoples. Rather, it is aimed at finding in those other views their most rational and constructive elements, which can then be taken as a basis for joint interstate efforts for protection of the biosphere.

V. Prevention in the USSR of military threats to the environment

The Soviet concept of nature utilization ranks weapons and military equipment, alongside military production and peacetime military activities, among the sources of gravest damage to nature. That is why a limitation of armaments and the curbing of further military production, research and development, are considered the most effective means of protecting the biosphere and of establishing harmony with nature. Including environmental protection among the major contemporary global problems makes it possible to consider efforts on behalf of nature as approaches to achieving favourable conditions for political, socio-economic and cultural development of humankind as a whole. Neither the theoretical foundations nor the functional orientations in the USSR in relation to environmental activities are locally nationalistic in essence, but rather universally humanistic. The USSR provides many convincing examples by its domestic actions as well as by its approach to international relations of how the large-scale problems facing humankind can be dealt with effectively. But it would be unwise to expect that these problems could be resolved alone by the efforts of the USSR and its allies. Only purposeful efforts by every country, in combination with constructive co-operation on a global scale, will open a way towards the solution of the contemporary global problems.

The political and philosophical foundations of the new outlook must, in the view of the USSR, contribute to the positive restructuring of international relations. It is necessary for all of humankind to co-operate politically, economically, scientifically and technically as a contribution to safeguarding peace and curbing the arms race, to protecting the biosphere and to solving other large-scale global problems. Such political co-operation would also lead to an increased scale of humanitarian and cultural co-operation, a prerequisite for establishing and sharing new values and new ethics in relation to nature.

The Constitution (Fundamental Law) of the USSR contains—alongside its basic principles of peaceful foreign policy—political, socio-economic, cultural and ethical principles in relation to nature. Thus, the Soviet Fundamental Law proclaims that (USSR, 1977, art. 18): 'In the interests of the present and future generations, the necessary steps are taken in the USSR to protect and make scientific, rational use of the land and its mineral and water resources, and the plant and animal kingdoms, to preserve the purity of air and water, ensure reproduction of natural wealth, and improve the human environment.' And the Fundamental Law further proclaims that (USSR, 1977, art. 67): 'Citizens of the USSR are obliged to protect nature and conserve its riches.'

An analysis of the Soviet concept of nature utilization against a background of the global ecological situation makes it possible to single out ecological imperatives for disarmament as being among the most urgent tasks of the day. Their accomplishment—by the joint efforts of political parties, trade unions, scientific, youth and other associations working in co-operation with governments and international organizations—will make it possible to reduce direct and indirect military dangers to nature. Their solution will additionally create favourable conditions for states to take measures—individually or co-operatively—to further protect the environment and to rationally utilize natural resources.

One of the primary ecological imperatives in the Soviet view is to limit further escalation of the arms race. The arms race has reached a militarily dangerous stage, slows down socio-economic progress, widens the gap between the developed and the developing countries and increases the probability of inflicting irreversible damage to nature. A second ecological imperative is to eliminate a large array of negative qualitative and structural consequences for the world economy caused by the one-sided employment of scientific discoveries, technological innovations, material resources and labour in the non-productive military sphere. Only under such conditions would measures to protect the environment have a real chance for success.

A third ecological imperative in the Soviet view is to reduce the negative impacts on nature from industrial production and other sectors of the national economy. Military research and development prevent the full transition of industry, agriculture, energy and other branches of the economy to more rational and ecologically benign methods of operation. Military industries in capitalist countries bear a grave responsibility for the aggravation of environmental problems. Apart from the growing contribution of military industries to air and water pollution, further development of the arms race raises an insurmountable barrier to the improvement of pollution-abatement equipment and technology.

Damage to the environment and to agriculture inflicted by such peacetime military activities as combat exercises and the movement of troops grows with every passing year. Such activity by armed forces spoils the topsoil, destroys vegetation and damages the landscape, thus negatively affecting the states of the economy and of human welfare. Still another consequence for the global biosphere of peacetime militarism is the more and more frequent accidents with weapons of mass destruction.

Ecological imperatives provide a theoretical basis for the limitation of all kinds of military activity. The USSR sees in these steps towards disarmament a tangible way of protecting the biosphere and of establishing harmonious relations between society and nature. Such a perspective conforms to the interests of all the states of the world. Important in this regard was the Soviet initiative of 15 January 1986 to eliminate nuclear weapons and other weapons of mass destruction by the year 2000 (Gorbachev, 1986b). In the words of General Secretary Gorbachev, '. . . continued testing causes tremendous and perhaps not yet fully studied harm to nature, to the environment in which we all live. Do we not feel obliged to show concern for our own home? And not only for ourselves, but for our children and grandchildren?' (Gorbachev, 1986a, p. 4).

Ecological imperatives of disarmament provide for a new approach to the 'limits of growth' concept, which was first proposed by the participants in Club of Rome projects. By the early 1970s Western scientists had, primarily through global studies of population growth, demonstrated the necessity of setting limits for the scientific, technological and socio-economic development of nations. However, in Soviet eyes it seems more expedient that limits to growth be set as a consequence of the normalization of international relations and the development of universal cultural norms that exclude military manipulation of the environment (Khozin, 1977).

For a proper understanding of the specific features of joint activity by governmental bodies and public organizations in the USSR for protection of the environment it is not sufficient to become acquainted with Soviet concepts of nature utilization, of Soviet legislative norms of regulated use and protection of natural resources or of Soviet governmental activities.

The present process of restructuring going on in the USSR—the move towards greater openness—could not but affect the central problems of nature utilization. It should be especially stressed that the current change towards openness, including wide discussions of the most urgent problems of environmental protection, had been prepared by active moves by many Soviet scientists, cultural workers and representatives of the public at large. It was they who attracted nation-wide attention to the problems of Lake Baikal, of the Aral and Caspian Seas and to the probably adverse consequences of large-scale transformations of river basins. It is primarily ethical and other cultural considerations of long standing that are determining the present ecological outlook of the public at large in the USSR. Such considerations are now also receiving more and more serious consideration on the part of those—at all levels of government—who participate in the important political and economic decisions.

By way of example, in August 1986 the Political Bureau of the Soviet Central Committee examined the problems connected with the planned diversion of a part of the flow of northern and Siberian rivers to the southern areas of the country and recognized the appropriateness of ceasing all of those activities (Micklin, 1986; Pravda, 1986). Among the determinants of this decision were the calls of the public for additional detailed analyses of ecological, economic and other large-scale consequences of such an ambitious undertaking.

It was openly stated at the 27th Communist Party Congress, held in Moscow during 25 February–6 March 1986, that the Soviet system, with its plan-governed organization and humane world outlook, is quite capable of imparting harmony into the relationship between society and nature. At the same time it was openly admitted that in a number of regions of the USSR the state of the environment is alarming. Thus it is clear that the opinions of writers, cultural workers and other representatives of the public who call for a more careful treatment of the land and its mineral resources, lakes, rivers, plants and animals receive wide support from Soviet officials and from the entire Soviet people.

Literary and publicist works by such authoritative scholars as Aitmatov (1980), Frolov (1982; 1983; 1986a; 1986b), Kapitza (1981) and Zagladin (1982; 1984) make it possible to bring together cultural and philosophical aspects of ecological problems. The efforts of such individuals not only bring to the consciousness of the peoples of the USSR and other states the concept that in further speeding up the arms race the progress of civilization is rendered impossible, but also the necessity of thinking in universal humanistic terms and as well in terms of both present and future generations.

One modern Soviet poet has called for all to put aside the rifle when entering the domain of nature. The peoples of the USSR are convinced that any kind of military activity—on land, on the surface or in the depths of the ocean or in the atmosphere or outer space—poses a great danger to the environment of the planet and innumerable threats to all forms of life. The single most crucial step towards harmony between society and nature will undoubtedly be removal of the burden of lethal weapons from humankind.

VI. Conclusion

Cultural norms in relation to military manipulations of the environment have developed in the USSR not as an independent trend, but within the general process of creating the multinational Soviet community. These norms are organically incorporated into the general philosophical and political concept of Soviet society—past, present and future. Soviet society declares as its primary goals satisfaction of the material and spiritual needs of all members of society, mutually beneficial relations with all states on earth and the complete elimination of war.

The USSR considers that in the course of moving towards the higher stages of civilization, humankind will not only perfect means of production on the basis of the growing capabilities of science and technology and harmonize its relations with nature, but will at the same time improve its way of life. This belief is based on the Soviet way of life that, together with the Soviet social system, determines the relation of society to the individual. The multinational peoples of the USSR call upon all of the peoples of the earth to elaborate by joint efforts a long-term strategy for creative activity by all of humankind.

Further progress of civilization will not be smooth, nor will it be free of contradictions, difficulties, losses and catastrophes. It is nevertheless impossible to agree with some Western researchers who suggest that further employment of the newest technologies will inevitably bring to humankind new victims and new disappointments. An advanced society will have to be able to foresee any negative consequences of its technological decisions and to minimize them by means of planned action.

All the knowledge that has been accumulated by humankind throughout its long history indicates that human development is a constant struggle between the old and the new, one that creates the prerequisites for mastering a higher stage of natural and social evolution. The history of nature—which is inseparable from the history of humankind—provides ample examples of devastating catastrophes. However, the greatest catastrophes in the history of planet earth have been wars: catastrophes initiated not by nature but by nations. Use in war of ever more elaborate means of destruction makes war the most dangerous of the planetary disasters. Indeed, the consequences of modern war for humans and nature can be so devastating that some future war might well mark the end of almost all forms of life on earth.

The peoples of the USSR profess an outlook of historic optimism, based on a belief in the unlimited capabilities of the human mind and of science. Such capabilities could provide for the progress of civilization guided by the most constructive ideals of humanism and harmony with nature. Such a civilization of the future will even be able to start the practical exploration of the universe. Looking into the future, while at the same time resolving the most urgent contemporary problems of humankind, implements the most noble ideals of the thinkers of all times and peoples. As to the elements of the biosphere which would be lost in the course of natural evolution or as a result of emergency economic actions, these must be restored or else replenished by the dedicated action of a humanity concerned with the destiny of its native planet.

A prominent Soviet scientist, Academician Vladimir Vernadsky, predicted that the triumph of human reason will make it possible to put an end to the military competition that deprives states of vital forces and resources and to channel all achievements of a steadily advancing science—indeed, all human talents—to the cause of progress and creation. It was as far back as the World War II period that Vernadsky (1945, pp. 8–9) recognized that: 'The historical process is being radically changed under our very eyes. For the first time in the history of [humankind] the interests of the masses on the one hand, and the free thought of individuals on the other, determine the course of life of [humankind] and provide standards for [people's] ideas of justice. [Humankind] taken as a whole is becoming a mighty geological force. There arises the problem of the *reconstruction of the biosphere in the interests of freely thinking humanity as a single totality*.'

Thinking in terms of the universal interests of humanity in our time implies fighting for peace and for elimination of the arms race. Only under such conditions will humankind be able to advance to new heights of progress and to save for future generations this unique and beautiful planet—earth.

References

Aitmatov, C. 1980. Peace: the supreme right of mankind. *Peace & Disarmament: Academic Studies,* Moscow, 1980:160–167.

Deevey, E. S., Rice, D. S., Rice, P. M., Vaughan, H. H., Brenner, M. & Flannery, M. S. 1979. Mayan urbanism: impact on a tropical karst environment. *Science,* Washington, 206:298–306.

Frolov, I. 1982. *Global problems and the future of mankind.* Moscow: Progress Publishers, 311 pp.

Frolov, I. T. 1983. [*Perspectives of man.*] 2nd edn (in Russian). Moscow: Politizdat, 350 pp.

Frolov, I. T. (ed.). 1986a. [*Horizons of ecological knowledge: social-philosophical problems*] (in Russian). Moscow: Nauka Publishers, 204 pp.

Frolov, I. 1986b. *Man-science-humanism: a new synthesis*. Moscow: Progress Publishers, 342 pp.

Goldman, M. I. 1972. *Spoils of progress: environmental pollution in the Soviet Union.* Cambridge, Mass.: MIT Press, 372 pp.

Gorbachev, M. 1986a. March 29 talk on Soviet television. *New Times*, Moscow, 1986(14):3–5.

Gorbachev, M. 1986b. Statement. *New Times* 1986(3):1–5.

Hardin, G. 1972. *Exploring new ethics for survival: the voyage of the spaceship Beagle.* New York: Viking Press, 273 pp.

Kapitza, P. 1981. Global problems, international solutions. *Bulletin of the Atomic Scientists*, Chicago, 37(1):40–43.

Khozin, G. S. 1977. Ecological imperatives for disarmament. *Peace & the Sciences,* Vienna, 1977(4):35–44.

Lebedev, A. 1977. *The itinerants: Society for Circulating Art Exhibitions (1870–1923)*. rev. edn. Leningrad: Aurora Art Publishers, 210 pp.

Micklin, P. P. 1986. Water diversion in the Soviet Union. *Science,* Washington, 234:411.

Pravda. 1986. [In the Politburo of the Central Committee of the Communist Party of the Soviet Union.] (in Russian). *Pravda*, Moscow, 1986 (16 Aug):1.

USSR. 1977. *Constitution (Fundamental Law) of the USSR*. Moscow: USSR Supreme Soviet. [Reprinted in: Lane, D. 1978. *Politics and society in the USSR*. 2nd edn. Oxford: Martin Robertson, 622 pp.: pp. 553–584.]

Vernadsky, W. I. 1945. The biosphere and the noösphere. *American Scientist*, New Haven, 33(1):1–12.

Zagladin, V. 1982. Peace and human progress. *Peace & Disarmament: Academic Studies,* Moscow, 1982:34–50.

Zagladin, V. 1984. Working-class parties and the anti-war struggle. *Peace & Disarmament: Academic Studies,* Moscow, 1984:131–147.

4. Gender as an influence on cultural norms relating to war and the environment

VIRGINIA HELD
City University of New York

I. Introduction

Human societies are structured along various lines. Among the most fundamental are the lines of gender. Nevertheless, the gender structure of society has until recently received little attention in the study of society. Explored in this chapter are the connections between gender and cultural norms regarding war and the environment. Singled out for analysis, following the establishment of some basic premises, are the topics of mothering, of politics, of weapons and of biological gender differences as they may affect these norms. Because of the lack of attention paid to these issues in the past, often the most that can be achieved so far are suggestions for useful research. The chapter builds to some extent upon a number of prior studies (Held, 1984; 1987a; 1987b).

II. Basic premises

Gender structures and divides society more deeply and fundamentally than does class or race (Harding, 1983; Jaggar, 1983). Thus gender can be expected to be a powerful influence on cultural norms of every kind, certainly on those concerning war and the environment. What have been taken to be the cultures of nations are in reality the cultures of males (Burris, 1973; Harding, 1983). Female culture exists, but it exists 'invisibly' and in subjection to male culture.

In virtually all known societies, men have been the dominant gender. They usually organize society in hierarchical ways such that some men have more power than others. The status of a woman depends upon that of the man with whom she is associated, but remains subordinate to his. All men appear to be united in a shared relationship of dominance over their women (Hartmann, 1981), which is the crux of a patriarchal society (Thorne, 1982).

Dominant cultural attitudes towards war are shaped in conjunction with the way men come to think of themselves as men and the way they feel about their masculinity. And prevailing cultural attitudes towards nature are developed by those who seek domination over women, whom they see as being more like nature than themselves.

III. Mothering

Although a few men are gradually coming to participate somewhat more in child care, mothering is traditionally an activity conducted almost entirely by women. This section is therefore devoted primarily to the influence of female mothering on cultural norms.

Mothering gives rise in the individual who is carrying out this activity to what Ruddick (1982) refers to as 'maternal thinking'. Such thinking is governed by interests in preserving the life of the child, in nurturing the child's growth and in having the child develop in acceptable ways. According to this view, it is not female anatomy or other aspects of female biology that gives rise to the peacefulness of mothers, but rather the complicated social activity of preservative love (Ruddick, 1983). Such development of preservative love is not restricted to biological mothers, but is also attainable by other women or men engaged in mothering.

Although maternal thinking is valuable, some defects in mothering can be observed (Ruddick, 1982). For example, the urge to preserve life can lead to excessive control; and the urge to guide the child's development can be influenced by the values of the dominant (male) culture. It also appears that the fact that mothering is performed almost entirely by women can have pernicious effects on the psychological development of children (Chodorow, 1978; Dinnerstein, 1976). Nevertheless, authentic maternal thinking is incompatible with violence, military destruction and domination of nature (Ruddick, 1983).

The peaceful tendencies associated with mothering are not yet in a position to bring about less militaristic public policies in most societies, but the potential for such influence does exist. It can be suggested that for motherly peacefulness to have a public impact, maternal practice will have to be recognized for its pacifism and then extended to wider domains. A social transformation will have to be achieved so that maternal thinking is no longer denigrated, but accepted as a pervasive guide to public policy. The presumption is made that if men would take part equally in mothering (as well as in caring for the sick and old and otherwise dependent) they too would develop more peaceful tendencies.

A maternal interest in peace at the global level is not direct (Ruddick, 1983). Especially in an individualistic, hierarchical and competitive society, mothering individuals may well see the good of their own children as being in conflict with the good of other children elsewhere. However, mothers can come to understand that the good of their own children is interrelated with the good of other children, for example, that a world at war would be a disaster for all children. Some tension between a concern for one's own children and that for all children will never disappear, but in a less hierarchical society such tension could be minimized.

In defence of maternal thinking, it must be emphasized that peacefulness is not at all the same as surrender or as complicity in being overpowered. Peacefulness involves a commitment to non-violence, not to the avoidance of all conflict. Necessary battles are to be fought non-violently and with the aim of reconciliation and the restoration of a sense of community (Deming, 1984, pp. 177–80). Maternal practice and its norms thus differ from military practice and its norms in that the latter accepts violence to achieve its aims, and also in that the latter places a higher value on victory than on reconciliation.

Conflict is a part of everyday maternal reality. Those who have taken on the responsibility of mothering routinely engage in battles with their children, with the other adults in the home and with the outside world. They also become involved in their children's battles with each other and with playmates and neighbours. But maternal practice involves a non-destructive and non-violent—that is to say, pacifistic—approach to the resolution of these conflicts. Even when such pacifistic behaviour is not achieved in the practice of mothering, it remains the fundamental criterion of maternal thinking (Held, 1987b; Ruddick, 1983). At the same time, when force is considered genuinely and inescapably necessary to defend the safety of children, mothers can be as resolute in using it as the situation requires. This observation is not inconsistent with the notion that women (the predominant motherers) tend to seek peace more firmly and patiently than do men (Brock-Utne, 1985).

Thus, the experience of women, and particularly of mothers, seems to be especially suitable as the basis of non-violent resistance, both in theory and in practice. Although the use of non-violent pressure may not always succeed against violence, it has been suggested that at least in the long run the casualties will be fewer through a non-violent approach (Deming, 1984). A major hindrance to the use of non-violent techniques seems to be the difficulty that men have in renouncing violence while still feeling manly.

IV. Politics

Men routinely use violence in their relations with each other, depersonalizing the violence rather than eliminating it (Stiehm, 1984). It is clear that the use of organized force—whether that of the outlaw, of the revolutionary or of a government—is a male problem. Sexism and the war system may arise from the same set of authoritarian and competitive constructs (Ås, 1982; Reardon, 1985). The profile of men who abuse women is similar to that of soldiers; this may be a deliberate and necessary similarity (Roberts, 1983). Indeed, military combat training uses woman-hating as part of its method of turning men into soldiers, a process in which the individual must learn to dehumanize other people and make them into targets (Enloe, 1983; Roberts, 1984).

The conceptualization of politics for the past 2500 years can be interpreted as an extension of the male barracks community of the ancient Greek warrior-heroes (Hartsock, 1982). Ever since the Athens of fifth century BC, politics has been constructed as a community of males united in opposition to supposedly threatening female forces. The forces thought to be threatening the masculine world have taken such different forms in different periods of history as 'the

Furies', as 'Fortuna' and, more recently, as 'Nature'; but throughout, such forces have been seen as female and as something men should conquer.

If, indeed, politics is an extension of the barracks community and composed of masculine fear of women and hostility towards them, then the equal participation of women in the political community requires either of two alternatives: (*a*) women must become warriors also; or (*b*) the nature of the political community must change. The first alternative is unacceptable to most women. The second alternative would require profound changes in the theory and conduct of politics. Among other things, there would have to be deep changes in the masculine hostility towards the female (Hartsock, 1982).

It is no argument against the views of the violent, anti-feminine and anti-environmental status of politics just put forth that some women are as militaristic as many men or that a few women have become the leaders of nations. Lone women are not allowed entry into the male domain of political life unless they learn its ways and are willing to follow them.

It is often suggested that men use violence against other men in order to protect women and children from harm. Such a notion is belied by the observation that in societies where much violence occurs among men, much violence is also used by the men against women (Roberts, 1983; 1984). Such violence against women, which includes the sexual abuse of girls, wife battering and rape, is widely accepted among men and to a substantial degree socially condoned. It would be highly useful—and feasible—to answer the empirical questions of whether societies which are able to curb domestic violence are more likely to be peaceful towards their neighbours, and whether less militaristic societies are also better at controlling male violence towards women.

Men and women appear to approach moral problems differently (Gilligan, 1982; Held, 1987a; Roberts, 1984). Males are trained to think abstractly, to strip problems from their contexts, to dissociate feeling from thinking and to rationalize. Such training provides both a moral and an emotional insulation that makes violence at any level more comfortable. It is thus important that there has been a growing understanding in recent years of the contribution that women should be making to the political process and to the search for peace. Thus, during the course of three United Nations conferences on women—in 1975 at Mexico City, in 1980 at Copenhagen and in 1985 at Nairobi—there was a progression from merely recognizing that opportunities should exist for women to take part in peace negotiations to the recognition that women might have a distinctive perspective and special contribution to make both in framing the issues concerning peace and in recommending solutions (Brock-Utne, 1986). It was ultimately seen to be insufficient to merely fit women into the international structures that have led to arms races and to international conflicts. It was also felt necessary to deal with the connections between violence against women and violence between nations, and to develop feminist approaches to non-violent conflict resolution that would find application at all levels.

Contemporary lamentations about the declines of authority and of the social order may well be indications of declines only of the conceptual order of the barracks community and of masculine supremacy. Far from being a cause for despair, such changes should be thought of as an exhilarating renewal, as women engage in the process of rebuilding almost everything.

V. Weapons and war

The visual similarity between missiles, guns and shells and an erect penis must certainly have an effect on cultural attitudes. Analogies between the penis and weapons seem to be deeply embedded in the male psyche. The English word 'vagina' is from the Latin word for scabbard or sheath. To conceptualize female genitalia in this way presumes a conceptualization of the male genitalia as a weapon. A synonym in Polish for the penis is the word for sword. Indeed, few images are as culturally familiar as that of the penis as weapon.

The acceptance by men of nuclear weapons may reflect inadequate male sexuality, a continuing need to prove virility and a primitive fascination with killing (Caldicott, 1986). The launching of a nuclear missile can be seen as a sexual event that is to reach its climax in an almighty orgasm. The men involved in planning nuclear-weapon systems, the men who develop strategic nuclear doctrines and the military men who deal with nuclear weapons all lace their discussions with sexual imagery (Caldicott, 1986; Cohn, 1987). At the same time, they use terms and perform actions which serve to domesticate their instruments of terror, as when they affectionately pat their missiles (Cohn, 1987).

Women are widely cast in the role of the protected, often being excluded from military service and almost always being excluded from combat. Although many men also do not engage in combat or even take part in military service, they are nevertheless able to identify with those men who do carry out these functions. Even though the protection that can be provided today is largely mythical, masculine identity remains tied to the image of protector, female identity to the image of protected. This serves to undermine a young man's hesitation to engage in violence and military pursuits, and to discourage women from seeking to protect themselves instead of relying on others (Stiehm, 1982).

The military sector plays a central role in the ideology of patriarchy because of the notion that combat is fundamental to the development of manhood and of male superiority (Enloe, 1983, pp. 13–14). Such connections lead to the militarization of society. Only in combat lies the ultimate test of man's masculinity; to be prepared for combat a soldier must be stripped of all his feminine attributes. And, being in possession of nuclear weapons, men attain a position comparable to that of a god: in possession of the power to destroy the earth.

Thus, the weapons of manhood seem to have reached their ultimate absurdity. But will males—who are socialized from childhood to be willing to use force, violence and destruction to achieve manhood—be able to recognize this?

VI. Biological gender differences

Given that the attitudes of men and women towards war may differ, the question arises of whether such gender differences reflect biological differences rather than social influences. To the extent that biological factors may be significant, they may affect the ways men and women value particular children (Held, 1987a). This, in turn, would affect their attitudes towards war and its potential or actual victims.

It is generally agreed by both men and women that all human beings have intrinsic value or worth and that in some sense any human life is irreplaceable. Although men and women may share a desire or an instinctive tendency to wish to reproduce—and even to have such a desire in equal measure—their attitudes towards a given child might nevertheless be very different. A mother has a greater biological stake in an existing child than a father because for her that offspring represents perhaps one-twentieth of all the children she could have, whereas for him the child represents only one in many hundreds (at least in his fantasy) that he could produce. Once having given birth to a child, the mother has already contributed many weeks of effort as well as considerable pain and danger, whereas the father has so far contributed only a few painless minutes.

Thus, since the father's biological contribution to the production of a child is far more readily replaceable than that of the mother's, it might be conjectured that the man will value his offspring proportionately less than the woman will value hers. Moreover, the value a man attaches to children would seem to be even further reduced in times of war because of his added opportunities for procreation—often, it has been reported, touted in war propaganda—through the raping of the enemy's women and through the sexual rewards awaiting his return home (Huston, 1982).

If it can, indeed, be established that the differing attitudes of men and women towards war are to a substantial extent grounded in biological differences, the question then arises of how to counteract the implied genetic deficiencies of men. To begin with, there should be societal encouragement for men to engage in mothering activities. Next, men could be required by law to do enough caring service to compensate for what may be their natural indifference towards children.

VII. The environment

Prior to the sixteenth century, there had existed a reluctance to violate nature, the earth being seen as a generative mother (Merchant, 1980). During the sixteenth century, earlier warnings against cleaving or otherwise injuring the earth continued to provide a considerable level of constraint on the disruption of nature. However, by the time of the seventeenth century sexual metaphors regarding the environment burgeoned: nature had come to be seen as a female to be dominated. Instead of earth as nurturing mother, the dominant imagery became that of earth as woman in need of being mastered (Merchant, 1980, pp. 170–89). In subsequent centuries, the image of nature as woman was overwhelmed by nature as device. The environment came to be imagined as a non-living mechanistic entity, which served to legitimate the destruction of nature altogether.

It has in recent years been suggested that important connections exist between the oppression of women by men on the one hand, and the way in which men dominate and misuse the environment on the other (Warren, 1987). Indeed, it is suggested that neither of these types of subordination can be comprehended without recognizing that they are embedded within a patriarchal framework and without understanding their connections.

It is important that women become involved in the interaction between humankind and nature. Women tend to think in more relational and holistic ways than is characteristic for men (Gilligan, 1982), and their experience is more shaped by caring. The perspective of mothering as it would develop in a non-patriarchal society is clearly a more promising one for the promotion of ecological concern than the extant perspective. Moreover, such specific environmental concerns as population growth are best seen in the context of gender: the most effective approach to this problem is to give women control over their reproductive capacities on the one hand and to improve their social and economic conditions on the other.

In short, it is suggested that if the patriarchal structure that today divides society into masculine and feminine could be transformed into a co-operative and co-equal arrangement, then conditions would not only be far more suitable for all human beings, but it can be further expected that the relation between humankind and its environment would become far more harmonious.

VIII. Conclusion

It is clear from the foregoing that the structure of society with reference to gender exerts at least some influence on cultural norms relating to war and the environment. It is therefore recommended that a considerable amount of energy be devoted to elucidating the connections between gender and societal attitudes towards war and the environment.

Women have long practised non-violent conflict resolution in their family lives (Stiehm, 1982); and they have long been active, and outstandingly so, in a wide variety of peace activities (Brock-Utne, 1985). It may well turn out that gender structure is the single most relevant feature of social life to be changed in order to reduce the risks of war and of environmental disaster. Perhaps the developing of feminist points of view, both at national and international levels, would contribute more to genuine national and international security than could any further expansion of arms. And feminist approaches to nature would seem to be similarly beneficial to environmental protection.

The more that is understood about the cultural norms of men and women linking gender, war and the environment, the greater is the hope for a transformation of society into a truly human society rather than a merely male one. Such a transformation would bring with it an understanding of how to overcome violence rather than admire it, and how to nurture the environment rather than rape it.

References

Ås, B. 1982. Materialistic view of men's and women's attitudes towards war. *Women's Studies International Forum*, Oxford, 5:355–364. [Reprinted in: Stiehm, J. H. (ed.). 1983. *Women and men's wars.* Oxford: Pergamon Press, 379 pp.: pp. 355–364.]

Brock-Utne, B. 1985. *Educating for peace: a feminist perspective.* New York: Pergamon Press, 175 pp.

Brock-Utne, B. 1986. *Development of the peace and peace education concepts through three UN women decade conferences.* Oslo: International Peace Research Institute, PRIO Working Paper No. 1/86, 25 pp.

Burris, B. 1973. Fourth world manifesto. In: Koedt, A., Levine, E. & Rapone, A. (eds). *Radical feminism.* New York: Quadrangle Books, 424 pp. + 12 pl.: pp. 322–357.

Caldicott, H. 1986. *Missile envy: the arms race and nuclear war.* rev. edn. New York: Bantam Books, 346 pp.

Chodorow, N. 1978. *Reproduction of mothering: psychoanalysis and the sociology of gender.* Berkeley: University of California Press, 263 pp.

Cohn, C. 1987. Sex and death in the rational world of defense intellectuals. *Signs*, Chicago, 12:687–718.

Deming, B. 1984. *We are all part of one another: a Barbara Deming reader* [ed. by J. Meyerding]. Philadelphia: New Society Publishers, 295 pp.

Dinnerstein, D. 1976. *Mermaid and the minotaur: sexual arrangements and human malaise.* New York: Harper & Row, 288 pp.

Enloe, C. H. 1983. *Does khaki become you?: the militarization of women's lives.* London: Pluto Press, 262 pp.

Gilligan, C. 1982. *In a different voice: psychological theory and women's development.* Cambridge, Mass.: Harvard University Press, 184 pp.

Harding, S. 1983. Why has the sex/gender system become visible only now? In: Harding, S. & Hintikka, M. B. (eds). *Discovering reality: feminist perspectives on epistemology, metaphysics, methodology, and philosophy of science.* Dordrecht: D. Reidel, 332 pp.: pp. 311–324.

Hartmann, H. 1981. Unhappy marriage of Marxism and feminism: towards a more progressive union. In: Sargent, L. (ed.). *Women and revolution: a discussion of the unhappy marriage of Marxism and feminism.* London: Pluto Press, 373 pp.: pp. 1–41.

Hartsock, N. 1982. Barracks community in Western political thought: prolegomena to a feminist critique of war and politics. *Women's Studies International Forum*, Oxford, 5:283–286. [Reprinted in: Stiehm, J. H. (ed.). 1983. *Women and men's wars.* Oxford: Pergamon Press, 379 pp.: pp. 283–286.]

Held, V. 1984. *Rights and goods: justifying social action.* New York: Free Press, 327 pp.

Held, V. 1987a. Feminism and moral theory. In: Kittay, E. F. & Meyers, D. T. (eds). *Women and moral theory.* Totowa, New Jersey: Rowman & Littlefield, 325 pp.: pp. 111–128.

Held, V. 1987b. Non-contractual society: the post-patriarchal family as model. *Canadian Journal of Philosophy,* Edmonton, Alberta, 13(supple.): forthcoming.

Huston, N. 1982. Tales of war and tears of women. *Women's Studies International Forum*, Oxford, 5:271–282. [Reprinted in: Stiehm, J. H. (ed.). 1983. *Women and men's wars*. Oxford: Pergamon Press, 379 pp.: pp. 271–282.]

Jaggar, A. M. 1983. *Feminist politics and human nature.* Totowa, New Jersey: Rowman & Allanheld, 408 pp.

Merchant, C. 1980. *Death of nature: women, ecology, and the scientific revolution.* San Francisco: Harper & Row, 348 pp.

Reardon, B. A. 1985. *Sexism and the war system.* New York: Teachers College Press, 111 pp.

Roberts, B. 1983. No safe place: the war against women. *Our Generation,* Montreal, 15(4):7–26.

Roberts, B. 1984. Death of machothink: feminist research and the transformation of peace studies. *Women's Studies International Forum*, Oxford, 7:195–200.

Ruddick, S. 1982. Maternal thinking. In: Thorne, B. & Yalom, M. (eds). *Rethinking the family: some feminist questions.* New York: Longman, 246 pp.: pp. 76–94.

Ruddick, S. 1983. Preservative love and military destruction: some reflections on mothering and peace. In: Trebilcot, J. (ed.). *Mothering: essays in feminist theory.* Totowa, New Jersey: Rowman & Allanheld, 336 pp.: pp. 231–262.

Stiehm, J. H. 1982. The protected, the protector, the defender. *Women's Studies International Forum*, Oxford, 5:367–376. [Reprinted in: Stiehm, J. H. (ed.). 1983. *Women and men's wars.* Oxford: Pergamon Press, 379 pp.: pp. 367–376.]

Stiehm, J. H. 1984. The man question. In: Stiehm, J. H. (ed.). *Women's views of the political world of men.* Dobbs Ferry, NY: Transnational Publishers, 231 pp.: pp. 205–223.

Thorne, B. 1982. Feminist rethinking of the family: an overview. In: Thorne, B. & Yalom, M. (eds). *Rethinking the family: some feminist questions.* New York: Longman, 246 pp.: pp. 1–24.

Warren, K. J. 1987. Feminism and ecology: making connections. *Environmental Ethics*, Athens, Georgia, 9:3–20.

5. The special challenge of our time: cultural norms relating to nuclearism

RICHARD A. FALK
Princeton University

I. Introduction

The connection between cultural norms and environmental protection is elusive, complex and almost totally unexplored. However, it is clear that the main flow of cultural energy in the West has been in the direction of unconditional destruction of the environment. Indeed, the New Testament book of the Revelation to John prophesizes the end of the world, relying on imagery that suggests an apocalypse. Fundamentalist interpretations go so far as to affirm the inevitability of a nuclear apocalypse as reflecting the will of god; and, accordingly, as a fate futile, and possibly even sinful, to resist. More broadly, this underlying apocalyptic expectation helps to explain the relative passivity of contemporary Western societies to the prospect of nuclear catastrophe.

The argument of this chapter is that restraints upon reliance on nuclear weaponry are vitally important to environmental stability and quality. As such, any contribution to the delegitimation of nuclear weaponry is a contribution to the overall protection of the environment in relation to military activities. Following the establishment of a basic orientation to the subject of nuclearism—that is, of the corpus of attitudes towards the nuclear arms race, nuclear proliferation and nuclear war—the chapter continues with discussions of relevant legal and cultural norms and how these might be strengthened. The presentation builds upon a number of past examinations of the subject (Falk, 1983a; 1983b; 1984; 1986a; 1986b; Lifton & Falk, 1982).

II. A basic orientation

There is an important body of literature that associates underlying attitudes and images of physical reality to the unfolding of an autonomous technology in a manner harmful to nature (Merchant, 1980; Winner, 1977). Nuclear weapons are the culmination of trends, initiated centuries ago, that build on evolving societal capabilities to produce more and more destructive technologies. The use of atomic bombs at the close of World War II, in order to assure a decisive and punitive defeat for Japan, suggests the overall willingness of governments to destroy in war whatever might contribute to the realization of state goals. That is, the diplomacy underlying war is unconditional. The only ethos that is generally respected is one devoted to victory at a cost that does not substantially weaken the resource base of the prevailing side. Such a view of military necessity gives the state a mandate to regard national security as an absolute. Nothing is rejected out of hand: not the mass destruction of unarmed civilians; not even the total destruction of life-sustaining biospheric stability.

This prevailing drift of technology, war and cultural identity is not the entire story. An ethic of limits and restraints operates at the same time, serving as a counterweight to the sheer calculations of power. Law, morality and prudence introduce some sources of constraint that have become significant. Even the state absolutists are rationalists in a framework that relates means to ends. Reactions to atrocities, massacres and threats to survival suggest that the major world cultures may, in fact, be getting ready to act defiantly so as to break the momentum of nuclearism.

The cultural norms in the West regarding the environment are complemented by pre-modern and non-Western traditions. Much support exists within these latter traditions to regard nature as sacred. It is not unreasonable to believe that the non-Western cultural traditions, with their more participatory view of the connections between humankind and nature, might mobilize against nuclear weapons as legitimate instruments of conflict (Kothari, 1984; Nandy, 1984). Indeed, such a posture has been struck by many Third World governments over the years, within the United Nations and elsewhere. Of course, counter-trends also exist in non-Western societies that emphasize the assimilation of the full plenum of Western attitudes and beliefs as a necessary pre-condition for modernization and, with it, prosperity and power. But the enthusiasm for such modernization has dimmed in many non-Western societies, partly as a consequence of some severe environmental disruptions that have been associated with modern technologies. The accidents that occurred in Bhopal, India in December 1984 (Bowonder *et al.*, 1985) and Chernobyl, USSR in April 1986 (Hohenemser *et al.*, 1986) have made a strong impact on social and political consciousness in many countries.

Any use of nuclear weapons entails environmental disruption to some degree. The large-scale use of such weapons threatens severe environmental damage, perhaps of a long-range character (Pittock *et al.*, 1985–86). It is possible to interpret recent concern over the health effects and environmental disruption associated with all aspects of nuclear weaponry as beginning to give rise to global cultural norms against nuclearism. The recent anti-nuclear-weapon stand of New Zealand is illustrative of this development (Anderton, 1986), as is the six-nation nuclear-weapon test-ban initiative of August 1986 (Goldblat, 1987, pp. 391–92).

III. Legal norms

An increasing consensus exists among legal scholars that all, or at least most, threats and uses of nuclear weapons violate existing standards of international law (Builder & Graubard, 1982; Falk, 1983b; Miller & Feinrider, 1984;

Weston, 1983). Bolstering such a view is a series of resolutions by the United Nations General Assembly, going back to 1961, declaring that any threat or use of such weapons is prohibited.

It must be noted that the prohibition on use, or threat of use, of nuclear weapons does not forbid their possession or development; nor is it clear whether retaliatory use in response to a prior nuclear attack would be illegal. For example, the USA, the United Kingdom and France all maintain the view that nuclear weapons are not illegal *per se* unless explicitly prohibited by treaty (Falk, 1975). They argue that legality can be assessed only after a use of such weapons, doing so by reference to the traditional criteria of military necessity and to the customary rules of international law that forbid indiscriminate, disproportionate or inhumane weapons and tactics. The USSR and China have subscribed to no-first-use positions, thereby giving implicit approval to possession and retaliatory use. Moreover, a number of nations—India, Israel, Pakistan and South Africa among them—seem to be reserving their nuclear-weapon options.

Two broad conclusions emerge from the foregoing discussion: (*a*) that the legal condemnation of nuclear weapons is controversial and incomplete, as well as ineffectual with respect to several governments that currently rely on nuclear weapons to uphold their national security; and (*b*) that a legal prohibition of use cannot assure environmental protection as long as the rights of possession and development exist and retaliatory options are retained.

IV. From legal norms to cultural norms

Existing patterns of cultural norms generally work against a policy of environmental protection against nuclear weapons. However, if certain currently marginal cultural norms could be strengthened, this would improve the climate of respect for the existing legal norms against nuclear weapons. Public pressures for more comprehensive and effective restraints would then increase.

The link between legal norms and cultural norms is not an obvious one and can differ widely from nation to nation. By way of example, in India the urban traffic laws are largely ignored both by the public and the authorities. In Canada, on the other hand, there is a great deference shown to such laws by all of the concerned parties.

A similar circumstance pertains in international political life. The existence of a treaty rule may or may not point to a pattern of compliance at the level of practice, or of a retaliatory response in the event of a detected violation. The existence of a legal rule is not by itself very important unless it generates strong spontaneous patterns of compliance. This is particularly important in relation to the law of war and peace. In general, structures of compliance are only operative where relatively strong reciprocal interests are perceived to exist. For instance, rules protecting prisoners of war tend to be upheld if the belligerents perceive themselves as equal. Compliance is less common if ethnic differences exist between the belligerents or if each side views the other as an illegitimate belligerent.

The proscription of weaponry is an especially problematic area of international law, especially where one side perceives an advantage arising out of use, or even where the armed services of one side are bureaucratically committed to a certain line of tactics. For example, the US Air Force can mount great pressure within governmental bureaucracies to bomb despite studies casting grave doubts on the military effectiveness of most past bombing campaigns.

Nuclear weapons present very formidable problems from these points of view. The policies governing their use are closely held state secrets. There is no overt procedure to guide and shape these policies. The possessors of nuclear weapons do not accept the authority of those organs that have so far condemned as illegal nuclear weaponry and much of the associated strategic doctrine.

Strengthening the legal régime after the fact of use is not a satisfactory approach because of the feared magnitude of devastation, even in the event of limited use. Furthermore, the effort to mobilize a legal régime of prohibition has not been very specific about its concern about environmental effects. Indeed, the relevant literature on international law is relatively insensitive to environmental concerns (Miller & Feinrider, 1984). For example, it is often accepted that the employment of nuclear weapons against a naval concentration on the high seas might be a legal use because there would not be inevitable large-scale damage to civilians. However, there is no consideration of whether marine ecosystems might be severely damaged; or, if so, whether this could be put forward as a legal objection.

Two possibilities of a mutually reinforcing character emerge. The first possibility is that the reach of legal prohibition should be extended to forbid weaponry that is calculated to have, or cannot avoid having, seriously disruptive environmental impacts. Such an extension of international legal consciousness might alter, possibly in a decisive form, the debate about whether there are ever legal grounds for the use of these weapons; and, if verification can be considered reliable, whether even their possession is tolerable. The second possibility is to accept that the existing legal régime on nuclear weapons is a comprehensive one, but to recognize that it must be reinforced socio-culturally to be elevated from nominal law to effective law. In this latter setting, effectiveness would be a matter of action from below, by popular movements that act as vehicles for transnational normative opinion.

As with cultural norms generally, there is no assurance that the overall effects of the suggested changes will be positive. The embrace of apocalyptic destinies, the acceptance that the other side is evil and the mandate to use destructive violence in the service of perceived good all work against restraint, whether legal or otherwise, in human affairs. This is aggravated in the setting of war where the cultural norms associate security with military prowess and virtue with victory. Nuclearism is so dangerous partly because *it is* sanctioned by the most relevant and powerful cultural norms, thereby being so difficult to overcome by legal prohibition or even by moral argument.

Yet there are some cultural norms that, if strengthened, could move society away from nuclearism. There is, above all, the submission of war itself to the discipline of instrumental rationality. For nuclear weaponry this discipline has produced a growing consensus that these weapons are never usable, indeed, that they are not even military weapons in a true sense (McNamara, 1983–84; 1986). The trouble is that notions of deterrence have come rushing to the rescue of nuclear weaponry, especially given the alleged irrationality of trust in an anarchic world of antagonistic sovereign states (Carnesale *et al.*, 1983; Mandelbaum, 1979; 1982; 1983; Nye, 1986).

Deterrence, in whatever form, provides the least objectionable scenario, and becomes the apotheosis of the rationalist's attempt to adapt to nuclearism: the *only* role of nuclear weapons is to *threaten* unacceptable destruction in the service of a policy designed to maximize the prevention of nuclear war. Such an approach is defended 'rationally' by the claim that peace has been achieved among major states and in Europe since 1945 despite severe conflict; and, further, that conventional warfare would be a very horrifying experience given the technology and deployment of existing non-nuclear weaponry. Thus has the perverting of rationality been disguised from the public (Lifton, 1979).

The image of nuclear rationality has been under attack from several distinct directions, and has been powerfully challenged. One significant challenge has been from mainstream religion. In the USA, the National Conference of Catholic Bishops, in an important pastoral letter on war and peace, has disputed the bland assumptions of nuclear deterrence from the perspective of the just-war framework, questioning both the character of nuclear violence and its disproportionateness (National Conference, 1983). Yet even this letter acknowledges the conditional acceptability of limited forms of retaliatory deterrence during a period of dedicated quest for a reliable means for moving towards a world without nuclear weapons.

Another source of challenge to nuclearism in recent years has been from professional groups, for example, groups of physicians and of lawyers. This challenge, which has been international in scope, has generally been limited to a containment of the arms race, not characteristically insisting upon an abandonment of deterrence.

A further challenge to nuclearism has been closely related to the transnational feminist surge. Women have been at the forefront of many peace-movement activities, arguing that war and nuclearism are expressions of an abusive patriarchal structure of society (Caldicott, 1986; McAllister, 1982). Some lines of feminist philosophy also embody a concept of the sacredness of the earth, thereby further resisting nuclearism, as a cause of enduring damage to nature. The women who have protested the deployment of US cruise missiles in the United Kingdom give expression to this multidimensional challenge to nuclearism (Cook & Kirk, 1983).

Yet the various normative reactions just catalogued seem to lack the capacity to overcome nuclearism in the near future. The state structures now in place, with their militaristic assumptions, have been able to dominate the debate about rationality. And even the champions of anti-nuclearism rest most of their case on anthropocentric consequences, not on any intrinsic or separable deference to the worth or sacredness of the environment (Stone, 1987). Nature remains in this critical sense incidental, even in the struggle against nuclearism. Ecological effects are described merely to emphasize the intolerable situation—even the impossibility of human existence—in a post-apocalyptic setting.

V. Towards a strengthening of anti-nuclear norms

Cultural norms act in complicated, ambiguous ways. The central question is thus posed as to whether constructive intervention is possible to strengthen cultural dispositions against the environmental risks and damage that could result from nuclearism. There is, in fact, some revulsion against nuclearism because it threatens the miracle of life and beauty on the planet even quite apart from any preoccupation with the human species. Nevertheless, deference to environmental quality as a source of restraint does not at this time seem separable from the overall effort to avoid nuclear war and the arms race. Hence, the topic needs to be mainly conceived indirectly. This implies that attention be given primarily to counter-nuclearist pressures regardless of whether they are explicitly concerned with the new environmental factor; or, as is more likely, whether they concentrate on the subject of human survival or well-being.

From the perspective of constructive intervention, then, those factors that discourage the arms race or dependence on nuclear weapons will have the secondary benefit of making environmental quality more secure. Mobilizing cultural norms to serve these goals is a neglected dimension of social policy. The main criterion of benefit here is what set of feasible policies most diminishes the prospects of major war being fought with nuclear weapons. A secondary concern is the avoidance of any use of nuclear weapons whatsoever (even for testing), whether deliberately or inadvertently, given the extant stockpiles, doctrines and safety practices.

Discussed below are four factors to be considered in the struggle against environmental disruption from nuclearism: (*a*) new social movements; (*b*) a shift in the balance of legitimacy; (*c*) an ethos of non-co-operation and resistance; and (*d*) nuclear disengagement.

For purposes of clarity, the focus here is narrowed to environmental protection from the hostile use of nuclear weapons. Threats of use—although troublesome from other perspectives (Lifton & Falk, 1982; Thompson, 1980)—are not damaging to the environment; nor, essentially, is possession or research. Even the environmental disruption from the testing of nuclear weapons is usually quite circumscribed, especially in the forms this now takes. Moreover, prospects for environmental disruption by the hostile use of nuclear weapons must be assessed in relation to the existing arsenals and to the arms race in progress. They must also take into consideration the possibility that dangers of such use might actually rise as the size of nuclear arsenals is decreased (Mandelbaum, 1977). Another problem arises from the impossibility of evaluating definitively the several contrasting lines of risk assessment. There are those who contend that the proliferation of nuclear weapons is inevitable, that it will even extend to non-governmental political groups, including those relying on terrorism, and that the maximum inhibition on the further spread of nuclear weapons is desirable. Conversely, there is the view that proliferation actually enhances overall stability, decreasing the prospects of the use of nuclear weapons (Waltz, 1981). However, the general consensus on this issue appears to be that the more fingers there are on the nuclear trigger, the more destabilized will the situation become.

New social movements

Various transnational social movements exist that are bearers of at least some ecological values: (*a*) the environmental movement itself; (*b*) the movement for the protection of indigenous peoples; (*c*) the overall women's movement; (*d*) the peace movement; and (*e*) the movement for human rights. These social initiatives overlap to a considerable degree, but they all have the effect of questioning the war system, statist priorities and technological momentum. Especially, the rise to recent prominence of indigenous people has brought with it a renewed appreciation of pre-modern cultures, and their specific wisdom regarding the human dependence on nature. Alongside the pre-modern have emerged the contours of a post-modern possibility associated with an extension of ecological priorities to all modes of existence, in what is coming to be referred to as 'deep ecology' (Devall & Sessions, 1985).

These several developments are potentially significant for the struggle against nuclearism. The increasing challenge being directed at modernism suggests an increasing influence for a cluster of cultural norms that find the reliance on nuclear weapons to be an intolerable social practice, expressive of unacceptable attitudes towards war, state power and technology.

A shift in the balance of legitimacy

The normative repudiation of nuclearism in recent years by physicians, lawyers, clergy, artists and even professional military personnel suggests a shift in the balance of legitimacy of nuclearism. It is a clear indication of the existence of cultural reinforcement for restrictive attitudes on the acceptability (and legality) of nuclear weaponry. However, the effects of such a shift can be perverse. The US government has proposed an escalation of nuclearism, in the form of a so-called strategic defense initiative, apparently in large part in order to deflect these emerging normative criticisms. Nevertheless, on balance there has been a normative turn against nuclear weapons during the past decade.

The anti-nuclear turn has been given greater immediacy as a result of recent initiatives by the Soviet government for achieving a world without nuclear weapons (Gorbachev, 1986; 1987). It has also been reinforced by the proposal of a number of prominent former US officials for the USA to shift its nuclear-weapon policy at least to one of no-first-use (Bundy *et al.*, 1981–82; Kennan, 1983; McNamara, 1986). Thus, there are some indications that the pro-nuclearist consensus is beginning to dissolve, and to do so in such a way as to challenge the institution of war itself.

An ethos of non-co-operation and resistance

The conflict between conscience and respect for political authority goes back at least as far as Sophocles's depiction of the refusal by Antigone to obey Creon in ancient Thebes. More recently, this conflict has been brought into sharp relief and extended by the post-World War II Nuremberg trials (Falk, 1986b). In prosecuting the defeated leaders of Germany (and, in the parallel trials at Tokyo, also those of Japan) the generalized concept was established that observance of the laws of war and peace takes precedence over an individual's duty to obey the laws of his or her state. Indeed, upholding the Nuremberg principles became established as the overarching duty of citizenship.

The change in normative climate initiated at Nuremberg has had a significant effect on the acceptance by individuals of governmental authority, reinforcing traditions of resistance based upon personal conscience or religious conviction. For example, hundreds of people in the USA have in recent years protested the testing or deployment of nuclear weapons, and have as a result been arrested and prosecuted. The impulse to protest has been especially strong when the nuclear efforts have been perceived as having first-strike (non-retaliatory) properties (Aldridge, 1983).

The critical relevance of such protests to cultural norms should be evident. The protests are an expression of warning—a normative challenge—that nuclearist patterns are encroaching upon society to an unacceptable degree. In such circumstances, more moderate tendencies are given the opportunity to help create the political space for denuclearizing moves on the part of government. The ferment from below creates fissures among leaders and within bureaucratic structures. This permits a transformative process by which the overall relationship between the state and its civil society is reversed, especially with respect to such salient dimensions as nuclearism and environmental protection. But one must not underestimate the pro-deterrence backlash that views as disquieting even the endorsement of an ultimate goal of a world free of nuclear weapons (Schlesinger, 1986–87).

Nuclear disengagement

For several decades the states associated with one superpower or the other went along with the nuclear implications of their relationship. The serious early effort at nuclear disengagement by Japan was regarded as a special case because of that nation's 'nuclear allergy' as a deferred symptom of the Hiroshima and Nagasaki experiences.

More recently, however, a number of opposition political parties—and even some elected governments—have tried to pursue a policy of nuclear disengagement. The refusal by New Zealand to permit entry into its territorial waters of naval vessels that were or might be armed with nuclear weapons provoked a crisis within the Pacific Security (ANZUS) alliance of 1951 (Anderton, 1986). New Zealand's anti-nuclear-weapon stance has enjoyed consistent support at home and has attracted sympathetic global attention. A number of Social Democratic parties in Western Europe have also reflected the growing weight of anti-nuclear-weapon sentiments.

It must be stressed that governmental disengagements from nuclearism embody a tilt in cultural balance against earlier practices of the public deferring to the state when it came to national-security policy. At the same time, however, strong resistances make it difficult for these newer cultural norms to emerge. In particular, the permanent bureaucracies of governments tend to oppose any break in the linkage with their superpower. The officials enjoy their access to privileged information, new technologies and so forth, even if their role in the alliance is very subordinate. Moreover, public anti-nuclear-weapon sentiments are directed less at bureaucrats than at elected politicians. And, of course, the superpowers have the ability to exert economic and other pressures on the smaller states.

VI. Conclusion

The connection between cultural norms and environmental protection proceeds in many directions. At present, an important shift appears to be occurring in the tectonic plates of civilizational orientation. For a variety of reasons, nuclearism appears to be on the defensive, but some events might lead to its recovery at the core of security policy. The US strategic defense initiative is expressive both of a rising tide of criticism of deterrence theorizing and an effort to adapt nuclearism to a new global political order.

At this stage, it may be useful to reinforce the normative shift away from nuclearism by organizing a number of undertakings on a formal, explicit level. One such undertaking would be to circulate a Nuremberg pledge by citizens in all walks of life, to work for accountability by leaders in and out of government to the existing international legal rules governing recourse to and conduct of war. This would reinforce the concept that individuals have a responsibility to implement international law even as against their own officials and policy-makers. Another such undertaking would be to support an international convention on ecocide that emphasizes the duty of leaders and policy-makers to take account of the distinctive threat to the coherence and durability of nature arising from the prospect of employing nuclear weapons (Falk, 1984).

What is important now is the strengthening of the anti-nuclear side of cultural norms so that such steps become more than mere gestures.

References

Aldridge, R. C. 1983. *First strike!: the Pentagon's strategy for nuclear war.* Boston: South End Press, 325 pp.

Anderton, J. P. 1986. Nuclear freedom in one country—how and why: a case study of the development of a nuclear-free policy in New Zealand. In: Perry, T. L. & Foulks, J. G. (eds). *End the arms race: fund human needs.* West Vancouver, Canada: Gordon Soules, 336 pp.: pp. 184–195.

Bowonder, B., Kasperson, J. X. & Kasperson, R. E. 1985. Avoiding future Bhopals. *Environment*, Washington, 27(7):6–13,31–37.

Builder, C. H. & Graubard, M. H. 1982. *International law of armed conflict: implications for the concept of assured destruction.* Santa Monica, Calif.: Rand Corporation Report No. R–2804–FF, 58 pp.

Bundy, M., Kennan, G. F., McNamara, R. S. & Smith, G. 1981–82. Nuclear weapons and the Atlantic alliance. *Foreign Affairs*, New York, 60:753–768.

Caldicott, H. 1986. *Missile envy: the arms race and nuclear war.* rev. edn. New York: Bantam Books, 346 pp.

Carnesale, A., Doty, P., Hoffmann, S., Huntington, S. P., Nye, J. S., Jr & Sagan, S. D. 1983. *Living with nuclear weapons.* Cambridge, Mass.: Harvard University Press, 268 pp.

Cook, A. & Kirk, G. 1983. *Greenham women everywhere: dreams, ideas and actions from the women's peace movement.* London: Pluto Press, 127 pp.

Devall, B. & Sessions, G. 1985. *Deep ecology.* Layton, Utah: Gibbs M. Smith, 266 pp.

Falk, R. A. 1975. Methods and means of warfare: counterinsurgency, tactics, and the law. In: Trooboff, P. D. (ed.). *Law and responsibility in warfare: the Vietnam experience.* Chapel Hill: University of North Carolina Press, 280 pp.: pp. 35–53.

Falk, R. A. 1983a. *End of world order: essays on normative international relations.* New York: Holmes & Meier, 358 pp.

Falk, R. 1983b. Toward a legal regime for nuclear weapons. *McGill Law Journal,* Montreal, 28:519–541.

Falk, R. A. 1984. Environmental disruption by military means and international law. In: Westing, A. H. (ed.). *Environmental warfare: a technical, legal and policy appraisal.* London: Taylor & Francis, 107 pp.: pp. 33–51 [a SIPRI book.]

Falk, R. 1986a. Nuclear weapons and the renewal of democracy. In: Cohen, A. & Lee, S. (eds). *Nuclear weapons and the future of humanity: the fundamental questions.* Totowa, New Jersey: Rowman & Allanheld, 496 pp.: pp. 437–456.

Falk, R. 1986b. Spirit of Thoreau in the age of Trident. *Ecologist,* London, 16:258–265. [Also: *Agni Review,* Cambridge, Mass., 23:31–48.]

Goldblat, J. 1987. Multilateral arms control efforts. *SIPRI Yearbook*, London, 1987:383–408.

Gorbachev, M. 1986. Statement. *New Times*, Moscow, 1986(3):1–5.

Gorbachev, M. 1987. Reality and guarantees for a secure world. *New Times*, Moscow, 1987(39):3–6.

Hohenemser, C., Deicher, M., Ernst, A., Hofsäss, H., Lindner, G. & Recknagel, E. 1986. Chernobyl: an early report. *Environment*, Washington, 28(5):6–13,30–43.

Kennan, G. F. 1983. *Nuclear delusion: Soviet–American relations in the atomic age.* rev. edn. New York: Pantheon Books, 265 pp.

Kothari, R. 1984. Peace in an age of transformation. In: Walker, R. B. J. (ed.). *Culture, ideology, and world order.* Boulder, Colorado: Westview Press, 365 pp.: pp. 323–361.

Lifton, R. J. 1979. *Broken connection: on death and the continuity of life.* New York: Simon & Schuster, 495 pp.

Lifton, R. J. & Falk, R. 1982. *Indefensible weapons: the political and psychological case against nuclearism.* New York: Basic Books, 301 pp.

Mandelbaum, M. 1977. International stability and nuclear order: the first nuclear regime. In: Gompert, D. C., Mandelbaum, M., Garwin, R. L. & Barton, J. H. *Nuclear weapons and world politics: alternatives for the future.* New York: McGraw-Hill, 370 pp.: pp. 13–80.

Mandelbaum, M. 1979. *The nuclear question: the United States and nuclear weapons, 1946–1976.* Cambridge, UK: Cambridge University Press, 277 pp.

Mandelbaum, M. 1982. Future of nuclear weapons. *Naval War College Review,* Newport, Rhode Island, 35(5):58–79.

Mandelbaum, M. 1983. *Nuclear future.* Ithaca, NY: Cornell University Press, 131 pp.

McAllister, P. (ed.). 1982. *Reweaving the web of life: feminism and nonviolence.* Philadelphia: New Society Publishers, 440 pp.

McNamara, R. S. 1983–84. Military role of nuclear weapons: perceptions and misperceptions. *Foreign Affairs,* New York, 62:59–80.

McNamara, R. S. 1986. *Blundering into disaster: surviving the first century of the nuclear age.* New York: Pantheon Books, 212 pp.

Merchant, C. 1980. *Death of nature: women, ecology, and the scientific revolution.* San Francisco: Harper & Row, 348 pp.

Miller, A. S. & Feinrider, M. (eds). 1984. *Nuclear weapons and law.* Westport, Connecticut: Greenwood Press, 415 pp.

Nandy, A. 1984. Oppression and human liberation: toward a Third World utopia. In: Walker, R. B. J. (ed.). *Culture, ideology, and world order.* Boulder, Colorado: Westview Press, 365 pp.: pp. 149–179.

National Conference of Catholic Bishops. 1983. *Challenge of peace: God's promise and our response.* Washington: US Catholic Conference, Publication No. 863, 103 pp.

Nye, J. S., Jr. 1986. *Nuclear ethics.* New York: Free Press, 162 pp.

Pittock, A. B. *et al.* 1985–86. *Environmental consequences of nuclear war. I. Physical and atmospheric effects. II. Ecological and agricultural effects.* Chichester, UK: John Wiley, 2 vols (359+523 pp.).

Schlesinger, J. 1986–87. Reykjavik and revelations: a turn of the tide? *Foreign Affairs,* New York, 65:426–446.

Stone, C. D. 1987. *Earth and other ethics: the case for moral pluralism.* New York: Harper & Row, 320 pp.

Thompson, E. 1980. Notes on exterminism, the last stage of civilization. *New Left Review,* London, 1980(121):3–31.

Waltz, K. N. 1981. *Spread of nuclear weapons: more may be better.* London: International Institute for Strategic Studies, Adelphi Paper No. 171, 32 pp.

Weston, B. H. 1983. Nuclear weapons versus international law: a contextual reassessment. *McGill Law Journal,* Montreal, 28:542–590.

Winner, L. 1977. *Autonomous technology: technics-out-of-control as a theme in political thought.* Cambridge, Mass.: MIT Press, 386 pp.

6. The law as a force in shaping cultural norms relating to war and the environment

CHRISTOPHER D. STONE
University of Southern California

I. Introduction

Recent developments in military technology have added the environment to the list of potential victims of warfare. The spectre of earth-as-casualty appears most ominously in connection with the 'nuclear winter' that a number of scientists predict would follow an extensive nuclear exchange (Ehrlich *et al.*, 1983; Sagan, 1983–84). But even hostilities on a more limited scale threaten to draw the environment into warfare in disturbing new ways. The Second Indochina War of 1961–75 demonstrated that, by at least the 1970s, the arsenals of advanced nations included such environmental modification techniques as chemical defoliation, massive mechanical landclearing and perhaps even rain-making (Falk, 1963; Westing, 1976). Far more disruptive weaponry may have been developed since, and certainly has been envisioned. Concern in the world community has prompted two international conventions aimed at restricting the hostile use of environmental modification techniques: the 1977 Environmental Modification Convention and the 1977 Protocol I Additional to the 1949 Geneva Conventions (Westing, 1984; see also appendices 2.XI & 2.XII). Additionally, a draft treaty on ecocide has been proposed for consideration (Falk, 1984, pp. 45–49).

These conventions and proposals have received, and continue to receive, careful critical analysis on their merit as techniques of arms control (Goldblat, 1977; Westing, 1984; Wunsch, 1980). But there is another perspective from which to review them, one that has not yet received comparable attention. The law-making activity can be regarded as part of a process of influencing world-wide cultural norms.

There are several reasons to reflect upon the relationship between the proposed weapon agreements and cultural norms. The first might be deemed a campaign strategy. Many nations have thus far declined to enter formal agreements limiting environmental modification techniques of warfare. Hence, the proponent of limitations, in quest of further accessions, may wish to present the case for controls in different justificatory terms to different nations, depending upon their predominant cultural norms. Second, the joining of a covenant is no guarantee of compliance. Abidance by the rules is calculated to improve, the more firmly the aims of the law find support in prevailing norms. Assuming that those norms are subject to change, one wants to know what has been, or could be, the role of the law—including the activities which surround law-making and adoption—in disposing those norms more favourably towards protection of the environment in times of war.

A conditioning of norms, if it affects the global political climate, will offer a two-fold reward: more nations entering the relevant conventions and more thorough-going compliance. Moreover, the environment is not threatened by warfare alone. Many of humankind's non-hostile tamperings with the environment are at least equally worrisome. Therefore, it is important to consider whether the law-making activity in the area of weapon control, with its ramifications on norm development, may not also have, as a side benefit, a heightening of environmental consciousness generally.

II. The interplay between cultural norms and the law

An inquiry into law as a force in shaping cultural norms reverses the usually assumed order of things. One ordinarily thinks of laws as arising out of, and as giving authoritative expression to, norms that already enjoy broad acceptance. Theft is criminalized because private property is valued. So viewed, laws reflect prevailing norms; they do not form them.

But the conception of laws as mere reflectors of cultural norms grasps only half the dynamic. Laws also contribute to the fashioning of the norms on which their success as moulders of conduct will ultimately depend. The evolution of various 'rights' movements in the USA provides a good illustration of such feedback on a national level. Such movements—whether seeking improved treatment of women, homosexuals, animals or the environment—typically originate with only fragmentary support in the mainstream mores. The initial campaign to kindle popular support is typically opened on a number of fronts: through the media, within educational and religious organizations and so on. At some level of growth the groups complain that the practices they oppose deserve not only moral censure, but also legal relief. Activity focuses upon proposed legislation or upon a vivid legal test case. The agitation of law reform unites the movement behind a tangible and often dramatic agenda. Moreover, it affords the reformers an opportunity to educate the public (as well as themselves) as to their exact position. Public consciousness is advanced so that an idea which might originally have been dismissed with contempt or humour—for example, that women are equal to men or that animals have rights—is received as a familiar and intelligible, if not yet compelling, alternative. The legal measure that results from this first stage will quite likely be less than what the advocates wanted. Nonetheless, even a token victory in a legislature or court authoritatively legitimates the advocates' concern. This initial legitimation strengthens and broadens support in the general culture, thereby advancing the prospects for a subsequent generation of proposals.

In the international arena, too, there are many instances in which laws and law-making can be regarded not as the product of pre-existent norms, but rather as an integral part of the process of norm development and substantiation. Before the 1982 Law of the Sea negotiations, it was unclear whether any nation, drawing upon its own cultural norms of ownership, would have conceived of the deep-ocean resources as belonging to the common heritage of humankind. Today that very norm, although not yet transformed into a universally acceptable institutional structure, has become a seriously entertained and broadly shared ideal, a viable talking point for further negotiations.

Consider, too, the history of whaling regulation. There is little doubt that when the International Whaling Commission was established in 1946, the prime moving force and the intended beneficiary was not an endangered category of animals, but rather an endangered industry (Siegel, 1985). But as the years passed, a shift could be discerned from commerce to conservation. After gradual reductions in the allowable catch, the Commission has come to the point of decreeing a total moratorium on whaling. True, the moratorium can be rationalized in marketing terms, and the Commission's constitution and mandate impel it to cite conventional, commercial justification; for example, that time is needed to examine catch and other data and to restore stocks for human consumption. But close followers of the Commission doubt whether the whole story is to be found in the official rhetoric (Birnie, 1985; Scarff, 1977, p. 338). Once an international juridical organ was endowed with power over whaling, it became a handy pressure point for conservationist energies in a world that was becoming, for various reasons, increasingly sympathetic to cetaceans. Pressures developed to which the Commission could not, and cannot, be oblivious. Viewed as an historical process of norm/law interaction, cultural norms regarding the killing of marine mammals are evolving in the direction desired by conservationists. The laws—and perhaps particularly, concentrated efforts to amend the laws—are not only symptoms of, but contributors to, that heightening of consciousness. The heightened consciousness, in turn, fuels support for new levels of legal intervention.

And, of course, among other examples of this feedback process operating on an international scale is one close to the subject at hand. Consider the line of development that runs from the 'just war' theories, through the conventions on warfare and the Nuremberg trials, and on further through the protests and laws against genocide and violations of human rights. Moral ideals have given rise to laws, and the laws, in turn, have shaped moral ideals from which further laws have risen.

The fact that such feedback scenarios have been played out on a municipal scale and, in some cases at least, on an international one, rather naturally suggests the following inquiry. Are there cultural norms regarding war and the environment? If so, how influential are they on human conduct? Are they subject to change; specifically, what role might the law itself play as a force in changing the pertinent cultural norms and in directing their influence?

III. Cultural norms relating to war and the environment

It is necessary to define at the start what is meant by a cultural norm, and to establish which norms, exactly, are to be examined. Depending on how the term 'cultural norm' is understood, there may be no authentic cultural norm specifically relating to war and the environment (or, equivalently, to the environment in times of war).

In some usages, a norm is essentially synonymous with a rule that, while commanding public support, has not been authoritatively enacted. Often, however, a cultural norm is distinguished from other rules, not by reference to its non-authoritativeness, but rather by reference to the unconsciousness of the force it exercises over human actions. In this sense, a cultural norm is a reason for action of whose content and roots the actor is less aware than he or she is of the ordinary rule. It is an attitude that is so well-entrenched through habit and ceremony, so broadly, even intuitively, honoured that it exercises its sway with minimal reflection. It has become a premise for conduct, one that seems not so much right or wrong as inevitable. The strongest of such norms, typified by those against incest, are able to intercept, repress and deflect desires before there is even an awareness of them. Other, weaker, norms edit thoughts less invasively; although they lack the force to head off 'wrongful' inclination at the subconscious level, they are able to intercept and interrogate doubtful options that migrate into awareness.

Perhaps the ultimate test for a cultural norm, whether of the public-external or private-internal sort, is that it be able to compete with law and law enforcement as a mode of modifying behaviour. Indeed, what keeps most people from committing serious offences in well-working societies is not the fear of formal sanctions; it is instead the force of attitudes about such things as fairness, possessions and the infliction of suffering.

If cultural norms are considered in this sense, any survey of civilization will reveal a host of cultural norms respecting labour, marriage and eating—the sorts of activities that govern everyday people in their everyday lives. In moving from society to society it may be possible to discern one set of norms respecting warfare and another respecting the environment. But does any culture really hold a deep-seated, broadly-shared set of principles and attitudes towards 'war and the environment', that is, towards a subject matter that is at once so specific and so recondite?

It is true that use of the environment in wartime received early, even primitive, attention, as demonstrated, for example, by the Old Testament (see appendix 4.I). But travesties of the order of the Roman salting of Carthage or of the 1938 dynamiting of the Huayuankow dike of the Yellow River (Huang He) (Westing, 1984, p. 6) fortunately have occurred only sporadically. The most sophisticated and worrisome techniques for the deliberate manipulation of the environment that the 1977 Environmental Modification Convention addresses are relatively untried, if not prospective. As a consequence there has been no opportunity for the customs and principles of any peoples to have responded with an authentic cultural norm for guidance, whether of the public/external or private/internal definition or emphasis. As explained more fully below, it is doubtful whether it is the sort of conduct concerning which specific norms are likely to evolve at the local cultural level.

It may thus be better to examine cultural norms not towards environment-and-war specifically, but rather towards the environment generally. An environmental focus appears warranted on the assumptions that: (*1*) the more a culture values the environment, the more reticent it will be to disrupt nature with either hostile or civil intentions; and (*2*) one way to change the culture—to reinforce or develop latent strains sympathetic to the environment within it—is through laws and legal reform. However, it must be noted that such a programme of inquiry rests upon two causal claims, both of which are open to question. First, a link is implied between culture and conduct. Do cultural norms regarding the environment influence conduct of the sort in question, in particular, impairments of the environment in the course of hostilities? Second, a link is implied between law and culture. Assuming that the environmental norms of a culture have an influence on martial conduct, to what extent and how can that influence be stimulated by law?

IV. Influence of cultural norms relating to the environment

It is not uncommon to claim that different cultures have embedded in them radically different attitudes towards the environment. On the one hand, Taoism and various of the native American religions are represented as encompassing world-views that idealize nature and even resist regarding human beings as an especially important part of it (De Loria, 1970, pp. 186–97; Goodman, 1980). By contrast, the Judaeo-Christian tradition is launched with god's determination to make humans in god's image, endowed with 'dominion over the fish of the sea, and over the birds of the air, and over the cattle, and over all the earth, and over every creeping thing that creeps upon the earth' (Genesis 1:26). Some would suggest that even if such an attitude has not impelled the destruction of the environment, it has blunted human sensitivity to its abuse (White, 1967). Drawing a contrast with Greek antiquity, White (1967, p. 1205) writes that: 'In Antiquity every tree, every spring, every stream, every hill had its own *genius loci*, its guardian spirit. . . . Before one cut a tree, mined a mountain, or dammed a brook, it was important to placate the spirit in charge of that particular situation, and to keep it placated. By destroying pagan animism, Christianity made it possible to exploit nature in a mood of indifference to the feelings of natural objects.'

In such vein, particular religious and philosophical ideas can be portrayed as conveying significant implications for the treatment of the environment. But caution must be exercised to distinguish between ideas that are championed by particular philosophers or religious leaders and those that have actually and effectively permeated the culture of those thinkers. Anyone bent on demonstrating that Western culture is ruthlessly anthropocentric can find many quotations with which to adorn the argument, for example, Johann Fichte's claim in 1847 that human freedom requires people to subjugate all non-rational nature to themselves and to rule over it freely according to their own law (Abrams, 1971, p. 359). But an isolated and obscure philosophical passage does not shape a cultural mainstream and may even constitute weak evidence of its course. A truly embedded cultural norm requires philosophical pronouncements to coalesce with literature, ritual and custom.

Let it be assumed here that native American religions, Taoism and the Judaeo-Christian ethic do constitute rival positions on the worth of nature, true exemplars of deeply embedded environmental norms. If the causal link is strong, one would expect to discover divergent patterns of behaviour regarding the environment as the relevant cultures are compared. But the evidence is not compelling. That is, even if the most strongly contrasting cultural attitudes towards nature that can be found are used as a starting point, corresponding contrasts in conduct are hard to identify. The native American environmental record, unromantically reviewed, is actually quite mixed and not always easy to distinguish from that of the European settlers (Regan, 1982, pp. 206–36). As for White's (1967) thesis, it is not clear how adequately 'pagan animism' protected the local countryside, rather than the limited demands of pagan populations and the limited capacity of primitive technologies to unshape it (Browne, 1987; Diamond, 1986). In the same vein, in China—Tao and *feng-shui*[1] notwithstanding—ruthless deforestation has been continuous (Murphy, 1971; Tuan, 1968).

Much work remains to be done on the influence of cultural norms on a community's environment-threatening action. However, it is doubtful that differences in conduct are nearly as significant as would be suggested by differences in cultural credo and ceremonies.

V. Influence of cultural norms in the context of warfare

The point emphasized thus far is that the supposed causal link between any society's ostensible cultural norms (as expressed in its philosophers' pronouncements or prevailing dogma and ceremony) and its environmental practices cannot be accepted too uncritically. A change in the one does not assure a change in the other. Others have been less sceptical (Toynbee, 1972). But wherever the truth lies—that is, whatever influence a culture's environmental norms may have on conduct generally—such influence is certain to prove particularly fragile when a nation is being asked to constrain its international conduct, or when an environmentally sympathetic norm is tested

[1] Literally 'winds and water', *feng-shui*, China's most influential pseudo-science, constituted a system of divination for determining the auspicious siting of human dwellings (Thompson, 1979, p. 22). The general effect was to encourage a preference for winding paths and for structures that seem to fit into the landscape rather than to dominate it (Tuan, 1968). The philosophical/religious texts of *feng-shui* regarding the environment did not prevent deforestation by needy populations, even though forests offered, among other advantages, a strategic defence against horse-riding barbarians.

on foreign soil in time of war. In their general application, environmental norms address situations of ordinary life. They deal with the cultural member's own lands; and, through such application, with relations to his or her own people, including descendants. War, by contrast, involves an extraordinary crisis situation that introduces shrill competitive norms of its own. Often when hostilities are conducted on foreign soil, the belligerent's environmentally disruptive actions can be confined to the opponent's territory. Thus, even doctrine and attitudes that operate influentially within a culture may waver at the border when tested in a hostile international context such as the one that the 1977 Environmental Modification Convention addresses. And, indeed, even in times of peace the environmental norm may be stifled by the larger, more Byzantine claims of geopolitics.

In itself, the fact that prevalent cultural norms fail to provide sturdy support for the threat envisioned by the 1977 Environmental Modification Convention and comparable measures is not fatal. Consciousness can evolve. Ideas that originate with negligible support can ascend into strong and influential cultural norms. The evolution is one to which the law may in some areas contribute. Is this one of those areas? Indeed, it is suggested below that the law be enlisted to participate in a norm-shifting effort. But to be realistic, any attempt to develop and transform environmental norms sturdy enough not to bend in the winds of war is a particularly formidable task.

One reason why the task of developing environmental norms is formidable can be illustrated by contrast. Until a few years ago in the USA it was generally unclear what were the legal, and probably even the moral, implications of computer 'hacking' (i.e., of electronically entering another's computer system in order to extract information or to tamper with it). Legally, the action did not fit conventional definitions either of theft or of breaking and entering, because no tangible thing was being taken or physically opened. Morally, it was often viewed as ambiguous, many teenagers apparently even regarding the practice as an entertaining test of their skills. Recently, however, a new set of statutes, fortified by well-publicized prosecutions, even of young persons, has unambiguously established the inappropriateness of computer hacking. This is the sort of situation in which it is fair to assume that the firm response of the law has clarified and developed cultural norms. But it must be noticed that in dealing with computer hacking, the law was drawing strength from strong pre-existent cultural norms about the sanctity of property. Moreover, in their pronouncements the laws were addressed to: (*a*) individuals; (*b*) matters over which millions of persons have personal power (whether regarded as stealing in general or computer crimes in particular); and (*c*) individuals in regard to their relations with members of their own culture.

By contrast, a law that prohibits the pursuit of war by the creation of earthquakes or storms not only involves extraterritorial impacts, but probably extra-cultural ones as well. It is addressing nations about actions that only nations have the technology in which to engage. Every individual has the opportunity to be either cruel or kind to animals in his or her personal conduct, and is thus disposed to absorb norms on the subject. But who has the power and opportunity to defoliate jungles or to precipitate tsunamis (seismic sea waves)?

Another obstacle to the law-driven formation of strong universal norms is that even under the most favourable of circumstances, there are limits to how far the law can transcend prevailing mores and lead a culture to new levels of awareness. It can be done, as attested to by many episodes in the history of the US Supreme Court; the school desegregation rulings are often cited. Indeed, the desegregation cases may have had more influence on US mores than on the racial composition of classrooms. However, that was a situation in which a domestic court was dealing with its own domestic culture. In the international sphere, such bold, norm-modifying strokes are destined to be even less common. For one thing, international legal organs, in their adjudicatory function, are more constrained than is the US Supreme Court to lead in declaring what is generally accepted and in advocating what ought to be. It is probable that in the making of treaties international law is not as tied to existent norms as it is in adjudication. But treaties face their own restricting mechanism, the requirement that consensus be obtained among different states.

Finally, norms involving the conduct of warfare are especially resistant to control. Historically, conventions dealing with warfare, signed in times of peace with the best of intentions, have had a salutary but only limited influence in times of war (Falk, 1963). That is true even though the traditional treaties have taken as their object the protection of natural persons, such as hostages and prisoners, not of natural landscapes. Is there any reason to believe that environmental norms might be more successful than the humane ones when they come into conflict with norms of national survival and self-survival, norms fortified by the principles that drew each belligerent into the maelstrom of hostilies? The question is not a rhetorical one. There may well be countries in which it is far harder to marshal support for the enemy than it is for a stand of trees. But overall, when hostilities erupt, one cannot be optimistic about the prospects of either.

VI. A positive programme

It can be argued that authentic, consciousness-pervading cultural norms on war and the environment do not, in fact, exist and, moreover, are not likely to emerge. The existence of environmental norms has to be recognized, but their potential influence, particularly on martial conduct, is clearly restricted. Norms are susceptible to change and strengthening; and international law-making procedures could, and quite possibly should, be summoned into that effort. But the leverage of international law over world-wide cultural norms is limited; growth in local cultural norms is typically glacially slow. In all events, the reflexive influence of local cultural norms on international affairs is uncertain, even should the former be modifiable.

In response to these obstacles, efforts at norm-shifting ought to take as their primary aim, not the various cultural norms of the world, but those of international conduct. If it is hard to penetrate local cultural norms, and if the reward for the effort is in all events doubtful, the implication is to focus directly on the attitudes and principles that govern nations, national leaders and world organizations. The details of the 1959 Antarctic Treaty and of the conventions on land and naval warfare are little known to most of the peoples on earth. Hence, whatever contribution they may make to the world's local cultural norms, at least at present, is indirect and remote. The direct object of treaties is to develop international norms. These international norms, the standards to which nations and national leaders are subject in the world arena, are distinct from the cultural norms examined earlier. They do not adhere to any particular local culture. They may address activities regarding which local, internal norms have nothing to say. Moreover, unlike true cultural norms, which exercise their grasp with only the barest of deliberate reflection, the norms that govern world leaders and world bodies, are not so likely to bypass conscious reasoning. An appeal to the world community to adopt and tolerate new norms is one that must be based upon reason.

To say that the appeal must be based on reason is not to mouth an obvious sentiment. In fact, it helps identify one of the difficulties that environmental modification conventions face, particularly when viewed as contributors to an educative process. A proposed law cannot promote education (whether the education be aimed at the masses or at world leaders) unless it is accompanied by a clear sense of its moral purpose. Perhaps this is true only by degrees. The proponents of conventions against the slaughter of non-combatants have little cause to specify their moral basis: everyone will grant such proposals to be morally intelligible on sight. But assuming that warfare is not unlawful, that the killing of humans is permissible and that bombs are not banned, why should nations restrict tampering with the environment? If triggering a storm, thereby turning a landscape to mire, will stave off a troop clash and consequently reduce human casualties, why is the conscription of natural forces to be rejected? Such questions are not rhetorical: the answers are unclear because the moral underpinnings are not in sharp focus. To what arguments does the proponent of limitations appeal? What moral message would assent to the proposals serve to reinforce in the world community?

It is not always clear what rationales were animating the drafters of the 1977 Environmental Modification Convention and the 1977 Protocol I Additional to the 1949 Geneva Conventions. For example, in regard to articles XXXV.3 and LV.1 of the latter (see appendix 2.XII), one wonders whether the environment is to be protected for its own sake (a position that raises the objection of how an uncaring environment can have a sake, or interest, of its own to protect). Or is the position an obliquely anthropocentric one, one in which the natural environment is protected only from such damage as is calculated 'to prejudice the health or survival of the population'?

A clearer, more consistent sense of purpose, if that is achievable, would possess more than the educational advantage of a clear and strong message. It would in addition assist in the interpretation of the treaties. For example, there is considerable dispute over how to interpret, and whether to retain, the triad of threshold conditions for application both of the 1977 Environmental Modification Convention (see appendix 2.XI, article I.1) and the 1977 Protocol I Additional to the 1949 Geneva Conventions (see appendix 2.XII, articles XXXV.3 and LV.1). Some of the issues appear impossible to resolve without further agreement on the underlying ethic that is being advanced. How otherwise can be judged what effects or damages are 'severe'? What is a prohibited change in the 'composition or structure of the earth . . . or of outer space'? If not every measurable variation, in any degree, is forbidden, by reference to what standards can the allowable be distinguished from the unallowable? If a forest is threatened, is the point of reference (of impermissibility) a threshold volume or mass of vegetation affected? Or is it the destabilizing of a habitat or ecosystem? Or is the key the lost economic value to contemporary human beings? Or should the cost of repairing the environmental damage be considered, that is, of restoring the forest to its pre-injury condition, perhaps even if the costs of restoration exceed the present value of the resource?

Blowing up an uninhabited, infertile atoll may cost humankind very little, if 'costs' are confined to opportunity costs. Is destruction of the atoll therefore permissible? Or are there other values to be considered? If so, what are they, and how are they to be entered into the analysis? Is it implied that killing combatants with the consequence of damaging the environment is permissible, but that precipitating the same environmental damage, as a means of killing combatants, is not—and if so, why not?

Questions such as these force further consideration of the fundamental issue: what *is* the basis for environmental protection? If the signature-gathering process is to be the occasion for dialogue and the inculcation of international norms, what are the norms which are to be inculcated?

The answer to these questions—the substance of an international environmental ethic—would advance and clarify the various anti-martial and environmental proposals by providing them with a more coherent objective. But there are independent, perhaps even larger reasons to enlist anti-martial and environmental sentiments into the cause of developing a global environmental ethic. Threats to the environment emanate not only from hostile actions and the arms race, but also from the civil sector (Westing, 1980). The global environment is in jeopardy from sheer negligence, and even from tamperings with nature that are undertaken with the most benign of intentions. In fact, deforestation, peacefully purposed, represents a far more immediate and far-reaching threat to the forests of the world than does military defoliation. There is transnational pollution, including radioactive discharges, with which to contend. More frequent releases into the environment of genetically tailored materials, whose menace remains uncertain, cause concern. Such non-military activities not only represent, in the aggregate, threats to the environment at least as realistic and weighty as those from warfare, they are also more amenable to international control. The containment of these non-hostile hazards may be advanced by the expanded employment of environmental impact assessments regarding conduct having extraterritorial effects, orderly procedures for the exchange and monitoring of environmental information and so forth. Public and state support for such efforts, as well as the support of such bodies as the United Nations Environment Programme (UNEP), would also gain from the development of a global environmental ethic and consciousness.

To invoke the spectre of non-hostile hazards is not to distract attention from the overriding questions of war and peace. Indeed, war and peace are part of a seamless web with all those things that are required to sustain a harmonious world: space, air, water, food, seemly surroundings and a sense of common fate and purpose. The point is merely that even if the drive for limitations on environmental modification proves to have only minor influence on the development and use of weaponry, the effort would still be warranted as part of the broader campaign to develop a world-wide environmentalism.

Nor should it be supposed that to define and proselytize an international environmental ethic is too idealistic. It is true that the task of sensitizing humankind to the environment is hard, particularly in a world pressed with ever more urgent demands for natural resources. But in some ways an international environmental ethic faces relatively less opposition than an international ethic on human rights. The proponents of international norms on human rights and genocide collide with long-standing doctrines about sovereignty and associated notions of what constitutes purely internal affairs. By contrast, there is no matter more fit for international accord than protection of the environment, particularly of global attributes or components—such as weather patterns, ocean and atmosphere—that play so clear a role in the indivisible fate of all nations and of all humankind.

But what is to be the normative basis for that accord? The question might be put this way: Why ought the environment be given special protection, whether in time of war or of peace?

VII. Normative foundations for a global environmental ethic

There are several approaches to dealing with the question of normative foundations for a global environmental ethic. Each of these approaches is in the form of a norm that implies somewhat variant directions for human conduct.

Norms that appeal to conventional human welfare

A straightforward and conventional anthropocentric argument can be invoked regarding environmental conservation: the environment should be protected simply as a means of advancing human interests. This is the view that some will trace back to the Old Testament book of Genesis. But it can find easy expression in a utilitarian vocabulary: the sole basis for judging an action is its consequences for human welfare, namely, that the morally best choice is that which produces the greatest good for the greatest number of persons. In the area of warfare and the environment, such a rationale is the support, for example, of the sort of husbandry principle found in the 1899 and 1907 Hague Conventions enjoining an occupying state to administer forests and so forth according to the rules of usufruct (see appendix 2.I, annex article LV; appendix 2.II, annex article LV).

Even this conservatively anthropocentric view may contain the foundation for more far-reaching, and not always so obvious, legal and administrative reforms. In many circumstances the received rules of international law are not competent to restrain environment-affecting actions destined to impinge upon human welfare (setting aside here their consequences on the environment *per se*). For example, if the environment is to be protected to a degree consistent with human needs there are doctrines of jurisdiction to overcome. In the absence of changes in international legal doctrine, standing to challenge impairments to what has been called the 'global commons' (the ocean, sea-bed and other features of the planet that lie beyond any sovereign competence) is problematical, even if such impairment threatens not nature alone, but human welfare as well (Soni, 1985, pp. 91–93; Springer, 1983, pp. 158–59). For example, a considerable amount of damage to the atmosphere that constitutes a human hazard can occur without the infringement of any sovereign interest as that term is presently understood, and hence without occasioning any legal relief. Moreover, in tampering with the environment, there is a real risk that before there develops evidence of a measurable, judicially cognizable level of harm to humans, the disruptions may have become irreversible.

It seems obvious that from the most narrowly anthropocentric perspective alone, arrangements should be made to provide legal protection from such circumstances. For example, the Food and Agriculture Organization of the United Nations, the United Nations Environment Programme, the World Meteorological Organization or some other appropriate agency could be empowered to act as legal guardian for various unowned resources, such as the atmosphere (including the climate) and the oceans. The guardian, staffed with experts, would be charged with gathering and assessing data relating to changes in its 'ward', and in reviewing environmental impact assessments of any state or other entity proposing actions that threaten to affect it. The guardian could in some circumstances be empowered to institute judicial review of any threatened disruption not otherwise provided for, from weapon tests to chlorofluorocarbon releases. If the laws were structured to reflect the conventional anthropocentric rationale, the judicial body would be authorized to enjoin or denounce the hazard on the basis of reasonably anticipated risks to human welfare, even if those risks had not yet risen to a level that would be recognized as actionable wrongs under existing rules of transnational pollution or the like.

To illustrate, the growing concern about depletion of the ozone layer has led to international conferences on the subject and to recommendations for treaties. Several alternatives are under consideration. The point is that one way to protect the present state of the ozone would be to recognize it as a jural person with a legal guardian to speak for it. Such an approach has many latent problems that need ironing out; however, it is one way to assure the review and restraint of harms before they reach a level that would make them cognizable by prevailing standards, and perhaps also irreversible (Stone, 1972; 1987b).

Norms that appeal to the interests of future generations

A norm with its own distinct implications involves appeal to the anticipated interests of future generations. Even if the environment *per se* has no interests, future generations of persons may have an interest in at least some features of the environment. If a future-generation norm is adopted, the expected interests of future generations are pooled with those of the present world population; then options can be assessed within the framework of familiar welfare theories. In this manner justifications can be derived for preserving the environment in ways not warranted if the welfare of contemporary populations is considered exclusively, in accordance with the prior norm discussed.

To illustrate, consider the question of how to dispose of nuclear wastes. The present world population, if it were to consider only the costs and benefits to it, would prefer a relatively inexpensive burial site on the assumption that by the time there is contamination of water systems and so forth none of the present population will be around to suffer the consequences. On the other hand, if an ethic is adopted that respects the projected interests of future generations (if submission of the issue to an inter-generational 'vote' is imagined) the outcome would presumably favour the bearing of some additional costs for more secure measures, that is, some subordination of the welfare of the present population for that of future persons.

A concern for the welfare of future generations runs through many international agreements. It is implied by the concept of a common heritage of humankind to be found, for example, in the 1982 Law of the Sea Convention, the 1972 World Heritage Convention (see appendix 2.X) and the 1979 Moon Agreement (see appendix 2.XIV). Moreover, a concern for future generations would appear to lie within the spirit of the 1977 Environmental Modification Convention and the 1977 Protocol I Additional to the 1949 Geneva Conventions, although it is a matter of interpretation whether the basis for such a rationale can be found within the texts themselves. Perhaps it turns upon—and determines—how lengthy 'long-lasting' and 'long-term' effects are understood to be.

In interpreting the triad of threshold conditions which have been established by the 1977 Environmental Modification Convention and the 1977 Protocol I Additional to the 1949 Geneva Conventions, as in fixing upon a general policy, the valuing of future generations is intuitively attractive as a normative principle. But if a future-generation norm is to be taken seriously, rather than merely as a noble sentiment, then it must be recognized that such acceptance implies restrictions of choice that many will find difficult to accept. To present a hypothetical case from the context of warfare, suppose that the strategic military choice is between (*a*) a manoeuvre that results in 10 000 burn victims now, but that entails no long-term consequences, and (*b*) one that results in only 100 victims now but that, after a 300-year latency period, will disrupt the environment for yet further centuries to come, with deleterious effects on many millions of remote descendants. Can the victimization of the 10 000 now be accepted as the lesser evil, notwithstanding that they be temporal 'neighbours'?

Norms that appeal to ideals of personhood

A norm that appeals to ideals of personhood has already been anticipated. Desires, whether of present or future persons, are not the only foundation on which moral reflection could be based. Historically, few moral theories have accepted without qualification what is wanted as being either given or good. More commonly, human desires have been regarded as a variable subject to—indeed, the precise target of—some disciplining virtues. Thus, an environmental norm might take the tack of asking whether there exist specific virtues of personhood for the attainment of which some features of the environment are instrumental or even necessary. If it is believed, for example, that persons are better off (happiness aside) for having had exposure to magnificent vistas, then there is reason to preserve for humankind that opportunity, independent of any present or future 'utility'. That is to say, a utilitarian (preference-satisfying) norm may warrant sacrificing a forest in the interests of more commodious housing; but a person who subscribes to anthropocentric idealism, whose notion of an ideal person includes exposure to wilderness, may feel morally committed to retaining the forest.

Norms that appeal to an intrinsic good of nature

All the normative foundations outlined thus far can be classed as fundamentally anthropocentric. The first two are anthropocentric in orienting towards the wants of present or future humans; the third, in orienting towards some ideal of what human beings ought to be and become. In the final analysis, the claims each makes on behalf of the environment are made dependent on the well-being (including spiritual well-being) of persons. There is also a more radical, because less deeply anthropocentric, normative viewpoint. It can be maintained that parts of the non-human environment are good intrinsically, that is, not by virtue of their causes (that god made them) or their effects (that they provide sustenance or pleasure to humans), but rather because that aspect of nature represents a good for independent reasons.

The supporter of such a norm confronts the task of identifying an intrinsic (non-instrumental) worth of something not human. Those who have taken up that challenge have drawn different dividing lines as to where moral considerateness ends. Some argue for the considerateness of all creatures capable of experiencing pleasure and pain, so as to include animals (Regan, 1983; Singer, 1975); others have widened the circle to include all life (Schweitzer, 1949; Taylor, 1986); still others, including this author, have argued for the moral considerateness even of some lifeless features of nature, according to appropriately tailored rules (Stone, 1987a). However, all such endeavours appear strained and unfamiliar, particularly when they are stretched to make a case for things that cannot be killed, frustrated or pained. Such endeavours seem hard to accomplish without assuming a somewhat dogmatic stance or without saying that 'X is a good because . . . X is a good'. Yet, all moral philosophies have their greatest difficulty at the very same starting point: identification of the basic (non-instrumental) goods. Utilitarianism adopts a particular psychological state, pleasure, as the intrinsic good—not, as we know, uncontroversially. Other philosophies adopt other goods, for example, as with Immanuel Kant (1785, p. 9), at times, the 'good will'.

The intuition that non-human, even inanimate, nature is inherently good does not lack intuitive appeal. Consider for a moment, from the 1972 Stockholm Declaration on the Human Environment the proclamation that 'of all things in the world, people are the most precious' (UNGA, 1973, pt I.5). Perhaps that sentiment appears obvious. But to put it to a test, suppose the choice had to be made between an earth with an additional thousand million persons, or one with an additional thousand million trees. Many people would certainly choose the latter, valuing the additional trees as more precious—and not only for the implications regarding human welfare. At present levels, more trees make for a more highly valued earth than do more people.

Has such an 'idealistic' norm any place in shaping international conduct? That is, is it feasible to prohibit certain changes in the environment *per se*, without a showing of: (*a*) a net loss to contemporary humans (as per the first norm presented above); (*b*) a net loss to contemporary plus future humans (as per the second norm presented above); or even (*c*) deleterious ramifications on human virtue (as per the third norm presented above)? Indeed, the acid test of the 'deep' ecology position is whether it is right—and, can humans be motivated—to preserve certain aspects of the environment even if doing so conflicts with the more familiar bases for judgement, that is to say, if it derogates from present or future human welfare.

The 1982 World Charter for Nature implicitly adopts an intrinsic-good norm as regards living things, namely in the preambular declaration that 'every form of life is unique, warranting respect regardless of its worth to man' (UNGA, 1982). That language is, of course, only aspirational. However, certain provisions of the 1959 Antarctic Treaty, may be read as actually embodying such an aspiration. The environmental *status quo* of Antarctica is preserved in ways that appear to go beyond the interests of human beholders (how many visitors can flock to the Antarctic?) or even of scientists; the framers of the Treaty seem to have been animated by a sense of awe of Antarctica's magnificent existence as one of the last great largely pristine areas on earth (Stone, 1987a). Moreover, in several of their recommendations, the participants of the 1984

SIPRI/UNIDIR Symposium on Environmental Warfare reflected a desire to adapt the laws of environmental warfare to an intrinsic-good norm, espousing a concern for humankind as well as for the global balance of nature, including species and habitats (Westing, 1984, pp. 83–88). As already suggested, if an intrinsic-good norm were adopted to govern the interpretation of the 1977 Environmental Modification Convention, it would be understood to protect ecosystems from certain effects *per se*, that is, without any showing of damage to humans, as long as the triad of threshold conditions could be otherwise met, for example, by reference to such factors as the toll on species or on non-sentient life, depending upon which non-anthropocentric ethic were being adopted.

It is worth noting a possible distinction in the present context between treaties limiting hostile and those limiting non-hostile disruptions of the environment. Many people will be prepared to accept an intrinsic-good norm as a basis for controlling the hostile disruptions from an underlying sense that no good can come of warfare. That is, if the possibility of a just war is rejected (a large and controversial assumption) then the benefits of warfare become nil. Those who feel this way will therefore be inclined to restrict environmental disruption without any cost-benefit accounting—restrict it, in other words, *per se*, a posture that is effectuated by counting the environment as a good that is intrinsically capable of protection. But when the disruption originates in non-hostile, presumably well-intentioned and beneficial activity, those assessing it will be less inclined to dismiss evidence of the impact on human welfare.

VIII. Conclusion

In general, laws and cultural norms are mutually reinforcing. Formal laws arise from cultures, and command obedience in proportion to their coherence with the fundamental beliefs of the culture. Cultures, however, are not static. Law, and especially the activities of law making and legal reform, are among the forces that contribute to cultural evolution.

It is not clear how well these general principles apply in the context of environmental warfare. True cultural norms concern matters of common, everyday experience, such as those which touch private property and theft. They are not as likely to surround employment of weaponry disruptive of the environment with the same familiarity or strength. World-wide, it may be possible to identify less specific popular cultural norms regarding the environment generally (e.g., a respect for all living things). But the effect on conduct of these general environmental norms, particularly on military conduct, is apt to be limited.

These obstacles are sobering; but they are no excuse for not pressing for the development of an international norm of environmental conduct. In one sense, the environmental treaties are themselves international norms. But what is meant here primarily is the less formal but no less influential analogue of cultural norms: the expectations and sense of right and wrong that constrain behaviour in the world community, and that will gradually produce—and govern the interpretation of—their formalized counterparts. The activity that surrounds discussion and ratification of outstanding proposals can be an important forum for clarifying the relevant normative foundations.

Four normative foundations have been suggested. Does it matter upon which of them an international environmental ethic is primarily based? Although the four entail different conclusions over some range of options, it must be granted that in most real situations, either all normative bases will point in the same direction, or else the first (the most straightforwardly anthropocentric one) is likely to dominate. The true value of a deep normative ethic then becomes problematical. For example, the arguments against nuclear war that are based simply upon immediate human suffering are so clear and strong that one wonders what an environmental philosophy can contribute. The query is not a rhetorical one.

There are perhaps two different audiences for which the 'death' or 'mortal injury' to the global ecosystem might have independent significance. There are those who simply cannot think about their own death—the thought is so horrible they dismiss it from mind—but who can dwell upon, and be sobered by, the thought of planetary 'death'. There are others who, on the contrary, may be prepared to contemplate and accept their own death and the death of others, but for whom the injury to the environment—a sort of 'brain death' of the planet—has a separate and supplemental poignancy. This is a group whose membership is apt to grow as the image of humans all living together on 'spaceship earth' becomes more widely shared. (And might not the law and law-making activities contribute to a broader sharing of this image?) Moreover, there is no logical reason why an argument against nuclear destruction may not proceed on the basis of appeals both to long-range human interests and to the principle that the environment is an intrinsic good, consequences for humankind aside. To take both routes is no more inconsistent than for a vegetarian to rest his or her case both on the welfare of animals and on the health of humankind.

In closing, treaty-making efforts in the field of military disruption of the environment should be conducted conscious of their normative basis. They should be part of a deliberate effort to develop, clarify and promulgate, at least among the community of nations, a global environmental ethic. Such an undertaking is not a commitment to deciding, finally and for all times and circumstances, which of the four bases developed above has to be the sole rationale for all international agreements. But moral growth, and moral influence, cannot take place without giving express attention to the issue: on an imperilled planet, what shall the community of nations adopt as the normative foundation for its conduct?

References

Abrams, M. H. 1971. *Natural supernaturalism: tradition and revolution in romantic literature.* New York: W. W. Norton, 550 pp.

Birnie, P. 1985. Role of developing countries in nudging the International Whaling Commission from regulating whaling to encouraging nonconsumptive use of whales. *Ecology Law Quarterly,* Berkeley, Calif., 12:937–975.

Browne, M. W. 1987. New findings reveal ancient abuse of lands. *New York Times* 1987(13 Jan):C1,C3.

De Loria, V., Jr. 1970. *We talk, you listen: new tribes, new turf.* New York: Macmillan, 227 pp.

Diamond, J. M. 1986. Environmentalist myth. *Nature,* London, 324:19–20.

Ehrlich, P. R. *et al.* 1983. Long-term biological consequences of nuclear war. *Science,* Washington, 222:1293–1300.

Falk, R. A. 1963. *Law, morality and war in the contemporary world.* New York: Praeger, 120 pp.

Falk, R. A. 1984. Environmental disruption by military means and international law. In: Westing, A. H. (ed.). *Environmental warfare: a technical, legal and policy appraisal.* London: Taylor & Francis, 107 pp.: pp. 33–51. [a SIPRI book]

Goldblat, J. 1977. Environmental warfare convention: how meaningful is it? *Ambio,* Stockholm, 6:216–221.

Goodman, R. 1980. Taoism and ecology. *Environmental Ethics,* Athens, Georgia, 2:73–80.

Kant, I. 1785. *Foundation for the metaphysics of morals* [ed. by L. W. Beck]. New York: Bobbs-Merill, 92 pp., 1959.

Murphy, E. F. 1971. Has nature any right to life? *Hastings Law Journal,* San Francisco, 22:467–484.

Regan, T. 1982. *All that dwell therein: animal rights and environmental ethics.* Berkeley: University of California Press, 249 pp.

Regan, T. 1983. *Case for animal rights.* Berkeley: University of California Press, 425 pp.

Sagan, C. 1983–84. Nuclear war and climatic catastrophe: some policy implications. *Foreign Affairs,* New York, 62:257–292.

Scarff, J. E. 1977. International management of whales, dolphins and porpoises: an interdisciplinary assessment. *Ecology Law Quarterly,* Berkeley, Calif., 6:323–427,571–638.

Schweitzer, A. 1949. *Philosophy of civilization* [translated by C. T. Campion; revised by C. E. B. Russell]. New York: Macmillan, 347 pp.

Siegel, A. J. 1985. U.S.–Japanese whaling accord: a result of the discretionary loophole in the Packwood-Magnuson amendment. *George Washington Journal of International Law & Economics,* Washington, 19:577–615.

Singer, P. 1975. *Animal liberation: a new ethics for our treatment of animals.* New York: New York Review of Books, 301 pp.

Soni, R. 1985. *Control of marine pollution in international law.* Cape Town: Juta, 301 pp.

Springer, A. L. 1983. *International law of pollution: protecting the global environment in a world of sovereign states.* Westport, Connecticut: Quorum Books, 218 pp.

Stone, C. D. 1972. Should trees have standing?: toward legal rights for natural objects. *Southern California Law Review,* Los Angeles, 45:450–501. Also: Los Altos, Calif.: William Kaufmann, 103 pp., 1974.

Stone, C. D. 1987a. *Earth and other ethics: the case for moral pluralism.* New York: Harper & Row, 320 pp.

Stone, C. D. 1987b. *Umwelt vor Gericht: die eigenrechte der Natur [Environment in court: the rights of nature].* Munich: Trickster Verlag, 163 pp.

Taylor, P. W. 1986. *Respect for nature: a theory of environmental ethics*. Princeton, New Jersey: Princeton University Press, 329 pp.

Thompson, L. G. 1979. *Chinese religion: an introduction.* 3rd edn. Belmont, Calif.: Wadsworth, 163 pp.

Toynbee, A. 1972. Religious background of the present environmental crisis: a viewpoint. *International Journal of Environmental Studies,* London, 3:141–146;4:157–158.

Tuan, Y.-F. 1968. Discrepancies between environmental attitude and behaviour: examples from Europe and China. *Canadian Geographer,* Montreal, 12:176–191.

UNGA (United Nations General Assembly). 1973. *Report of the United Nations Conference on the Human Environment, Stockholm, 5–16 June 1972*. New York: UN General Assembly Document No. A/CONF.48/14/Rev.1, 77 pp.

UNGA (United Nations General Assembly). 1982. *World charter for nature.* New York: UN General Assembly Resolution No. 37/7 of 28 Oct. 1982, 5 pp.

Westing, A. H. 1976. *Ecological consequences of the Second Indochina War.* Stockholm: Almqvist & Wiksell, 119 pp. + 8 pl. [a SIPRI book]

Westing, A. H. 1980. *Warfare in a fragile world: military impact on the human environment.* London: Taylor & Francis, 249 pp. [a SIPRI book]

Westing, A. H. (ed.). 1984. *Environmental warfare: a technical, legal and policy appraisal.* London: Taylor & Francis, 107 pp. [a SIPRI book]

White, L., Jr. 1967. Historical roots of our ecologic crisis. *Science,* Washington, 155:1203–1207.

Wunsch, C. R. 1980. Environmental modification treaty. *A.S.I.L.S. International Law Journal,* Washington, 4:113–131.

7. Formal education as a force in shaping cultural norms relating to war and the environment

BIRGIT BROCK-UTNE
Universities of Oslo & Dar es Salaam

I. Introduction

It is a thought-provoking fact that the same countries responsible for the main threats facing humankind today—ecocide and genocide—are also the ones having the populations with the highest levels of formal education. One cannot assume that this statistical correlation is a causal one, that the more formal education a population receives, the more it will start polluting the environment and producing arms. Yet the correlation warrants reflection upon the type of formal education given in the highly industrialized world today: what is the role of schooling in shaping norms relating to war and the environment?

For analytical purposes the factual knowledge transmitted in schools, the official curriculum, is in this chapter distinguished from the attitudes and norms shaped or strengthened in schools, mostly through what might be called the hidden curriculum (Brock-Utne, 1982; Brock-Utne & Haukaa, 1980). In reality, it is difficult to make such a division because all factual information also conveys attitudes and norms. If history is taught as a long series of wars, youngsters may learn that wars have always existed, that violence pays, maybe even that wars are exciting. If science is taught 'for its own sake' (Brock-Utne, 1985, p. 116), without its detrimental effects taken into account, this teaching may merely strengthen cultural norms previously conveyed to youngsters, especially boys, of disregarding danger (Brock-Utne, 1986b; 1987; Nader, 1981; Sabo, 1985).

The first part of this chapter deals with the more cognitive aspects of the knowledge transmitted in schools, not disregarding that this knowledge, given or not given, also shapes attitudes and norms. Questions are asked about the teaching of non-violent solutions to conflict. Are youngsters taught the necessary skills to handle conflicts non-violently? Could such teaching be made part of the curriculum? What about the role of non-violent solutions to conflicts in the teaching of history? Questions about science teaching are also raised: Is there reason to believe that youngsters are taught a narrow-minded science where the human, ecological and ethical consequences of scientific and technological innovations are not taken into account? What about an integrated, interdisciplinary form of teaching? Does it have a foothold anywhere in the formal educational system, at any level? Is conservation taught in schools at all? Are youngsters taught to take care of the environment, to maintain and repair rather than to use and discard?

The second part of this chapter deals with the entire structure and set-up of education. Knowledge, along with attitudes and norms, is of course shaped by any actual information given or not given. But norms are also significantly shaped through the entire educational structure. To what extent does the structure of education encourage the critical thinking needed in people who would restore ecological balance and put the world on the road to disarmament? Is there reason to believe that the hierarchical structures of school systems encourage obedience and loyalty instead of critical thinking in regard to authority? Is formal education an oppressive system where the main function of the teacher, no matter what the official curriculum says, is to sort pupils, to create winners and losers among them? Are schools places where youngsters are taught to compete against each other, that life is a rat race one must win? Are they taught that the important thing is to be ahead of the others, to be stronger, braver, faster? Are they taught that they get ahead by stepping on other people? Are they taught that detrimental effects on their surroundings do not count as long as their own success is enhanced? Are they taught to think in dichotomies rather than in connections?

Patriarchal thinking is a belief system in which a few men hold power over other men, women, children and nature. It is a system of values developed through male experience: competition, hierarchy, aggression, alienation from the earth, denial of emotion and the objectification of 'other', whether this be sex, race or class (Reardon, 1985, p. 37). These values are not unlike those characteristic of the militaristic mind: victory, defeat, supremacy, strength, destruction, threat, revenge, loyalty and obedience (Skjelsbaek, 1979). There is reason to believe that formal education is a force shaping norms conducive to patriarchal and militaristic thinking.

The third and last part of this chapter suggests the possibility that education could create or foster values, norms and concepts that are non-congruent with the militaristic mind, norms such as trust, forgiveness, construction, connectedness, reconciliation and empathy. To what extent could education plant seeds of doubt about the direction in which the world is heading? This part of the chapter makes use of a distinction between the traditional concept of power as dominance—'power-over'—and a feminist concept of power as competence, sharing, joy—'power-to' (Brock-Utne, 1986c; 1987; Carroll, 1972; Eisler & Loye, 1986; French, 1985; Vellacott, 1982). It can be argued that the traditional concept of power—power as dominance over other human beings and nature—is ultimately an expression of powerlessness or 'sourcelessness'; as separation from the source of life, creation and joy, as from the human spirit and co-operation (Brock-Utne, 1987; Stiehm, 1982; Vellacott, 1982). The whole concept of power should be replaced by a concept of pleasure in that 'power-to' primarily increases pleasure, whereas 'power-over' increases violence and pain (French, 1985, p. 478). Finally it is suggested that there is the chance that schools could become places where pleasure is experienced, where youngsters are taught the joys of sharing, are taught to take care of each other, of the weak ones in society, of plants and animals, of nature.

II. The official curriculum

In a well-known song the US songwriter Tom Paxton (1963) asks:

What did you learn in school today,
  dear little boy of mine?

And the boy answers:

I learned that war is not so bad,
I learned about the great ones we have had,
We fought in Germany and in France,
And some day I might get my chance. . . .

Is this what youngsters are taught in schools, that wars are not so bad, that they are exciting, that they are what makes the world go round? And—if they are boys—that they may even get their chance to participate in this excitement, to prove their strength and virility? Do they get the impression that wars have always existed and are efficient means of solving conflicts? Not only the news media (Eysenck & Nias, 1978; Schmid & Graaf, 1982), but also history books (Kruegler & Parkman, 1985), consistently focus on results achieved by violence. Moreover, history books give more attention to violent struggles that fail to achieve their objectives than to non-violent struggles that succeed (Kruegler & Parkman, 1985).

Unfortunately, it cannot be assumed that formal education in itself will lead to creative problem-solving. On the contrary, studies show that formal schooling may tend to slow down creative thinking. The capacity of literate and illiterate workers to provide new and creative solutions to technical problems has been compared. The illiterate workers were seen to display far greater creativity in their problem-solving than the literate ones (Schuman *et al.*, 1967). Indeed, literacy seems to have little to do with social development, but more to do with control of workers (Graff, 1981). In Africa at least, illiterate women seem to have much more time, energy and enthusiasm for political work than literate ones, who seem to have become politically passive (Boulding, 1986).

It cannot be concluded that literacy necessarily leads to political passivity, to less capacity for conflict resolution and problem-solving. However, the findings mentioned do necessitate a closer look at the type of education given. Has formal education led to the development of certain human capacities to the detriment—maybe even loss—of other human capacities? There is reason to believe that formal education develops mostly that part of human intelligence which has to do with narrow technological and rational thinking, a trend that is now being furthered by the introduction of computers (Boulding, 1986; Gardner & Perkins, 1982). Other parts of human intelligence, those which have to do with imagination, vision, problem-solving and conflict resolution, are underdeveloped. This may be part of the reason why people in the industrialized world, especially in the West, have a pessimistic view of the future and are often unable to envision a disarmed world.

Formal education, it seems, does little to teach youngsters non-violent solutions to conflict or to train their capacity for visionary thinking. As history is presently taught, important phenomena, such as the effective use of non-violence and the important role of women in society, are rendered invisible, hidden, forgotten (Spender, 1982). If a woman has devoted her life to non-violent conflict solving, to peace and disarmament, she is often invisible, if not to her own generation then to future ones. Such has been the fate of one of the great heroes of peace of this century, the Austrian writer and political activist Bertha von Suttner [1843–1914] (Suttner, 1889; 1909). Without her suggestion and urging there would have been no Nobel Prize, yet it is Alfred Nobel (who bequeathed the money for the prize from his profits on weapons and dynamite) who is the one remembered (Brock-Utne, 1985, pp. 37–45). There seems now to be at least some literature emerging on von Suttner's fascinating life and work (Hamann, 1986). Is there hope that she will be introduced into history books?

Natural science is another important school subject shaping cultural norms regarding technical progress, scientific research and the use of the environment. It has been suggested that every advance in methods of mass destruction has been made, not in response to demands from the armed services, but from proposals put forward by men of science (Oliphant, 1982). All nuclear weapons are said to have originated in this way, as perhaps have all the guidance systems for the vehicles designed to deliver them. Indeed, in relation to the nuclear-arms race, which feeds on the continuous input of scientific innovation and technological skill, these factors appear to have acquired a momentum of their own. Thus it seems that technology dictates policy, that new weapon systems emerge, not because of any military or security requirements, but because of the sheer impetus of the technological process (Zuckerman, 1980).

Most scientists proceed with what they regard as an interesting and challenging task without much concern for the social, political or economic consequences of their success. Scientists who are not concerned about the ethical and political implications of their research should be referred to as alienated scientists (MacBride, 1978). The scientific revolution that has overtaken humanity since World War II has not been matched by the development of a counterbalancing sense of moral responsibility. Thus, science unaccompanied by moral and ethical responsibility has, in itself, become a threat to human survival.

The real obstacle to social responsibility in science is not that natural scientists are peculiarly ignorant or insensitive about ethical questions, but that they acquire an armoury of precepts by means of which they defend themselves from the discomforts and dangers of social action (Ziman, 1982). These precepts become entangled in a web of rationalization picked up by scientists in the course of their education and used automatically to shield their consciences from attack. The peculiarity of science is that the principles that are used to excuse social irresponsibility have been elevated into a coherent ideology (Ziman, 1982).

The basic principle of the ideology of natural science is that the pursuit of knowledge is the most worthy of all human activities. A scientist is perceived as duty-bound to explore the universe to its utmost limits, to leave no stone unturned, to follow every curious circumstance, regardless of any ethical or political consideration. Scientists lean heavily on a mystique of personal devotion to research in order to maintain high standards of performance, just as good soldiers lean heavily on the mystiques of obedience to orders and personal devotion to duty. But such mystiques are essentially myths that ignore the social significance of whatever is done in their name. Scientists as well as soldiers often excuse their own behaviour by claiming that they are not responsible: they are just doing their duty to their country, to their corporation, to the furthering of science. This apolitical attitude seems to have been epitomized by the scientist Wernher von Braun who developed large rockets, first for Germany and then for the USA. The US satirist Tom Lehrer (1981, pp. 124–25) puts these words into his mouth:

Once the rockets are up,
  who cares where they come down?
That's not my department,
  says Wernher von Braun.

Other scientists—for example, Samuel Cohen, the so-called father of the neutron bomb—are known to hold similar attitudes. In an interview in which Cohen was asked about the development of weapons for mass killing and mass destruction he responded that he looked at this work only as an intellectually stimulating activity, as a great challenge and as a very fascinating job (Kirkerud, 1982).

The scientific revolution of the seventeenth century was a revolution that put men in charge of nature (Easlea, 1981; 1983; Merchant, 1980). It was not enough to understand nature: men of science had to master 'her'. The language used had very clear sexual overtones, of which—it should be noted—Francis Bacon, the celebrated father of modern science, approved: 'For you have but to follow and as it were hound nature in her wanderings, and you will be able, when you like, to lead and drive her afterwards to the same place again. . . . Neither ought a man to make scruple of entering and penetrating into these holes and corners, when the inquisition of truth is his sole object . . .' (Bacon, 1623, p. 296). Nature was looked upon as a woman to be conquered, subdued, mastered and penetrated by men of science. The ancient identity of nature as a nurturing mother links women's history with the history of the environment and ecological change (Merchant, 1980). The 'female' earth was central to the organic cosmology that was undermined by the scientific revolution of the sixteenth and seventeenth centuries and the rise of a market-oriented culture in early modern Europe. The mechanistic world view of science sanctioned the exploitation of nature, unrestrained commercial expansion and a new socio-economic order that subordinated women. This was a science and a world view that sanctioned the domination of both women and nature.

Nature, as just noted, is regarded as feminine, and the scientific quest as an essentially virile, masculine adventure with penetration as the key to manly success. The men behind the seventeenth-century scientific revolution saw nature as a woman passively awaiting the display of male virility and the subsequent birth of a series of inventions and machines that would, in Francis Bacon's words, 'conquer and subdue her' and even 'shake her to her foundations' (Merchant, 1980, p. 172).

As a 'new' science it would be constructive to see the development of a 'female' science, one based more on fitting into an ecological framework than on conquering nature (Easlea, 1981, p. 25). The necessity for this is suggested by the following anecdote about a woman who participated in a committee on nuclear and alternative energy systems of the US National Academy of Sciences all or most of whose other members were men (Nader, 1981). When, after six months of committee meetings and memoranda she remarked that no one in her 'synthesis panel' had ever used the word 'solar', she was informed by another participant that research on solar energy was not very intellectually challenging. The woman was forced to conclude that in order for something to be intellectually challenging to such professionals it had to be complicated, hazardous, difficult and risky. Conservation appeared to be considered 'feminine', and thus nuclear pursuits 'masculine'.

The dominant science of our time can be seen to be a merger of mind, nature and masculinity (Keller, 1985). The history of science gives evidence of tension between scientific explanations that stress hierarchies, control and unidirectional causal patterns—masculine science—and those that stress interconnectedness, reciprocal interactions and multidirectional paths—feminine science. Masculine science, epitomized by Francis Bacon, implies mastery of man over nature. Feminine science, epitomized by Plato, implies that humans are a part of nature.

Ecology can be defined as the study of the balance of all life on earth. The feminine principle, as presented in feminist philosophy, is the striving towards balance and interrelationship (Leland, 1983). It follows from this that feminism and ecology are inextricably connected.

Several scholars have tried to outline what a female science would encompass, some on a theoretical basis of 'green' politics (Spretnak, 1986; Spretnak & Capra, 1986) and others on one of 'eco-feminism' (Caldecott & Leland, 1983; King, 1983; Leland, 1983). Eco-feminism is based on connectedness and wholeness of both theory and practice and asserts the special strength and integrity of every living thing. Female science would involve an appreciation of the complexity of all phenomena, a perception of change as the only constant and the taking into account of social and ecological factors (Bleier, 1984; Keller, 1985). The career of the plant geneticist Barbara McClintock serves as an indicator of the direction female science might take (Bleier, 1984, p. 206; Keller, 1985, p. 163). Her research endeavours have been based on a respect for the complexity and interrelations in nature, a regard for individual differences and an appreciation of her own feelings and intuition.

It appears that if physics were taught in a manner in which the social and human consequences of scientific and technological innovations were taken into account, girls would be much more interested in physics than they are today and would not drop out of the subject (Lie & Sjöberg, 1984; Sjöberg, 1982). Thus, when girls drop out of physics in great numbers there might be something wrong with the physics rather than with the girls. Physics should be taught with an approach that is integrated with the humanities (Kapitza, 1982). Not doing so appears to lead to symptoms of fear and apathy, as suggested by the escapism and lack of interest shown in some countries by the younger generation. The emergence of irrationality can perhaps be traced to defects in modern education, that is, to a lack of a more general scientific and social outlook, without which it is very difficult to start thinking in a new way not only on matters of disarmament, but on the social impact of science and technology.

It should be added that the lack of interdisciplinarity is much more pronounced at the higher levels of formal education than at the lower ones. The most holistic and integrated teaching can be found in the kindergartens and the lower levels of elementary schools; the most narrow and compartmentalized in the universities and other institutions of higher learning. Moreover, some of the most holistic subjects carry the least prestige. For example, home economics is a subject in which maintenance and care of the environment is often taught. This subject is usually a curricular option, one most often chosen by girls.

Some promising international efforts to create a greater understanding for the care of the environment and for ecological principles should be mentioned. Among the recommendations of the 1972 United Nations Conference on the Human Environment was an important series on education (UNGA, 1973, recommendations 95–101). Largely in response to one of these recommendations (No. 96), the United Nations Educational, Scientific and Cultural Organization (UNESCO) together with the United Nations Environment Programme (UNEP) in 1975 launched an International Environmental Education Programme (Holdgate *et al.*, 1982, pp. 561–90). A 1975 workshop of this programme proposed as guiding principles that environmental education should (Holdgate *et al.*, p. 563):

—consider the environment in its totality—natural and [anthropogenic], ecological, political, economic, technological, social, legislative, cultural and aesthetic;
—be a continuous life-long process, both in school and out of school;
—be interdisciplinary in its approach; emphasize active participation in preventing and solving environmental problems;
—examine major environmental issues from a world point of view, while paying due regard to regional differences;
—focus on current and future environmental situations;

—examine all development and growth from an environmental perspective; [and]
—promote the value and necessity of local, national and international co-operation in the solution of environmental problems.

Several of these principles fit well into the concept of the new female science discussed earlier.

The UNESCO/UNEP International Environmental Education Programme sponsors international conferences (e.g., UNESCO, 1980), provides curricular help to teachers (e.g., Sinha *et al.*, 1985), publishes *Connect* (Paris), a quarterly newsletter available in five languages, maintains a computerized data base and provides financial and technical assistance to a number of pilot projects in different parts of the world. Nevertheless, these efforts will not suffice if learning in the classroom remains hierarchical in structure and if grades continue to be given on the basis of reproducing factual knowledge. The hidden curriculum is often stronger than the official one.

III. The hidden curriculum

When history is taught as a series of wars and natural science is taught without taking ecological and human consequences into account, such teaching naturally influences the attitudes and the norms that are being transmitted. The actual content of textbooks would not be such an issue if formal education encouraged critical thinking, opposition to authority and an independent search for knowledge by students and teachers together. Again, such pedagogy can be found in good kindergartens, but is found less and less often the higher one climbs up the ladder of formal education. It is a common observation, often made by student teachers in teacher training, that the number of spontaneous questions coming from a child decreases rapidly the further the child progresses in the school system. When a child first enters school he or she asks the adult all sorts of questions out of curiosity. The child is asking someone who is presumed to know more about matters about which he or she would like clarification. However, after some years of schooling questions are no longer asked out of curiosity. The child has learned that in school it is the teacher who asks the questions, not the pupil. And teachers ask questions to which they themselves already know the answers. They do not ask out of curiosity, but mostly in order to ascertain whether their students have acquired the right 'deposits' in their brains (Freire, 1972, p. 46). Or the teachers ask questions to 'motivate' the pupils with reference to the learning that is meant to take place. The teachers (who, unlike the pupils, know what this learning is meant to be) ignore those answers that fall outside the intended learning domain, but respond to those that conform to it (Unge Paedagoger, 1979). The type of questions encouraged in students are mostly of the sort asking for further information, not those which are truly critical of the learning process taking place. Indeed, the latter class of question is looked upon as an interruption of the learning process and even as a sign of disobedience.

Through the years of schooling students learn to become obedient because, if they are not, they can be subjected to various types of sanction, the worst being the lowering of their school grades, which reduces the chance of progressing up the educational ladder. Conformity to rules, obedience and loyalty seem to constitute a large part of the hidden curriculum of formal education (Altvater & Huisken, 1978; Brock-Utne, 1982; Illeris, 1976). Through the threat of sanctions the 'right' kind of information is stored in students, 'deposited' as in a bank, thereby leading to a necrophilic adjustment to the world (Freire, 1972, p. 51).

That obedience to authority and loyalty to rules make up a large part of the hidden curriculum of formal education is not normally admitted to by those administering the educational system. The desire is expressed that schools foster values in children, such as democratic thinking, co-operation, creativity and critical awareness, yet it is not recognized that the means used in schools are incongruent with such aims. And—as, for example, in disarmament negotiations—the means are more important than the aims because it is the means that form the ongoing reality.

The major difference between training for loyalty and obedience within the formal school setting and within the military sector is that in formal education this training is part of the hidden, not official, curriculum (where it may even be denied), whereas in the military sector this training is part of the official curriculum. The purpose of basic military training is not so much to teach the recruits military skills, but rather to inculcate in them the values of obedience and loyalty (Arkin & Dobrofsky, 1978); 'I guess you could say we brainwash them a little bit', in the words of a US Marine Corps drill instructor (Dyer, 1985, p. 105).

Though the values of co-operation may be stressed in official school curricula, the system of examinations, grades, awards and class ranking defeats such an aim; instead it furthers the value of competition. In many Western capitalist countries grades are given according to a normal distribution curve, which means that a certain percentage of the student body must receive failing or otherwise bad grades. In practice this means that the student who is constantly getting one of these poor grades is unable to advance unless someone else is downgraded, that is, unless he or she steps on someone else. The hidden lesson here is that in order for students to get ahead they must do so at the expense of their classmates. Thus, structural violence is built into the system.

Competition, one-upmanship, seems to be one of the key norms regulating behaviour within the formal educational system, mostly taught through the hidden curriculum. And competition increases during the school years as the sorting of students into their proper places in society gains momentum. In some countries, for example, in the Nordic ones, grading is kept to a minimum during the first years of schooling. In Norway no grading is supposed to take place during the first six years of elementary school. In spite of this official stricture, some teachers have second- and third-grade (eight- and nine-year-old) pupils solve as many mathematical problems as they are able to within a certain limited period of time and then rank the pupils according to their performance. And what do these youngsters learn? Not merely to solve a mathematical problem, but also whether they are 'good' students, better than the others, or 'bad' students, worse than the others. They learn to compete with others and that time is important. Not only are feelings of superiority and inferiority created, but also a situation of stress.

Competition in elementary and secondary schools has the effect of sorting youngsters, both horizontally and vertically. The youngsters are sorted into boxes that fit into the social structure. It may be in this way that schooling is a major factor responsible for oppression.

By the time that the higher levels of education are attained the basic sorting has already been accomplished, but the competition still goes on. And it carries over into adult life: a race among individuals and among groups of individuals; among states and among groups of states. The race continues for higher prestige, for more money; it continues to be important to win, to be best and to be strongest. In many of the explanations given for the continuing arms race, competition is suggested as the main driving force. Such competition may exist between military blocs; alternatively, it may exist within one bloc; or else it may exist independently within each bloc, a phenomenon that could be referred to as bilateral autism (Wiberg, 1981).

Competition between the USA and the USSR certainly plays a large part in the accelerating arms race, but there is also reason to believe that the notion of such a competition is fostered in part in order to motivate taxpayers to spend more money on the perfection of instruments of death and destruction. It seems that the competition going on within each of these two superpowers—both among scientists and among military branches—plays an even larger role than the competition between them (Mansueto, 1983). In the case of nuclear weapons, the USA is so far ahead of the USSR in almost every aspect of the technological race that the former does not really have to compete with the latter. The formal educational systems in both the NATO and the Warsaw Pact countries are highly competitive and are likely to produce individuals questing to be discoverers, heads of laboratories or chief researchers. Thus the concept of bilateral autism is supported by a consideration of the two formal educational systems.

When Virginia Woolf (1938) maintained that universities shape norms that might easily lead to war, she was writing about the harsh competition in those institutions together with the segmented kind of knowledge taught in them.

IV. Towards more benign norms

Formal education, as it is outlined here, may seem like a dark tunnel filled with suffering, pain and structural violence. Is there some light to be seen somewhere in that tunnel? Is there some place where at least part of that vision of the new approach to education advanced by Virginia Woolf (1938) has come true?

Woolf (1938) tells about a woman who was asked by an educated man how women could help men prevent war. The woman decided that it would be necessary for women to be educated so as to be in a position to prevent war, but not through an education of the sort then being given. She envisioned a new type of university in which there would be no grades and no competition, a university where the aim would not be to specialize and segregate knowledge, but rather to integrate it, with desirable consequences for the human condition. In such a university, ideas, joy and pleasure would be shared; animals, plants and other living beings cared for. There would not be the traditional power plays associated with dominance and competition.

As it is indicated in the first part of this chapter, a number of scholars are doing research into the non-violent resolution of conflict. Their number should be drastically increased and their findings be made part of the teaching of history. History books and curricula should be rewritten and the now hidden history of non-violence and of the lives of women be illuminated. Youngsters could be taught that wars are relatively new phenomena in the history of humankind. Human beings have existed on the earth for at least 300 000 years and there have been weapons for hunting for the past 200 000 of these. On the other hand, wars seem to have existed for only the last 9000 years and thus can be suggested to be cultural phenomena (Mansfield, 1982; Moberg, 1986). Youngsters could learn more about the non-violent solutions to conflict and less about the violent ones. This would also necessitate more research on non-violent conflict resolution and a rewriting of history books. In fact, there is a vast history of non-violent sanctions, that is, pressures that do not kill or threaten physical harm but which, nonetheless, thwart opponents' objectives and cause them to alter their behaviour (Sharp, 1970; 1980, p. 289). Some 85 major cases have been described (Sharp, 1970). Yet the conflicts which have been solved through non-violent means are both inadequately researched and made invisible in history. When both a violent and a non-violent action have been used in a conflict, the violent one is the one which is described in history (Kruegler & Parkman, 1985). In the case of the uprising against the dictatorship of Maximiliano Hernandez Martínez in El Salvador in 1944, the violent action of 2 April was not successful in obtaining the resignation of the dictator whereas the non-violent one of 9 May was. Yet it is 2 April that is celebrated, not 9 May.

When violent sanctions fall short of achieving their objectives the conclusion is not drawn that violence has been tried and found wanting. Instead military analysts ask what conditions favoured the winner and where did the loser go wrong? The assumption is not made that there is something totally wrong with the use of violence. However, when non-violent struggles are not successful, it is easily concluded that non-violence is not useful. Questions need to be asked about ways of improving non-violent means of conflict resolution.

In most cases where non-violent sanctions have been used they have been improvised under harsh conditions with little or no advance preparation on the part of those using them. It is important to teach non-violent solutions to conflict at all levels of formal schooling and in adult education so that non-violent methods become the normal means of conflict resolution (Boulding, 1982; 1986). A declining civilian competence in conflict resolution can be discerned and the whole educational system should be geared towards creating more confidence and competence in conflict resolution by means other than violent ones (Boulding, 1982). When the capabilities for the non-violent solution of problems are not developed at the lower levels in the educational system, it becomes more difficult to develop them later. It can be suggested for the USA, at least, that legal personnel are called in too often in conflicts which people could have solved themselves or through mediation (Boulding, 1982).

It appears possible for educated Westerners to train their social vision through participating in special seminars (Boulding, 1986). The social or natural scientists in such a seminar group must be asked at the outset to forget their accumulated knowledge as it could block new and visionary thinking. The group is asked to envision a disarmed world 30 years from now. Such an exercise would be almost impossible if the participants were to plan for disarmament in the world as it is today. To work with this task, the participants must already have spent considerable time in training their minds to recall past events and to be able to imagine possible future situations. It is hard work to envision a disarmed world 30 years from now, but even harder to work back from that future vision to the present time in five-year intervals, suggesting at each step what the world would look like if the disarmed 30-year vision had, indeed, come true. Yet such seminars increase competence and pleasure, lead to the empowerment necessary as a substitute for the norms of dominance or 'power-over'. It is recommended that such teaching of constructive thinking and conflict management be made a part of the traditional school curriculum. There are books which could be used for such teaching (e.g., Masters & Houston, 1972); these should be translated into several languages and adapted to various levels of schooling. It would also be a good idea to have educators and historians from various countries meet in order to select some good examples of non-violent solutions to conflict. Such exercises, when done by dedicated and competent people, could be incorporated into very useful textbooks that give an appropriate outlook on history.

Non-violent solutions to conflict can also be taught within a traditional school setting where the teacher uses her or his own class as a laboratory. By way of example, a Norwegian teacher in a lower secondary school has shown how a class containing a high percentage of working-class children plus children of immigrants can solve problems they meet in their daily lives, whether in the classroom, during breaks or in the school corridors (Halvorsen, 1982). Becoming conscious of conflicts among themselves, and between them and parents or teachers, helps such children to find solutions to their conflicts; and, in general, to train their imagination regarding conflict. That teacher minimized the use of grades in her class, but did not eliminate them since the children had to pass the regular school examinations. In the process, the children were made aware of what grades do to the climate of a classroom.

The success of peace education in schools can perhaps be judged more by the way pupils behave towards one another in the schoolyard and the classroom than by the amount of learning they are able to reproduce about the arms race or disarmament (Röhrs, 1983, p. 193).

Another light is shown in the dark tunnel of the first part of this chapter in the envisioning of a new 'female' science. Scientists of either sex critical of the traditional approach to science education and in sympathy with this new vision should be given time and money to work together in order to permit the development of a new natural science, a science built upon connectedness and relatedness, upon respect for nature and ecological balance. The UNESCO/UNEP International Environmental Education Programme described above is also a clear step in the right direction. It is to be hoped that the philosophy and guiding principles from this programme will gain wide acceptance and will be able to permeate the educational system. The governments of the world should provide more funds for the programme so that it can be expanded and the results of pilot projects disseminated widely.

Within traditional peace research there seems to be too much mindless weapon counting, too little research on the human and social consequences of the arms race and too little research on non-violent conflict resolution (Boulding, 1981). Another light in the dark is that since 1981 the International Peace Research Association has benefited from the infusion of feminist theory and studies (Brock-Utne *et al.*, 1986).

In the second part of the chapter no example is given of formal education shaping norms conducive to the necessary questioning of, and even disobedience towards, authority; or of the furthering of co-operation, sharing and joy instead of competition. Some examples could have been given of small private schools where parents and teachers strive to realize other values than those that permeate traditional school systems. However, these schools are mostly at the elementary level and their numbers are very limited and their effects uncertain. Additionally within the formal educational system there have been experiments in co-operation and sharing, in team-work among teachers, in group-work among pupils, and in the keeping of grading to a minimum. For example, in one four-year study a comparison was made between two lower secondary schools that belonged to the same formal educational system, were located in the same municipality, and had available the same economic resources—one of them traditional and the other progressive (Brock-Utne, 1981). The traditional school gave many examinations and had separate subjects; the progressive school placed little emphasis on examinations and had an integrated approach to teaching. When teachers in the upper secondary schools received students from these two schools they could always tell from which one they had come on the basis of the questions the students asked. Those from the traditional school asked only questions which would assure that they understood their homework assignments. By contrast, the students from the progressive school would ask questions such as: Why do you want us to learn that? What is the point of that? Why study that subject at all?

There are also examples of college and university studies built on co-operating and sharing, where the studies are interdisciplinary and problem-oriented, where students work and even take their examinations in groups and where the only grades given are 'pass' or 'non-pass' (Brock-Utne, 1986a).

V. Conclusion

It has been claimed that those who try to create green oases in the grey educational desert are just deluding themselves (Callawaert & Kallos, 1976). Education, it is suggested, will always be a function of society, an instrument for the state and for the élite to control. Education cannot change unless the whole structure of society changes. Thus a task for educational researchers might well be to analyse how education functions in maintaining the existing power structure of society, the ruling values and norms. However, attempts to initiate change in this system are seen by some as futile and even counter-productive.

To such criticism one must answer that educational structures are built up of people and that changes must be striven for simultaneously at all levels. Personal changes achieve political significance and political changes have personal consequences. Moreover, even if one wishes to analyse how formal education functions in maintaining the *status quo*, one important way to approach that would be to create alternatives (green oases) within the system. Not only would this test the limits of the system, it might well simultaneously produce some individuals who possess critical faculties, individuals of the sort that are sorely needed.

References

Altvater, E. & Huisken, F. (eds). 1971. *Materialen zur politischen Ökonomie des Ausbildungssektors [Materials regarding the political economy of the educational sector]*. Erlangen, FR Germany: Politladen, 468 pp.

Arkin, W. & Dobrofsky, L. 1978. Military socialization and masculinity. *Journal of Social Issues,* Ann Arbor, Mich., 34(1):151–168.

Attenborough, R. 1982. *Gandhi*. Hollywood, Calif.: Columbia, 35 mm color film, 188 min.

Bacon, F. 1623. Of the dignity and advancement of learning. In: Spedding, J., Ellis, R. L. & Heath, D. D. (eds). *Works of Francis Bacon. IV*. London: Longman & Co., 498 pp.: pp. 275–498, 1860.

Bleier, R. 1984. *Science and gender: a critique of biology and its theories on women.* Elmsford, NY: Pergamon Press, 220 pp.

Boulding, E. 1981. Perspectives of women researchers on disarmament, national security and world order. *Women's Studies International Quarterly* [now *Women's Studies International Forum*], Oxford, 4(1):27–41.

Boulding, E. 1982. Education for peace. *Bulletin of the Atomic Scientists,* Chicago, 38(6):59–62.

Boulding, E. 1986. *Från vision till verklighet [From vision to reality].* Stockholm: Fredsårsdelegationens Skriftserie No. 2, 31 pp.

Brock-Utne, B. 1981. *Ungdomsskoler i utvikling: rapport fra et prosjekt [Secondary schools in development: report from a project].* Oslo: Universitetsforlaget, 254 pp.

Brock-Utne, B. 1982. Hidden curriculum of the Norwegian compulsory school. *Tidskrift för Nordisk Förening för Pedagogisk Forskning,* Lund, 1982(1–2):33–45.

Brock-Utne, B. 1985. *Educating for peace: a feminist perspective.* New York: Pergamon Press, 175 pp.

Brock-Utne, B. 1986a. Broren på Lillehammer [The brother at Lillehammer]. *Oppland Distriktshøgskoles Skriftserie,* Oppland, Norway, 1986(60):255–269.

Brock-Utne, B. 1986b. *En mors tåre: vi som mister våre barn på veiene [A mother's tears: we who lose our children on the highways].* Oslo: Ida Forlag, 186 pp.

Brock-Utne, B. 1986c. *Feminist perspectives on peace research.* Oslo: International Peace Research Institute, PRIO Report No. 11/86, 23 pp.

Brock-Utne, B. 1987. Sports, masculinity and education for violence. Oslo: International Peace Research Institute, PRIO Report No. 1/87, 16+5 pp.

Brock-Utne, B. & Haukaa, R. 1980. *Kunnskap uten makt: kvinner som laerere og elever [Knowledge without power: women as teachers and pupils].* Oslo: Universitetsforlaget, 221 pp.

Brock-Utne, B., Traylor, J. & Aas, S. (eds). 1986. *Women, militarism and disarmament.* Oslo: International Peace Research Institute, PRIO Report No. 6/86, 213 pp.

Caldecott, L. & Leland, S. (eds). 1983. *Reclaim the earth: women speak out for life on earth.* London: Women's Press, 247 pp.

Callawaert, S. & Kallos, D. 1976. Den rosa vågen i svensk pedagogik [The pink wave in Swedish pedagogy]. *Forskning om Utbildning,* Stockholm, 3(1):31–38.

Carroll, B. A. 1972. Peace research: the cult of power. *Journal of Conflict Resolution,* Beverly Hills, Calif., 16:585–616.

Dyer, G. 1985. *War.* New York: Crown Publishers, 272 pp.

Easlea, B. 1981. *Science and sexual oppression: patriarchy's confrontation with women and nature.* London: Weidenfeld & Nicolson, 314 pp.

Easlea, B. 1983. *Fathering the unthinkable: masculinity, scientists and the nuclear arms race.* London: Pluto Press, 230 pp.

Eisler, R. & Loye, D. 1986. Peace and feminist theory: new directions. *Bulletin of Peace Proposals,* Oslo, 17:95–99.

Eysenck, H. J. & Nias, D. K. B. 1978. *Sex, violence and the media.* New York: St Martin's Press, 306 pp.

Freire, P. 1972. *Pedagogy of the oppressed* [translated from the Portuguese by M. Bergman Ramos]. London: Sheed & Ward, 186 pp.

French, M. 1985. *Beyond power: on women, men, and morals.* New York: Summit Books, 640 pp.

Galtung, J. 1981. Disarmament education: a partial answer. In: Haavelsrud, M. (ed.). *Approaching disarmament education.* Guildford, UK: Westbury House, 280 pp.: pp. 269–272.

Gardner, H. & Perkins, D. 1982. Harvard's Project Zero studies the numerous artistic 'intelligences'. *Behavior Today,* New York, 13(17):1–2.

Graff, H. J. (ed.). 1981. *Literacy and social development in the West: a reader.* Cambridge, UK: Cambridge University Press, 340 pp.

Halvorsen, A. 1982. Krig, fred, nedrustning angår alle ungdomsskolelärere [War, peace, disarmament concern all secondary school teachers]. In: Hansjordet, H. (ed.). *Skole for fred [Schools for peace]*. Oslo: Det Norske Samlaget, 128 pp.: pp. 56–70.

Hamann, B. 1986. *Bertha von Suttner: ein Leben für den Frieden [Bertha von Suttner: a life for peace]*. Munich: Piper Verlag, 551 pp.

Holdgate, M. W., Kassas, W. & White, G. F. (eds). 1982. *World environment 1972–1982: a report by the United Nations Environment Programme.* Dublin: Tycooly International, 637 pp.

Illeris, K. 1976. *Problemorientering og deltagerstyring: oplaeg til en alternativ didaktik [Problem-orientation and participatory learning: proposal for an alternative didactic]*. Copenhagen: Munksgaard, 271 pp.

Kapitza, S. 1982. Social consciousness and education for disarmament: how to learn and think in a new way. In: Rotblat, J. (ed.). *Scientists, the arms race and disarmament.* London: Taylor & Francis, 323 pp.: pp. 245–254.

Keller, E. F. 1985. *Reflections on gender and science.* New Haven: Yale University Press, 193 pp.

King, Y. 1983. Eco-feminist imperative. In: Caldecott, L. & Leland, S. (eds). *Reclaim the earth: women speak out for life on earth.* London: Women's Press, 247 pp.: pp. 9–14.

Kirkerud, B. 1982. Forskerens ansvar [Researcher's responsibility]. *Samtiden,* Oslo, 1982(4):2–7.

Kruegler, C. & Parkman, P. 1985. Identifying alternatives to political violence: an educational imperative. *Harvard Educational Review,* Cambridge, Mass., 55(1):109–117.

Lehrer, T. 1981. *Too many songs.* London: Methuen, 144 pp.

Leland, S. 1983. Feminism and ecology: theoretical connections. In: Caldecott, L. & Leland, S. (eds). *Reclaim the earth: women speak out for life on earth.* London: Women's Press, 247 pp.: pp. 67–72,229.

Lie, S. & Sjöberg, S. 1984. *Myke jenter i harde fag [Soft girls in hard science]*. Oslo: Universitetsforlaget, 122 pp.

MacBride, S. 1978. Brainwashing with a good clean bomb. In: M'Bow, A.-M. (ed.). *Suicide or survival?: the challenge of the year 2000.* Paris: UNESCO, 192 pp.: pp. 89–94.

Mansfield, S. 1982. *Gestalts of war: an inquiry into its origins and meanings as a social institution.* New York: Dial Press, 274 pp.

Mansueto, C. 1983. Take the toys from the boys: competition and the nuclear arms race. In: Thompson, D. (ed.). *Over our dead bodies: women against the bomb.* London: Virago Press, 253 pp.: pp. 108–119.

Masters, R. E. L. & Houston, J. 1972. *Mind games: the guide to inner space.* New York: Viking Press, 246 pp.

Merchant, C. 1980. *Death of nature: women, ecology, and the scientific revolution.* San Francisco: Harper & Row, 348 pp.

Moberg, E. 1986. *Är krig naturligt? [Is war natural?]*. Stockholm: Fredsårsdelegationens Skriftserie No. 1, 24 pp.

Nader, L. 1981. Barriers to thinking new about energy. *Physics Today,* New York, 34(2):9,99–104.

Oliphant, M. 1982. Comment on the social responsibilities of scientists. In: Rotblat, J. (ed.). *Scientists, the arms race and disarmament.* London: Taylor & Francis, 323 pp.: pp. 191–196.

Paxton, T. 1963. What did you learn in school? *Sing Out!*, New York, 13(4):15.

Reardon, B. 1981. Militarism and sexism: influence on education for war. *UME [United Ministries in Education] Connexion,* Valley Forge, Pennsylvania, 9(3):6–10.

Reardon, B. A. 1985. *Sexism and the war system.* New York: Teachers College Press, 111 pp.

Röhrs, H. 1983. *Friede—eine pädagogische Aufgabe: Idee und Realität der Friedenspädagogik [Peace—a pedagogical assignment: concept and reality for peace pedagogy].* Braunschweig, FR Germany: Agentur Pedersen, 397 pp.

Sabo, D. 1985. Sport, patriarchy and male identity: new questions about men and sport. *Arena Review,* Las Vegas, 9(2):1–30.

Schmid, A. P. & Graaf, J. de. 1982. *Violence as communication: insurgent terrorism and the Western news media.* London: Sage Publications, 283 pp.

Schuman, H., Inkeles, A. & Smith, D. H. 1967. Some social psychological effects and noneffects of literacy in a new nation. *Economic Development & Cultural Change,* Chicago, 16:1–14.

Sharp, G. 1970. *Exploring nonviolent alternatives.* Boston: Porter E. Sargent, 161 pp.

Sharp, G. 1980. *Social power and political freedom.* Boston: Porter E. Sargent, 440 pp.

Sinha, S., Jangira, N. K. & Das, S. 1985. *Environmental education: module for pre-service training of social science teachers and supervisors for secondary schools.* Paris: UNESCO Environmental Education Series No. 9, 123 pp.

Sjöberg, S. 1982. Soft girls in hard science? *Tidskrift för Nordisk Förening för Pedagogisk Forskning,* Lund, 1982(1–2):55–63.

Skjelsbaek, K. 1979. Militarism, its dimensions and corollaries: an attempt at conceptual clarification. *Journal of Peace Research,* Oslo, 16:213–229.

Spender, D. 1982. *Women of ideas and what men have done to them: from Aphra Behn to Adrienne Rich.* London: Routledge & Kegan Paul, 586 pp.

Spretnak, C. 1986. *Spiritual dimension of green politics.* Santa Fe, New Mexico: Bear, 95 pp.

Spretnak, C. & Capra, F. 1986. *Green politics: the global promise.* Santa Fe, New Mexico: Bear, 257 pp.

Stiehm, J. H. 1982. The protected, the protector, the defender. *Women's Studies International Forum,* Oxford, 5:367–376. [Reprinted in: Stiehm, J. H. (ed.). 1983. *Women and men's wars.* Oxford: Pergamon Press, 379 pp.: pp. 367–376.]

Suttner, B. v. 1889. *Die Waffen nieder!: eine Lebensgeschichte [Down with weapons!: a biography].* Dresden: E. Pierson's Verlag, 2 vols (309+324 pp.). English-language edn: *Lay down your arms: the autobiography of Martha von Tilling* [translated from the German by T. Holmes & rev. by the authoress]. London: Longmans, Green, 435 pp., 1892.

Suttner, B. v. 1909. *Memoiren [Memoirs].* Stuttgart: Deutsche Verlags Anstalt, 553 pp.

UNESCO. 1980. *Environmental education in the light of the Tbilisi conference.* Paris: UNESCO, 100 pp.

UNGA (United Nations General Assembly). 1973. *Report of the United Nations Conference on the Human Environment, Stockholm, 5–16 June 1972.* New York: UN General Assembly Document No. A/CONF.48/14/Rev.1, 77 pp.

Unge Paedagoger. 1979. *Projekt Skolesprog: skoledage [Project school language: school days].* Kongerslev, Denmark: GMT, 2 vols (744 pp.).

Vellacott, J. 1982. Women, peace and power. In: McAllister, P. (ed.). *Reweaving the web of life: feminism and nonviolence.* Philadelphia: New Society Publishers, 440 pp.: pp. 30–42.

Wiberg, H. 1981. Dilemmas of disarmament education. In: Haavelsrud, M. (ed.). *Approaching disarmament education.* Guildford, UK: Westbury House, 280 pp.: pp. 129–144.

Woolf, V. 1938. *Three guineas.* San Diego, Calif.: Harcourt Brace Jovanovich, 188 pp.

Ziman, J. 1982. Basic principles. In: Rotblat, J. (ed.). *Scientists, the arms race and disarmament.* London: Taylor & Francis, 323 pp.: pp. 161–178.

Zuckerman, S. 1980. *Science advisers, scientific advisers and nuclear weapons.* London: Menard Press, 16 pp.

8. The news media as forces in shaping cultural norms relating to war and the environment

DAVID M. RUBIN
New York University

I. Introduction

The competition between the USA and the USSR is commonly scored by comparing the numbers of new weapon systems developed and deployed, or by counting the dollars and roubles spent on defence. However, maintaining the military balance depends on more than the comparative sizes of nuclear and conventional arsenals. Each side must convince the other of its grim resolve to actually use weapons of mass destruction. With psychology and perception an integral part of strategy, the journalist becomes every bit as important in this competition as the general, the scientist or the political leader.

Although journalists do not make military policy in either the USA or the USSR, they do frame these issues for their respective audiences. Since the two societies have little direct interaction, what is known about 'the enemy' comes almost exclusively from the media, whether directly or via governmental officials speaking through the media. What journalists choose to report, and how they report it, is as much a component of the arms race as a new missile or warhead.

Over the last 40 years the media in both the USA and USSR have, willingly or not, worked with their respective governments to condition the public to accept the inevitability of nuclear weapons and of their possible use. Given that the basic strategic relationship between the USA and USSR has changed little over this period—each holding the other (and the rest of the world) hostage in a nuclear embrace—both systems of media have, for their own reasons, been reliable partners with government in this undertaking.

Could it be otherwise? Could the media be independent forces for change, challenging the nuclear policies of their governments? The power of the media to shape public attitudes and cultural norms is much celebrated. Could that power be put to use to change the way the peoples of the world view the arms race and its likely impact on the environment?

This chapter is an examination of the constraints that bind the systems of media in both the USA and USSR—and, to a great extent, all such systems—when they approach this unique subject. These constraints include: (*a*) governmental and ownership controls over the content of the media; (*b*) nationalistic or patriotic impulses of journalists, who are naturally bound by their own cultural experience; (*c*) historic definitions of what and who makes news; and (*d*) limits on the power of the media to change public attitudes.

Not surprisingly, it must be concluded that it is difficult for any press system—libertarian or authoritarian—to challenge the enormous power of government in shaping the views of its citizens on questions of war, peace and environmental destruction. Change, if it is to come at all, will not come easily. Yet, developments in both the East and West foreshadow that such change must eventually come.

II. News media and the protection of national security in the USA

Libertarian theory argues that one of the obligations of the press in a free society is to act as a check on the power of government (Siebert, 1963). In providing this check, the press has been called a fourth branch of government (Cater, 1959) or an adversary of government (Rivers, 1970).

In the nuclear era, the first important test of the willingness and ability of the media to play the role of adversary came in the weeks after the atomic explosions at Hiroshima and Nagasaki. While the US administration struggled to define a strategy to cope with the political, military and scientific problems created by the atomic bomb (Manoff, 1983), the news media in the USA were filled with the views of clergymen, scientists and other citizens who questioned the ethics of the attack on Japan and debated who should control the new technology.

Once the US administration set its nuclear course and decided not to share the atomic secret with the USSR, these adversarial voices gradually disappeared from the media. The 'civil' voice, which for a short time made itself heard through the news media on the management of the bomb, was quickly crowded out by the voice of the state. It is this 'statist' view that has come to dominate coverage of the US–Soviet superpower relationship (Manoff, 1983).

National-security journalism is the severest test of the adversarial relationship between press and government, and also the best measure of the robustness of freedom of the press in a society. A journalist who would attempt to use the news media to shape the norms of the culture towards war and its likely impact on the environment must be prepared to enter this territory and investigate the combat strategies of government and the uses to which weapons are to be put. Such information, essential to any public debate about governmental policy in a free society, is closely held by the decision-makers and is amongst the deepest secrets of the culture.

The ethic of the press as the fourth branch of government has produced many journalists in the USA who have, from time to time, peeled back the secrets of the nuclear régime. For example, William Broad of the *New York Times* has reported on the accuracy of verification of underground nuclear-weapon tests (Broad, 1986). The same reporter has exposed many of the problems confronting scientists at work on the US strategic defense initiative (Broad, 1985). The *Washington Post* has demonstrated how the current US administration is preparing to fight a protracted nuclear World War III, despite public assertions to the contrary (Hiatt, 1986).

The above examples of adversarity are, in fact, atypical of day-to-day national-security journalism in the USA, which is controlled by the state to serve its own needs. The US government is able to use the law, or its own considerable powers of persuasion, to circumscribe coverage of the nuclear régime. It can also limit the journalist's access to information, so that freedom to publish is undercut by the inability to gather information worth publishing. Journalists who persevere against governmental objections risk damaging their careers by seeming to be either unpatriotic or dupes of the enemy. Journalists make the task of government easier by the way they have chosen to define 'news' in the national-security setting. Only a small circle of past and present officials—all with 'statist' views—are accorded a hearing on the nuclear-arms race and superpower relations.

Governmental constraints on journalists in the USA, discussed in some detail below, make it highly unlikely that even the adversarial US press can present its own sustained vision of a world free of the threat of total war, and to thereby help in changing the views of the public towards war and the destruction of the environment.

Limits imposed by the law

Of all the measures a government may employ to restrict the press, prior restraint is the most damaging since it keeps information from ever reaching the public. Beginning in 1931 the US Supreme Court (in its case 'Near *vs* Minnesota') limited the use of prior restraint to situations posing a clear and present danger to the national security, situations in which the sailing dates of military transports or the number and location of troops would be revealed. Prior restraint is, therefore, legally acceptable, if rare, in the US system.

On a handful of occasions in the years since 1931, the US government has tested the tolerance of the courts—and, ultimately, of the public—for the prior restraint of national-security information. In 1971 the government tried through use of an injunction ('USA *vs* New York Times Company') to stop further publication of a series of articles based on secret documents about the origins of the Second Indochina War. In 1979 the government similarly moved to halt publication of a magazine article (Morland, 1979) about the construction of hydrogen bombs ('USA *vs* Progressive'). In each case the press ultimately prevailed and published the information; nevertheless, the threat of prior restraint overhangs the national-security field. A permanent injunction against publication awaits only a set of facts that will permit the government to meet its heavy burden of proof that such publication (or broadcast) of sensitive information would pose a grave threat to national security.

Journalists and their potential sources in the US government are made aware of the areas of greatest sensitivity by an elaborate system of secrecy classification that serves to compartmentalize information and to limit its flow to the press and public. Penalties that may be assessed against governmental officials who traffic in classified information run the gamut from loss of job to prosecution under such statutes as the 1954 US Atomic Energy Act (which limits unauthorized disclosures about nuclear technology) or the US Federal Code of Civil Law (title 18, section 798 of which makes it a crime to publish or disclose any classified information about US or foreign code-making, code-breaking or eavesdropping). Moreover, one governmental employee has been successfully prosecuted for violating the espionage laws (Yoder, 1985), by providing classified photographs to a magazine (Jane's, 1984). Employees of the US Central Intelligence Agency, and other bureaucracies where secrecy is prized, are particularly constrained in what they may reveal to the public (see, e.g., the 1972 lawsuit 'USA *vs* Marchetti' and the 1980 lawsuit 'USA *vs* Snepp').

Journalists themselves have not as yet been prosecuted in the USA under the prior-restraint laws because of the legal uncertainty about whether limiting publication in the mass media was the actual intent of the legislators. None of these laws seems to have been intended originally to limit the performance of the press. However, the prosecution of a journalist might be awaiting only the right set of facts and a suitably irate public.

The rigour with which violations of the US system of secrecy classification are pursued varies from administration to administration. The leaking of classified information is not easy to police because so much secret material exists; and also because the practice of leaking is, for a variety of motives, solidly entrenched in Washington at all levels of government (Hess, 1984, pp. 75–94). Neither the US government nor US journalism, as they are now practised, could proceed without it.

Although it is not possible to predict precisely which stories with national-security implications will arouse the ire of the US government, it is safe to hypothesize that information about combat plans and the capabilities of specific weapon systems are high on the list of forbidden topics. As a result, the government has a virtual monopoly over information on these subjects, and can shape or restrict public debate on them as it likes. Journalists who seek to break that monopoly risk at least a wall of silence or, if they are successful, prior restraint and prosecution. However, such information is essential to any informed public discussion of warfare and its effects on the environment.

Extra-legal limits imposed by government

Just the threat of legal action, and the inherent power and prestige of the presidency in the USA, permit the executive branch of the US government to warn off journalists from national-security stories. The most celebrated example of such restraint occurred during the 1962 Cuban missile crisis when the *New York Times* uncovered information about Soviet missile installations in

Cuba and the likely response of the US administration to them. The president telephoned the publisher of the newspaper and asked that the story be held up so as not to give the USSR advance notice of the US strategy. The *New York Times* agreed, and the president later gave credit to the newspaper for its contribution to the success of the operation (Aronson, 1973, pp. 77–78).

Even when the US press and government do not agree on the necessity for secrecy, the government can usually get its way. In 1986 the director of the US Central Intelligence Agency was concerned that press coverage of the case of accused spy Ronald Pelton would compromise secrets about US intelligence gathering and provide information to the USSR. He warned the press to avoid even public speculation about Pelton's activities. Representatives of the Central Intelligence Agency, the National Security Agency, the Federal Bureau of Investigation and the National Security Council met frequently with editors and reporters of the *Washington Post* in order to read drafts of one particular story before its publication. After a call from the US president to the publisher of the newspaper, the Pelton story that eventually appeared did not contain certain information objectionable to the government (Bradlee, 1986).

The rules of this game are difficult to establish. Journalists and editors evaluate each US government request for secrecy on its own terms. They weigh the sensitivity of the information, the foreign power that would stand to benefit, the public's need to know, competitive pressures from other news organizations, the likelihood that their willingness to co-operate would achieve the government's desired end, the public standing of the president and more. In the end, the decision to publish rests with the journalist and newspaper, but it is a decision that can lead to post-publication penalties or diminished access to sources and information. If journalists decide too often to ignore requests for secrecy from government, then government may exercise, or seek to expand, its legal options.

Source control of national-security journalism

As useful as legal and extra-legal tools are in controlling the press, the US government can, in addition, almost always manipulate the flow of information on national-security questions because it is the most important—often the only—source for journalists to consult. For example, it would be exceedingly difficult to cover underground nuclear-weapon testing without access to the US Department of Energy; or to cover the US strategic defense initiative without contacts among scientists at the Los Alamos and Livermore national weapon laboratories.

Sources are essential to journalists no matter what subject they cover (Hess, 1984; Sigal, 1973). The best journalists generally have access to the best sources, and conscientious journalists attempt to present some approximation of the truth in their stories by gathering and presenting the views of as many diverse sources as possible.

The more complex the subject, the more dependent are journalists on their sources. This has been demonstrated in how the press covered two serious nuclear power plant accidents: first at Three Mile Island in Pennsylvania, USA in March 1979 (Rubin, 1979), and then at Chernobyl in the Ukraine, USSR in April 1986 (Hohenemser *et al.*, 1986). In both cases the many errors that appeared in press accounts were usually traceable to sources who were either uninformed or misinformed or who were intentionally shading the truth. Under the pressure of daily deadlines that leave little or no time to check conflicting accounts, and without alternative sources to consult, journalists are virtually powerless to avoid manipulation by their sources. This is equally true in the national-security field.

Journalists should not be limited to a thin layer of top government sources, who provide a purely 'statist' view of the nuclear régime. The highly respected US journalist I. F. Stone was celebrated for relying solely on documents and primary source materials—together with his own analytic and intuitive skills—to report the doings of government, and not on leaks from high-level, usually unnamed, officials. This permitted Stone to identify and discuss the many real splits in the bureaucracy, thereby shedding light on the policy-making apparatus. It must be added that Stone's brand of journalism—one in which the journalist defines what is news—should not be confused with the journalism that records the public, almost ritualized, splits between policy-making élites. In the latter case journalists are merely being used as weapons for the waging of bureaucratic warfare, often by means of leaks.

Journalists without the ability or the time to adopt I. F. Stone's work habits nevertheless need not be rigidly limited to government sources. A number of alternatives are worth exploring: the political opposition in the USA; politicians from allied countries; officials in the USSR; and members of citizen-activist groups. However, for a variety of reasons, journalists rarely make imaginative use of these sources to expand the marketplace of ideas.

Government officials in the USSR are suspect as sources because the USSR is the declared enemy. Much of what the USSR says is termed propaganda by US government officials. US journalists who rely too heavily on Soviet sources run the risk of being labelled either naive or unpatriotic. This is precisely what happened to the ABC television network in 1986, when its news department was criticized by the US administration for permitting a lengthy rebuttal by a Soviet spokesperson to a presidential speech on defence spending (Cannon & Carmody, 1986).

Opposition party members in the USA (be they Republicans or Democrats) are not particularly useful to journalists because debate over arms-control policy or Soviet–US relations is extremely narrow in the USA. It is not conceivable that a serious politician would run for national office on a platform of eliminating the nuclear arsenal or of radically redefining US relations with the USSR. The US national-security establishment is sufficiently daunting as to limit the rhetoric and imagination of all national political figures. As a result, press coverage of political campaigns or of the congress does not elicit new perspectives for the public.

Notions radical in the US context are not received hospitably when they come from European politicians. The indifferent to negative reception journalists accorded the proposals of the leader of the British Labour Party (Neil Kinnock) regarding a non-nuclear United Kingdom when he visited the USA in 1986 are testament to that (Dugger, 1986–87).

The views of citizen-activist groups have gained a hearing in the press on many issues, including especially environmental ones (Dykstra, 1987). However, on issues of arms control or US–Soviet relations such sources have little credibility with the press.

In 1986 the Council of Bishops of the United Methodist Church in the USA rejected the mutual terror of nuclear deterrence and argued against the concept of justifiable war (White *et al.*, 1986). The Council's so-called foundation document, an official resource for the United Methodist Church, included language explicitly linking war and the environment (White *et al.*, 1986, p. 11): '. . . creation itself is under attack. Air and water, trees and fruits and flowers, birds and fish and cattle, all children and youth, women and men live under the darkening shadows of a threatening nuclear winter. . . . It is a crisis that threatens to assault not only the whole human family but planet earth itself. . . .'

Whereas these powerful words of the Methodist bishops did appear in the *Los Angeles Times* story (Goldman, 1986), they were absent from most other news accounts (Buursma, 1986; Hyer, 1986; Pace, 1986). Furthermore, the views of the Methodist bishops were covered only by religion writers or general-assignment reporters, not by the arms-control specialists of higher status who, moreover, might integrate such thoughts into their own reporting.

In the *Washington Post* account of the Methodist bishops' teaching statement, the reporter asked one of the bishops why the clerics were 'meddling' in arms-control policy (Hyer, 1986). The reporter's use of the word 'meddling' is revealing. It provides an accurate if unsettling insight into how most 'statist' journalists view citizens who have the temerity to confront their government on the nuclear *status quo*.

When the nuclear freeze movement in the USA was at its height in the early 1980s, the press was attracted to it not for its arms-control proposal (which the press did not take seriously), but because the movement threatened to play a role in US electoral politics. Once the freeze movement lost its perceived political power after the 1984 elections, the press lost interest in it.

Only a handful of private persons outside the government—principally those with special technical expertise in verification, intelligence gathering or weapon development—gain access to the media to challenge statist views. These persons are generally associated with such organizations as the Union of Concerned Scientists (Cambridge, Massachusetts), the Federation of American Scientists (Washington), the Brookings Institution (Washington) or the Carnegie Endowment for International Peace (Washington). Journalists will also accept as sources former high officials in past administrations, especially those who negotiated with the USSR or who made defence policy. Everyone else is in a journalistic purgatory—particularly those likely to make radical connections between military actions and environmental protection.

Even in a country like the Federal Republic of Germany, where the anti-nuclear movement is broader and more visible than in the USA, the press can be similarly hostile. During the demonstrations there in the early 1980s against the installation of US medium-range missiles, some editors ordered their reporters not to cover various activities of the demonstrators, and to portray them as communist-infiltrated or communist-inspired (Michel, 1986).

A content analysis of coverage of the arms race in a number of Hungarian, French and Austrian newspapers revealed that the views of peace movements were by no means regularly present in the newspapers analysed; indeed, the ideas and proposals of peace movements and their strategies and tactics aimed at arms limitation and disarmament were rarely presented to the reader (Terestyeni, 1986).

Private ownership and state control: their impact on national-security journalism

One reason for the enduring nature of the statist view of the arms race, in both the West and East, is the pattern of ownership and the economic base of the media. Where the media are directly controlled by the state (as is the case in the USSR and elsewhere in the nations of the Warsaw Treaty Organization), it is obvious that the mass media can play no independent or adversarial role in shaping cultural norms. This is not to say that state-controlled media could not be used by government to accomplish such a task (see below).

In the West, where private ownership and the need to attract advertisers and an audience is the rule, the media are also unlikely to be adversarial, but for different reasons. The capitalist system in the USA has served the press well. The three major US television networks are all parts of large and profitable corporations, including one—NBC—that is owned by a major defence contractor, General Electric. The daily newspaper industry is dominated by a small group of large chains (e.g., Gannett, Knight-Ridder, Times Mirror); these chains are all publicly held companies with strong records in the investment community. It is to be expected that the owners and chief operating officers of such corporations share their government's unenthusiastic view of the Soviet system.

Because television in the USA is a mass medium supported entirely by advertising, it must be able to deliver large numbers of contented viewers to those advertisers. This has produced a timid medium that avoids controversy in its efforts to attract and hold the lowest common denominator among viewers (Gitlin, 1983, pp. 24–26,61). Challenging the US government on nuclear policy or on its relations with the USSR is not the best way to achieve this goal. Whenever television does challenge the government on a national-security issue, unwelcome controversy results. For example, the congress investigated CBS for its documentary on *The Selling of the Pentagon*, which outlined the public-relations efforts of the military sector (Aronson, 1973, pp. 149–50). ABC was criticized for airing the film *The Day After*, which some on the political right saw as anti-nuclear propaganda because it portrays the ghastly outcome of a nuclear attack on a US city (Bianculli, 1986; Onosko, 1987). ABC was attacked from the political left for its series *Amerika*, which presented a frightening view of a Soviet takeover of the USA (Bianculli, 1986; Onosko, 1987).

To make matters even more difficult, in the USA television is a medium licensed by the federal government and subject to a complex web of regulations, some of which are aimed squarely at the content of news and documentary programmes (e.g., the 1949 US Federal Communications Commission 'Fairness Doctrine'). In such a regulatory climate, US television cannot be sufficiently distanced from government to provide a forum for new ideas about the nuclear régime.

Newspapers have greater freedom than television, but the owners and managers—overwhelmingly white, male and economically advantaged—share the same world view as the US civil and military officials that their reporters cover, and they identify strongly with the governmental and economic systems that have given them their success.

None of what has been presented above is peculiar to the USA among Western countries. British television is similarly wary of confrontation with its government on matters military, as its devotedly patriotic coverage of the Falkland/Malvinas War of 1982 demonstrated (Eldridge, 1983). As long as the major media in any society are in the hands either of large communication conglomerates or of the state itself, the military culture is unlikely to be challenged (Luckham, 1984).

Taken together, the legal and extra-legal controls at the disposal of the state, deference shown by journalists to official sources (and the hostility shown to everyone else), and the big-business ownership of the media have together produced a press system in the USA (and in many of its allied countries) that is 'free' to challenge the nuclear régime, but is generally unwilling to do so. On national-security subjects, the result is a US press that most often functions as an arm of the state. The degree to which such a press can independently challenge its audience to adopt new attitudes towards war and the environment is therefore quite limited.

III. Coverage by the US news media of nuclear winter

If an event were to be created that would permit—even encourage—the news media to discuss in compelling fashion nuclear warfare and how it might conceivably lead to the nearly total destruction of the environment, the theory of nuclear winter is that event. Nuclear winter became a major news story in 1983 after articles describing this possible phenomenon appeared in *Parade Magazine,* which is distributed as a supplement to many Sunday newspapers in the USA (Sagan, 1983), in *Science* (Turco *et al.*, 1983) and elsewhere.

These articles suggested that one by-product of a nuclear attack overlooked in previous modelling was the smoke produced by burning cities and forests. This smoke, the authors argued, would block out sunlight and produce a serious drop in temperature, leading to crop failures, famine and the possible extinction of combatant and non-combatant populations, along with most plant and animal life. The authors raised once again Herman Kahn's (1961) image of a doomsday machine: the attacker in a nuclear exchange would be committing suicide, and at the same time would be dooming the rest of the planet to death by starvation.

The notion of nuclear winter made the potential effects of a nuclear war less abstract to the general public and provided the opportunity for prominent individuals to discuss in the news media the responsibility of the superpowers for the protection of the planet. One example of this, among many, was physicist Freeman Dyson's statement to the *Boston Globe* that 'The discovery of nuclear winter has given a new starkness to the responsibility for the survival of mankind' (Saltus, 1986).

It is possible to imagine nuclear winter occasioning a searching national debate in the USA about the uses to which a nuclear arsenal can actually be put, and the appropriateness of the combat strategies that have been adopted by the two superpowers. For as one critic makes clear, if the thesis of nuclear winter is, indeed, valid, it would threaten to make nonsense of every notion that the war planners have managed to come up with in 40 years of trying to devise a sensible way to fight a nuclear war (Powers, 1984).

Few subjects are more enshrouded in secrecy than the so-called US Single Integrated Operational Plan (SIOP), which assigns strategic tasks to each of the nuclear warheads deployed by the USA. Not surprisingly, in light of the constraints on the press outlined above, no such national debate occurred over the significance of the nuclear-winter theory. The classification of relevant information as secret, a lack of alternative sources, government silence and the absence of a tradition in the USA of discussing such issues all combined to keep a significant debate from breaking out in the US mass media.

It must be noted that nuclear winter did not disappear entirely from the US news media after the first flush of interest. However, the focus was not on nuclear weapons and their impact on the environment. Rather, it shifted to the accuracy of the projections of the scientists who advanced the theory, and the degree to which they may have overstated the dangers. As a news story, nuclear winter evolved from a problem for military planners into a dispute among scientists. The US government assisted in this evolution by supporting further scientific research (certainly a legitimate course) and by remaining silent on the strategic implications of the theory (thus reducing the sources available to the press who might keep the strategic angle afloat). The questions before the public therefore became: If the superpowers use nuclear weapons, does the world face a nuclear winter, or just a nuclear 'autumn' (a word with a much less menacing ring)? And to what extent did the political views of the theory's proponents produce bad science (Gleick, 1986; 1987; Schneider, 1986;

Seitz, 1986; Turco *et al.*, 1986)? The question was *not*: How can the superpowers change their combat strategies to minimize the effects of nuclear weapons on the environment, given a variety of smoke-producing scenarios?

The quality of the science and computer modelling associated with nuclear winter is, of course, an important and newsworthy question, as is the intermingling of science and politics. However, from the US government's perspective these are much safer questions. Long-running and inconclusive scientific disputes are among the most difficult stories for the press to report (Nelkin, 1987) and for the public to digest. The likeliest results of such coverage would be public rejection of the nuclear-winter thesis on scientific grounds, public confusion about the degree to which nuclear winter ought to change thinking about nuclear war or public suspicion about the motives of the scientists involved. The result would not be—and has not been—a public call in the USA for rethinking US nuclear strategy in order to minimize the environmental damage likely to result from a nuclear attack. This could only happen if the focus of public interest became the military planners rather than the scientists.

Nuclear winter is only one case, but the pattern of coverage so neatly conforms to what one would expect, given the nature of the constraints on the US press in the national-security area, that one must question the possibility of covering such a story in any manner more challenging to government.

IV. The Soviet press as an arm of the state

The focus thus far has been on the US media because the limits to freedom of the press in the USA in the national-security context are not well defined, and because many of the possibilities suggested by that freedom are so rarely explored. A similar inquiry into the Soviet system does not raise as many contradictions or possibilities.

The Constitution (Fundamental Law) of the USSR proclaims that (USSR, 1977, art. 50): 'In accordance with the interests of the people and in order to strengthen and develop the socialist system, citizens of the USSR are guaranteed freedom of speech [and] of the press. . . . Exercise of these political freedoms is ensured by . . . the opportunity to use the press, television, and radio.' Nonetheless, the Soviet concept of freedom of the press is very different from the US view. In the USA, freedom of the press is freedom from government control, but not freedom from economic-class or advertiser control. In the USSR, the press is theoretically free from class control, but certainly not free from government control. Indeed, the US notion of the press acting as a fourth branch of government in order to provide an independent check on authority is not possible within the Soviet system.

The press is perhaps the most powerful institution available to the Soviet government to socialize and educate its citizens. The Soviet press is not a private business venture reflecting the views of reporters and editors, nor is it a mirror of public opinion. Rather, it is a major social force to facilitate the goals and interpret the doctrine of the government (Inkeles, 1961; Schramm, 1963,

p. 110). Stalin called the press the 'driving belt' between the masses and the government; Nikita Khrushchev called it 'our chief ideological weapon' (Inkeles, 1961, p. 221). More recently, speaking to the 27th Congress of the Communist Party in 1986, General Secretary Mikhail Gorbachev noted that the Central Committee of the Communist Party sees the mass media as 'an instrument of creation and an exponent of the Party's general viewpoint' (Gorbachev, 1986, p. 45).

This is not to say that the Soviet press never criticizes the workings of the bureaucracy. It does. One role of the press is that of safety valve, providing a forum for citizen complaints and frustrations through the publication of letters and investigative articles (Mickiewicz, 1981, p. 49). In recent years the Soviet press has vigorously condemned pollution of the environment, raising environmental protection to an issue of national importance (Kramer, 1983). This can be seen in angry newspaper articles about the despoliation of Lake Baikal in Siberia (Rasputin, 1986) and about the siting of an electric power plant in an Armenian nature preserve (Bablumyan, 1986).

The Soviet newspaper *Pravda* has made it quite clear that Soviet government officials must respond to press criticism of their policies: 'It cannot be considered normal when local officials do not react to articles in the press by front-ranking workers, innovators and respected people. . . . In our practice, it is accepted and established that a critical article in a newspaper must be answered. This is done not for the sake of the newspaper itself but for the sake of public openness, for the sake of the cause, so that people will be informed about how shortcomings are being eliminated' (Pravda, 1986). This should not be seen as criticism *of* the state; rather, it is criticism—within bounds—set *by* the state, for purposes of the state.

US journalist Robert Kaiser, who covered the USSR for the *Washington Post,* suggested a decade ago that there was a list of subjects not to be covered in the Soviet press, including information about local crime, drug use, natural disasters, censorship, security intelligence, arms sales abroad and special payment of athletes (Kaiser, 1976, p. 236). In the present Gorbachev era [1985–] this list has become out of date. Many subjects are now being explored by the press that were out of bounds during the era of Leonid Brezhnev [1964–82], among them domestic disasters such as the one at the Chernobyl nuclear power plant alluded to earlier.

A selective reading of the Soviet press makes clear that little is published in the national-security area; and it is rare, indeed, for published reports on national security to challenge Soviet government policy, even in the currently improving climate for criticism known as *glasnost.* One notable exception was a column in *Moscow News* by the respected Soviet commentator Alexander Bovin (1987), the last paragraph of which asked why his government was willing to remove intermediate-range missiles from Europe after it had gone to all the trouble and expense of deploying them in the first place. Bovin was answered by a military man in a subsequent issue (Lebedev, 1987). However, this exchange between journalist and official was polite by US standards.

Descriptions of Soviet strategic thinking, the size and deployment of the Soviet nuclear arsenal, the status of Soviet intelligence gathering and the like are all off limits. Calls in the Soviet press to establish nuclear-free zones (Kostikov, 1986; Mikhailov, 1986) or to outlaw chemical weapons (USSR, 1986) are common. But these are general appeals, stated in broad policy terms. There is far more to be learned about the Soviet military sector or the deployment of Soviet nuclear weapons from the US press than from the Soviet.

Neither the Soviet nor the US government wants its media to challenge nuclear policy and to create a citizenry at odds with the leadership on the management of its nuclear arsenal. The Soviet government does not confront such problems because the press is an instrument of its policy. The US government reduces the chance of such a challenge by exploiting the shared values of policy makers and of owners of the media, by limiting access to information, by providing misinformation, by appealing to the patriotic instincts of journalists or, if all else fails, by threatening legal action.

If either the Soviet or the US government were to make a decision to use the mass media in a campaign to educate the public about the dangers of total war, and to raise the level of public concern about combat strategy and environmental damage, how successful would it be? The discussion to follow suggests that the media are indeed powerful, but not as powerful as many assume or, perhaps, would like to believe. Soviet leaders might be marginally more successful than their US counterparts, but neither would find the press to be a perfect instrument for changing public attitudes or expectations.

V. Limits on the power of the press, both US and Soviet

Polls that explore what the US public knows about the arms race, and US–Soviet relations generally, find broad knowledge of the most basic facts, but general ignorance of all else, including the issues that divide these two superpowers and the conditions under which nuclear weapons might actually be used (Rosen, 1986–87). A recent poll suggests that 86 per cent of the people in the USA know that the USA and the USSR each possess thousands of nuclear weapons (Rosen, 1986–87). Yet only 22 per cent know that it is US policy to use nuclear weapons if the USSR were to invade Europe; and, in general, just 19 per cent are aware that the USA does not have a no-first-use policy for nuclear weapons (Rosen, 1986–87).

A 1980 survey in an industrialized city in southern Russia, USSR revealed that about 25 per cent of the people did not understand the word 'colonialism'; about 40 per cent could not define 'dictatorship'; almost 50 per cent did not know what 'imperialism' meant; and of the order of 70 per cent did not know the terms 'reactionary' and 'liberal' (Mickiewicz, 1983, p. 106). Similarly depressing statistics of public knowledge are available as well for the citizenry of other countries. Such indications of limited public knowledge suggest that the power of the media to change attitudes—or even merely to inform—is quite limited. Mass media usually work to reinforce existing attitudes of their audiences. Thus they are more often a force for preserving the *status quo* than a force for change (Sandman *et al.*, 1982, p. 17).

Communication researchers have learned that attitude change is difficult to achieve because of all the 'noise' in the channels inhibiting the smooth transmission of messages. The audience throws up its own barriers, including: (*a*) selective attention (willingness to expose itself only to communications that are liked); (*b*) selective perception (interpretation of communications to make them coincide with its current belief structure); and (*c*) selective retention (remembrance only of what it wants to remember) (Sandman *et al.*, 1982, p. 2). The tendency for people to be selective in assimilating information is reinforced by their additional tendency to avoid the discomfort of cognitive dissonance by selecting messages from the media that reinforce their convictions, and by rejecting those that challenge their beliefs (Festinger, 1957). As it is difficult to imagine a subject to consider that is more uncomfortable than the use of nuclear weapons and their likely impact on the environment, it is probably safe to assume that the mass media face particular difficulties in attracting and holding the attention of the public on this general issue.

Certain characteristics of the mass media in both the USA and the USSR can work to overcome some of the audience resistance referred to above. The audience is immersed in media. Messages are repeated often, and over considerable periods of time. The same messages may be communicated through different media in different ways. In the volume of messages, Western media may have an edge. But the Soviet media are more co-ordinated with the educational system (Jones, 1985, p. 160).

Although the US media are unlikely ever to be as co-ordinated in their content as the Soviet media, the marketplace of ideas in a libertarian society is much more uniform than one would suspect. Journalists move from story to story as a group, with all the mighty resources of the press focused on a very few predictable events, many of which are orchestrated by government. This notion of 'pack' journalism is a familiar and accepted one in Washington (Hess, 1981, pp. 61,130–32). The US media are also remarkably homogeneous in content because of a lack of daily-newspaper competition in local markets, the growth of newspaper chains, the shared news values of the four virtually identical nation-wide television news operations, the prevalence of wire-service material in the media, and the lack of diversity among owners of the media or among newsroom employees (Sandman *et al.*, 1982, pp. 102–35).

If harnessed by government, the media of both the USA and the USSR are capable of exercising limited power to change public norms and attitudes in the area of national security. But the option to employ the media in such a fashion in both cases belongs to government.

VI. Press systems other than US or Soviet

This chapter focuses almost entirely on the news media of the USA and the USSR because the superpowers possess most of the weapons fully capable of destroying the fragile global ecosystem. However, a brief review of other systems of media suggests that the lack of journalistic independence found in the USA and USSR in the face of the nuclear régime is probably worldwide.

An examination of newspaper coverage of the Eighteen Nation Disarmament Committee (now, the Committee on Disarmament) meeting in Geneva in 1968 revealed that the newspapers of one bloc generally ignored the proposals of the other bloc; and that coverage showed a bias towards national interests and the interests of allies (Gould, 1969). Most significantly, a bias was found in favour of nuclear weapons. Moreover, two important papers—*Rudé Právo* (Prague) and *Le Monde* (Paris)—provided so little coverage of the meeting that no conclusion could be drawn about their coverage.

A study of press coverage of disarmament and armament in the Federal Republic of Germany concluded that the information provided by the newspapers in the sample was insufficient to permit the public to evaluate national military policy (Becker, 1983). A study of the media in Finland led to the conclusion that the terms for debate on matters of security and disarmament are very much determined by a so-called security-policy élite (Varis, 1983). Such an élite is composed of a few military experts, defence committees and other closed organizations; experts outside this élite remain marginal.

Thus it seems that news media elsewhere than in the USA or the USSR, if not around the globe, are also unlikely to break with their governments by opening their news columns and television programmes to fresh thinking about combat, disarmament and the environment.

VII. Conclusion

The degree to which the press mirrors and reinforces government policy in the nuclear-weapon field (even when government begins to edge away from its own policies) can be seen in the aftermath of the meeting between the US and Soviet leaders at Reykjavik in October 1986. The two leaders placed on the negotiating table the fleeting possibility that all nuclear weapons could be destroyed in stages; or, at least, that all strategic missiles might be eliminated. That opened to the press the opportunity to explore how the two superpowers might move towards establishing a non-nuclear world, with a significantly decreased threat to the ecosystem. This would seem to be a newsworthy story.

Yet, with the exception of the *Christian Science Monitor* (Boston)—which alone among major US newspapers published a series of articles on a world without nuclear weapons (18 to 24 November 1986)—the press in the USA viewed the idea with the same scepticism as did US military and political leaders. One 'military analysis' article in the *New York Times* concluded that without a rebalancing of conventional forces, a world with fewer atomic weapons would be *more* dangerous than the current stand-off (Trainor, 1986). The US government as a whole quickly retreated to such a position, and the opportunity for the press to pursue that extraordinary turn of events in Iceland was lost. Nor were such articles forthcoming from the major Soviet organs in the months after the summit. For a variety of reasons, neither the US nor the Soviet government (and neither press system) appears to be interested in this path—or perhaps any path—to a world without nuclear weapons.

In its combat strategy, the USA has gradually been expending more and more munitions against larger and increasingly ill-defined target areas, with consequently higher levels of environmental damage (Westing, 1980, pp. 3–5). Westing (1980, p. 193) has suggested that restraints on such behaviour will have to be based on ecological, moral or ethical considerations that will presumably be expressed in the form of legal sanctions of an international character. However, such considerations do not at present appear to affect the combat strategies of either superpower; and, as a result, they are absent from coverage of the arms race by the media.

The recent fragile flowering of openness in the Soviet press under General Secretary Mikhail Gorbachev, and the great strides the US press has made in recent years in covering environmental, medical and women's issues, suggests that change in journalistic performance is indeed possible. A first step would be for journalists to recognize the need for change. However, fully 60 per cent of the ethical codes promulgated by journalistic organizations around the world fail to say anything at all about covering subjects that bear on peace and national security (Nordenstreng & Alanen, 1981). Journalists might well begin with a rigorous self-study and an explication of the ethical obligations of their profession in the nuclear era.

Galtung (1986) has called on the world's press to report on how arms control proposals are perceived by *both* sides, in order to avoid the dangerous reaction of presenting only the side with which one sympathizes. He suggests that at present the media lead the public to believe that war is exciting and that peace is a rather dull state of affairs. He urges that the media portray more clearly the benefits of peace—to make peace a more compelling concept. Journalists might also modify the definition of 'news' so as to pay somewhat less attention to the statist view and more attention to the civil view. The US press has shown that it is capable of this as regards the evolving story of Black independence in South Africa. This is not a story that the current US administration has wanted on the front pages of newspapers or on the evening television news day after day, yet the news media have reached out to embrace all manner of official and unofficial sources in order to report it, thereby keeping pressure on the US government to formulate new policy.

Beginning in the late 1960s, US journalists were willing to expand their definition of news and confer credibility upon environmental activists as legitimate sources, thereby transforming and dramatically improving coverage of such environmental issues as air or water pollution (Rubin & Sachs, 1973). In so doing, the news media assisted in putting the destruction of the environment on the agenda of the US government. The next logical step for journalists will be to link warfare, and particularly nuclear warfare, to their newly found concern for the environment.

Military tactics change as a result of battlefield experience. Change has certainly come in the operation of nuclear power plants in both the USA and the USSR. The accidents at Three Mile Island and Chernobyl provided the 'battlefield' experience necessary to stimulate changes in operating standards and procedures. The mass media of both countries played an important role in facilitating a spirited public debate about the technology. Although neither superpower has abandoned nuclear power plants, they both have taken steps to limit damage to the public and the environment that might occur in case of accident.

Military leaders of the two superpowers have not yet been drawn into a detailed debate of the above sort about the environmental effects of nuclear weapons; nor, for that matter, have they discussed damage to the environment exacted by non-nuclear munitions. Until such a debate breaks out, either within the armed forces or among their civilian leadership, the mass media are likely to be little more than bystanders. Painful as it is to contemplate, additional 'battlefield' experience in the nuclear realm may be the necessary condition for full participation by the mass media in the transformation of cultural norms towards war and the environment.

References

Aronson, J. 1973. *Deadline for the media.* New York: Bobbs-Merill, 327 pp.

Bablumyan, S. 1986. [Studying democracy: concerning a preserve] (in Russian). *Izvestia,* Moscow, 1986(11 Aug):6.

Becker, J. 1983. Methodological problems of dealing with disarmament in the press. *Current Research on Peace & Violence,* Tampere, 6:29–51.

Bianculli, D. 1986. 'Amerika' sparks controversy early. *Philadelphia Inquirer* 1986 (17 Oct):Fl,F8.

Bovin, A. 1987. World on my personal computer: breakthrough. *Moscow News* 1987(10):3.

Bradlee, B. 1986. The Post and Pelton: how the press looks at national security. *Washington Post* 1986(8 Jun):F1,F4.

Broad, W. J. 1985. Science showmanship: a deep 'star wars' rift. *New York Times* 1985(16 Dec):A1,B12.

Broad, W. J. 1986. Bomb tests: technology advances against backdrop of wide debate. *New York Times* 1986(15 Apr):C1,C3.

Buursma, B. 1986. Bishops assail military policy. *Chicago Tribune* 1986(30 Apr, Sect. 1):4.

Cannon, L. & Carmody, J. 1986. Reagan says ABC news erred. *Washington Post* 1986(28 Feb):A1,A8.

Cater, D. 1959. *Fourth branch of government.* New York: Vintage Books, 194 pp.

Dugger, R. 1986–87. U.S. press and Neil Kinnock's non-nuclear Britain. *Deadline,* New York, 1(6):4–7.

Dykstra, P. 1987. Unbalanced coverage: the failure of the U.S. media. *Greenpeace,* Washington, 12(1):7–9.

Eldridge, J. 1983. War and peace news on British television. *Current Research on Peace & Violence,* Tampere, 6:3–28.

Festinger, L. 1957. *Theory of cognitive dissonance.* Stanford, Calif.: Stanford University Press, 291 pp.

Galtung, J. 1986. On the role of the media for world-wide security and peace. In: Varis, T. (ed.). *Peace and communication.* San José, Costa Rica: Editorial Universidad para la Paz, 305 pp.: pp. 249–265.

Gitlin, T. 1983. *Inside prime time.* New York: Pantheon Books, 369 pp.

Gleick, J. 1986. Less drastic theory emerges on freezing after a nuclear war. *New York Times* 1986(22 Jun):A1,A20.

Gleick, J. 1987. Science and politics: 'nuclear winter' clash. *New York Times* 1987(17 Feb):C6.

Goldman, J. 1986. Methodists reject nuclear deterrence. *Los Angeles Times* 1986(30 Apr, Sect. 1):11.

Gorbachev, M. 1986. Political report of the CPSU Central Committee to the 27th congress of the Communist party of the Soviet Union. . . . February 25, 1986. *New Times,* Moscow, 1986(9):13–48.

Gould, L. N. 1969. *ENDC and the press.* Stockholm: SIPRI, Stockholm Paper No. 3, 77 pp.

Hess, S. 1981. *Washington reporters.* Washington: Brookings Institution, 174 pp.

Hess, S. 1984. *Government/press connection: press officers and their offices.* Washington: Brookings Institution, 160 pp.

Hiatt, F. 1986. Building a post-World War III force. *Washington Post* 1986(27 Jul):A1,A16.

Hohenemser, C., Deicher, M., Ernst, A., Hofsäss, H., Lindner, G. & Recknagel, E. 1986. Chernobyl: an early report. *Environment*, Washington, 28(5)6–13,30–43.

Hyer, M. 1986. Methodist bishops blast SDI, A-arms. *Washington Post* 1986(30 Apr):A1,A22.

Inkeles, A. 1961. Mobilizing public opinion. In: Inkeles, A. & Geiger, K. (eds). *Soviet society: a book of readings.* Boston: Houghton Mifflin, 703 pp.: pp. 219–228.

Jane's. 1984. Satellite pictures show Soviet CVN towering above Nikolaiev shipyard. *Jane's Defence Weekly,* London, 2:171–173.

Jones, E. 1985. *Red army and society: a sociology of the Soviet military.* Boston: Allen & Unwin, 230 pp.

Kahn, H. 1961. *On thermonuclear war.* 2nd edn. Princeton, New Jersey: Princeton University Press, 668 pp.

Kaiser, R. G. 1976. *Russia: the people and the power.* New York: Atheneum, 499 pp.

Kostikov, M. 1986. [Commentator's column: for a nuclear-free northern Europe] (in Russian). *Pravda*, Moscow, 1986(20 Aug):5.

Kramer, J. 1983. Environmental problems. In: Cracraft, J. (ed.). *Soviet Union today.* Chicago: University of Chicago Press, 348 pp.: pp. 153–161.

Lebedev, Y. 1987. World on my personal computer: why SS–20 missiles have appeared. *Moscow News* 1987(11):3.

Luckham, R. 1984. Of arms and culture. *Current Research on Peace & Violence,* Tampere, 7:1–64.

Manoff, R. 1983. Covering the bomb: press and state in the shadow of nuclear war. In: Rubin, D. & Cunningham, A. (eds). *War, peace and the news media.* New York: New York University, Center for War, Peace, and the News Media, 285 pp.: pp. 197–237.

Michel, L. P. 1986. The topic 'war and peace' in the mass media of the Federal Republic of Germany. In: Varis, T. (ed.). *Peace and communication.* San José, Costa Rica: Editorial Universidad para la Paz, 305 pp.: pp. 67–98.

Mickiewicz, E. P. 1981. *Media and the Russian public.* New York: Praeger, 156 pp.
Mickiewicz, E. 1983. Feedback, surveys, and Soviet communication theory. *Journal of Communication,* Philadelphia, 33(2):97–110.
Mikhailov, V. 1986. [International review: after Suva] (in Russian). *Pravda,* Moscow, 1986(17 Aug):4.
Morland, H. 1979. The H-bomb secret: to know how is to ask why. *Progressive,* Madison, Wisconsin, 43(11):14–23.
Nelkin, D. 1987. *Selling science: how the press covers science and technology.* New York: W. H. Freeman, 225 pp.
Nordenstreng, K. & Alanen, A. 1981. Journalistic ethics and international relations. *Communication,* London, 6:225–254.
Onosko, T. 1987. Only in 'Amerika'. *Chicago Tribune* 1987(4 Jan, Sect. 13):6–7.
Pace, E. 1986. Methodist bishops approve paper denouncing use of nuclear arms. *New York Times* 1986(30 Apr):A15.
Powers, T. 1984. Nuclear winter and nuclear strategy. *Atlantic Monthly,* Boston, 254(5):53–64.
Pravda, 1986. [Newspaper's critical word] (in Russian). *Pravda,* Moscow, 1986(14 Jun):1.
Rasputin, V. 1986. [Invitation to Moscow: we have only one Baikal] (in Russian). *Izvestia*, Moscow, 1986(17 Feb):3,6.
Rivers, W. L. 1970. *Adversaries: politics and the press.* Boston: Beacon Press, 273 pp.
Rosen, J. 1986–87. Public knowledge/private ignorance. *Deadline,* New York, 1(6):1–4.
Rubin, D. M. 1979. *Report of the public's right to information task force.* Washington: White House, President's Commission on the Accident at Three Mile Island, 308 pp.
Rubin, D. M. & Sachs, D. P. 1973. *Mass media and the environment: water resources, land use and atomic energy in California.* New York: Praeger, 320 pp.
Sagan, C. 1983. Nuclear winter. *Parade Magazine,* New York, 1983(30 Oct):4–5,7.
Saltus, R. 1986. Physicist calls abolition of nuclear arms feasible. *Boston Globe* 1986(15 Apr):6.
Sandman, P. M., Rubin, D. M. & Sachsman, D. B. 1982. *Media: an introductory analysis of American mass communications.* 3rd edn. Englewood Cliffs, New Jersey: Prentice-Hall, 525 pp.
Schneider, S. 1986. Nuclear autumn. *Wall Street Journal,* New York, 1986(25 Nov):29.
Schramm, W. 1963. Soviet communist theory. In: Siebert, F. *et al.* (eds). *Four theories of the press.* Urbana: University of Illinois Press, 153 pp.: pp. 105–153.
Seitz, R. 1986. Melting of nuclear winter. *Wall Street Journal,* New York, 1986(5 Nov):36.
Siebert, F. 1963. Libertarian theory. In: Siebert, F. *et al.* (eds). *Four theories of the press.* Urbana: University of Illinois Press, 153 pp.: pp. 39–71.
Sigal, L. 1973. *Organization and politics of newsmaking.* Lexington, Mass.: D. C. Heath, 221 pp.
Terestyeni, T. 1986. Case of Nepszabadság, International Herald Tribune, Le Monde, and die Presse. In: Varis, T. (ed.). *Peace and communication.* San José, Costa Rica: Editorial Universidad para la Paz, 305 pp.: pp. 112–125,289–294.
Trainor, B. E. 1986. Cutting A-arms: safer or more dangerous world? *New York Times* 1986(17 Oct):A9.
Turco, R. P., Toon, O. B., Ackerman, T. P., Pollack, J. B. & Sagan, C. 1983. Nuclear

winter: global consequences of multiple nuclear explosions. *Science*, Washington, 222:1283–1292.

Turco, R., Toon, O. B., Ackerman, T., Pollack, J. & Sagan, C. 1986. Nuclear winter remains a chilling prospect. *Wall Street Journal*, New York, 1986(12 Dec):29.

USSR. 1977. *Constitution (Fundamental Law) of the USSR*. Moscow: USSR Supreme Soviet. [Reprinted in: Lane, D. 1978. *Politics and society in the USSR*. 2nd edn. Oxford: Martin Robertson, 622 pp.: pp. 553–584.]

USSR. 1986. [Soviet government statement] (in Russian). *Pravda,* Moscow, 1986(31 May):1.

Varis, T. 1983. Media coverage of disarmament-related issues. *Current Research on Peace & Violence*, Tampere, 6:52–64.

Westing, A. H. 1980. *Warfare in a fragile world: military impact on the human environment.* London: Taylor & Francis, 249 pp. [a SIPRI book]

White, C. D. *et al.* (United Methodist Council of Bishops). 1986. *In defense of creation: the nuclear crisis and a just peace*. Nashville, Tennessee: Graded Press, 96 pp.

Yoder, E. 1985. New wave spying. *Washington Post* 1985(4 Nov):15.

9. The arts as forces in shaping cultural norms relating to war and the environment

ROSALIND J. MARSH
University of Exeter

I. Introduction

Since time immemorial war has been a major theme in art and literature, because for the last 9000 years war has been a fundamental and widespread aspect of human existence. Until the twentieth century war was generally accepted in human society, which made the occasional rejection of war by artists and writers particularly striking. The human relationship with nature has also been an enduring concern of Western art and literature, although it was not until the twentieth century that the devastation of nature through warfare and pollution became a prominent theme. The arts have a special contribution to make in relation to war and the environment, because they engage the emotions and imagination as well as the intellect, and thus can exert an influence which transcends the compass of rational argument or political debate. For this reason, however, the role of the arts throughout history has been an ambivalent one: the arts have possessed great power through words or images either to celebrate war or to condemn it.

This chapter explores the history of the arts relating to war in Western culture from earliest times to the present, in order to illustrate their dual role. The main focus of the chapter is 'high culture', especially painting and literature, but reference is also made to 'popular culture' or 'mass culture', particularly that of the twentieth century—film, 'pop' music, photography, television, popular novels and science fiction—which may act as a countervailing force to the 'high culture' created by outstanding individuals. A special section is devoted to Soviet literature since the time of World War II, in order to compare the way the themes of war and the environment are handled in a literature stringently controlled by the state with their treatment in the Western democracies where the arts are subject largely to commercial pressures. The chapter: (*a*) demonstrates how attitudes to war and the environment have changed throughout time; (*b*) analyses whether the arts are able to form cultural norms, and to what extent they merely reflect views prevalent in the societies which engender them; and (*c*) discusses what, if any, influence artistic works exert on the policies of governments.

II. War in the arts before the twentieth century

From the dawn of civilization poets, artists and musicians of all countries have celebrated courage and heroism (Jones, 1968; Keegan & Darracott, 1981; Silva *et al.*, 1963; Stallworthy, 1984), partly because people of ideas have always been fascinated by people of action, and partly because, without celebration in words, pictures or music, heroism would fade from memory for lack of an audience. Already in prehistoric rock paintings, such as the Archers of Tassili in the Sahara, war figured as a major theme (Silva *et al.*, 1963, pp. 15–16). In the ancient civilizations of the Near East, emperors, kings and conquerors promoted the celebration of their military exploits on a monumental scale: the art of ancient Egypt and Mesopotamia commemorates the victory of the absolute ruler over his enemies as a triumph of the forces of righteousness over the forces of evil. In Europe, Christianity became adopted by the state and came to accept war. With the exception of biblical themes, war was the main concern of medieval art; and although art of the Renaissance moved towards portraiture and landscape, it also continued to celebrate man as warrior and conqueror. Music too has from the earliest times been associated with European military traditions, since alarms and calls were essential to the day-to-day running of armies; and military marches and patriotic songs played a valuable part in stimulating a martial mentality in time of war. By the seventeenth century drums, fifes, bugle horns and trumpets had become the common property of all European military musicians. The military musician's calling was an honourable one, and he was an esteemed member of all royal households (Olson, 1981).

Artists and sculptors have frequently emphasized the glory of war because of their dependence upon powerful patrons. In the seventeenth and eighteenth centuries artists often chose military themes because they were employees of an imperial court, like Diego Velázquez; or because they had military subjects commissioned, like Albrecht Altdorfer's *The Battle of Issus* [1529] (Silva *et al.*, 1963, pp. 41–43). The French Revolution and Napoleonic wars coincided with the neoclassical movement, which, with its interest in Greek and Roman history and legend, produced much heroic war art, notably the paintings of Jacques-Louis David. The romantic movement, with its concern for individualism and extreme emotions, and the fashion for 'historical' subjects in the second half of the nineteenth century also inspired much writing and painting on military themes. Such heroic poems as 'Casabianca' by Felicia Hemans ('The boy stood on the burning deck . . .') and Alfred Tennyson's 'The Charge of the Light Brigade' [1855] (Stallworthy, 1984, pp. 115–16) became widely popular.

The value of military art for propaganda purposes was recognized by the Medici and sponsored by a succession of conquering kings and emperors, from Charles V to Napoleon. In the aggressively nationalistic atmosphere of late nineteenth-century and early twentieth-century Europe, the artist and writer continued to play an important part as influential political agents of the state.

The late nineteenth century saw the emergence of a school of specifically military artists who, acting as war correspondents, were given facilities by campaigning armies to depict events, in words or pictures, which could be rapidly circulated to a wide audience. During the two world wars all the belligerent governments commissioned artists to work at the front and record their visions of the scene. In Hitler's Germany and Stalin's USSR the role of the artist, writer and musician as servant of the state rose to its apogee.

There is another, opposing theme running through world literature and art: protest against war and the desire for peace (Bates, 1969; Bruckner *et al.*, 1984; Ferguson, 1972). Certain religious traditions have provided a powerful source of pacifist sentiment throughout the ages: the Judaeo–Christian tradition, which dates from the Jewish anticipation of a Messiah and which has become increasingly ethical and universal throughout history; the Chinese or Taoist tradition, which dates back to perhaps the third century BC and has spread throughout the East; and the Buddhist tradition, which merges with the latter. Other sources of anti-war thought are secular: the rationalist tradition, inherited from ancient Greece, which flourished again in the Middle Ages and Renaissance; and the 'purely human', individual response of poets, artists and others in contact with war in any age and country, both of which merge with the Jewish and Christian traditions to form a significant part of contemporary Western thought.

Anti-war art has always been very personal; occasional, since it has represented a response to a particular threat of war; and, up to the twentieth century, highly unusual (Keegan & Darracott, 1981). In the ancient world, where it was taken for granted that the well-being and security of the state rested on the army, there were few unambiguous denunciations of war. However, some writers were prepared to attack specific wars: in the fifth century BC Euripides' tragedy *The Trojan Women* [415 BC] and Aristophanes' comedy *Lysistrata* [411 BC] condemned the 27-year conflict between Athens and Sparta. In Homer's *Iliad* [*ca.* eighth century BC] Nestor, speaking to the assembled Achaeans on the plain before Troy, had earlier launched a more general attack on (Pope, 1867, p. 157):

That wretch, that monster, that delights in war:
Whose lust is murder, and whose horrid joy
To tear his country, and his kind destroy!

Similarly, in Vergil's *Aeneid* [19 BC] the poet and his hero constantly complain that fighting is a terrible duty imposed by omnipotent gods; yet both poets celebrate the great wars that shaped their countries' origin and destiny.

The first unambiguous condemnation of war in the ancient Western tradition is probably *De Rerum Natura* [*On the Nature of Things*; first century BC] by the Roman poet Lucretius, which blasphemed against the established order by repeatedly describing the war god Mars as a stupid brute. Lucretius' work contains several themes that have become prevalent from the nineteenth century to the present day: an awareness of the connection between religious intolerance and violence; the view that it is fine to watch a life-and-death struggle as long as the observer is in no danger; and compassion for the families of dead soldiers.

Western art and literature possess a rich tradition of images of peace, which has often been associated with the natural world. The ancient myths of the 'golden age' and of the Garden of Eden evoke a joyful time when humans and animals lived in harmony with one another and with nature (Clark, 1977). The Old Testament book of Isaiah contains (in chapter 11) one of the most beautiful and familiar expressions of this vision. The idea of a peaceable kingdom does not, however, necessarily mean the advocacy of an end to war: often the kingdom, even a spiritual one, is achieved by means of a successful war, as, for example, in ancient Asian and modern Muslim cultures.

War has frequently been seen as the potential destroyer of both human beings and the natural world. The New Testament book of Revelation to John (the Apocalypse) has provided an important source of anti-war thought and imagery in the literature and art of the West from the second century to the present times. Pieter Brueghel's *The Triumph of Death* [*ca* 1564] (Keegan & Darracott, 1981, pp. 210–11), which shows soldiers in vain combat with the forces of destruction, ostensibly represents a sermon against sinners, but it could also be interpreted as propaganda against the harshness of Spanish rule in the Netherlands. The apocalyptic paintings of Hieronymus Bosch and of Matthias Grünewald in the late fifteenth century were inspired by the general fear of the end of the world, which seems to take possession of Western society every 500 years (Clark, 1976, p. 239).

Throughout the ages the frightening aspects of war gradually became dominant in art. Sculptors and artists came to dwell more on the miseries than the glories of war, depicting the agonies of the defeated as well as the pride of the victors. The Thirty Years' War of 1618–48, embroiling many of the nations of Europe, was marked by the first widespread resistance to war and the emergence of art which unequivocally condemned war. The engraver Jacques Callot, in his two series on the *Miseries of War* [1633] (Bruckner *et al.*, 1984, pp. 23–25) depicts war as a monstrous engine devouring living human beings (although his work could also be interpreted in more personal terms as an expression of the hostility felt by an inhabitant of Lorraine for the French). The first great German picaresque novel, *The Adventuresome Simplicius Simplicissimus* [1669] by Hans von Grimmelshausen, a survivor of the Thirty Years' War, describes a world where human values are degraded, where murder, rape, looting and kidnapping are everyday events and where combatants and civilians neither know nor care on which side they are. Francisco Goya's (1863) famous series of prints *The Disasters of War*, executed between 1812 and 1826, expresses the artist's revulsion at the brutalities and famine during the Napoleonic Wars in Spain. Very few of Goya's prints, which so graphically condemn the folly of war, were published in his lifetime. Another skilful anti-war artist who was frequently in trouble with the authorities was the cartoonist Honoré Daumier, whose lethal visual images suggested that European security after the fall of Napoleon was being precariously maintained by militarism, fraud and exploitation. Daumier was perhaps the first artist to link an anti-war stance with the new cosmic vision of the planet as a whole, notably in his famous cartoon of 1867 depicting Galileo trying to tiptoe across a globe bristling with bayonet points (Bruckner *et al.*, 1984, pp. 36–39).

An anti-heroic attitude towards war emphasizing the hard lot of the common soldier dates back to the complaints of a miserable Egyptian foot-soldier around the fifteenth century BC (Bates, 1969, p. 92), and has been echoed since in countless folk songs and soldiers' songs handed on from one war to the next (Ferguson, 1972, pp. 21,55). Shakespeare in *Henry IV* created two archetypal characters embodying opposed attitudes to war: Hotspur, the incarnation of honour; and Falstaff, who upholds cowardice as a means of ensuring personal survival. Some nineteenth-century novelists, such as 'Stendhal' (Marie Henri Beyle) in *La Chartreuse de Parme* [1839] and Leo Tolstoy in *War and Peace* [1862–69], evoked the confusion and human suffering that war entails, presenting the battles of Waterloo and Borodino in realistic terms as a muddled, frightening series of isolated episodes. A similar anti-heroic attitude was championed by George Bernard Shaw in the play *Arms and the Man* [1894].

In the nineteenth century some pacifist writers began consciously to use fiction as a means of mobilizing people in the struggle for peace. Tolstoy devoted his long life of literary creation and public activity to the fight against violence and war. Tolstoy had a high regard for the Austrian writer Bertha von Suttner (1889), whose novel *Die Waffen nieder*! was widely read in her day. Subsequently von Suttner played an active part in the peace movement, and in 1905 was awarded the Nobel Peace Prize, which she herself had encouraged Alfred Nobel to establish (Brock-Utne, 1985, pp. 37–45). However, the concerted efforts of writers, intellectuals and pacifist-minded political leaders proved powerless to avert the outbreak of World War I.

III. War and the environment in the arts of the twentieth century

War and peace

War in the twentieth century has become more all-embracing, affecting the whole civilian population of belligerent nations as well as the armed forces. World War I, with its huge casualty rate—perhaps 45 million altogether, including 15 million or more dead—was a crucial event in world history which totally changed humankind's view of war. It banished the ideas of progress which had dominated human thinking during the previous century, reversed the traditional mythology of heroism and the hero, and created an ironic response which has conditioned the understanding of war throughout the twentieth century. The impact of World War I became so widely communicated that it has exerted a fundamental political, rhetorical and artistic influence on the response of humankind to warfare ever since (Fussell, 1975).

In the twentieth century individual responses to war, often opposed to government policy, have dominated art and literature in the Western world. However, it is important to distinguish between 'popular culture', which usually reflects the dominant cultural values of the society which engenders it, and the 'higher culture' of outstanding individuals who may oppose the values of their age.

The experience of World War I demonstrated that the arts can be used either to support or to condemn war. Throughout the war, poetry, especially poetry from the front, was in great demand. Some collections of poor poetry became extremely fashionable, for example, *Ardours and Endurances* [1917] by the mediocre poet Robert Nichols, who saw active service for a brief period (Bergonzi, 1965). The only other soldier poet to be widely read during the course of the war was Siegfried Sassoon, whose work developed from patriotic idealism to ironic realism, and finally to the extreme of angry, anti-heroic protest in such poems as 'Does it matter?' (Sassoon, 1918, p. 28) and 'Suicide in the Trenches' (Bates, 1969, pp. 84–85; Sassoon, 1918, p. 31). Sassoon's single-handed campaign against military authority and the continuation of the war culminated in his defiant statement of July 1917 that 'I believe that the War is being deliberately prolonged by those who have the power to end it. . . . I believe that this War, upon which I entered as a war of defence and liberation, has now become a war of aggression and conquest' (Ferguson, 1972, p. 217). By 1918, the public mood was ready for what he had to say, and Sassoon found admirers in surprising places: Winston Churchill, the then British Minister of Munitions, approved of Sassoon's poems because he believed that they would finally bring home to the civilian population the suffering that the troops at the front had to endure. Sassoon's bitter poems were not regarded as a moral protest, but rather as the result of shell-shock. His revolt was hushed up: he was not court-martialled, but committed to a psychiatric hospital. Sassoon's experience demonstrates that the establishment could blunt the public protest of anti-war artists by incorporating their views and turning them into a subtler form of pro-war propaganda (Bergonzi, 1965).

Wilfred Owen, killed in action at the age of 25, was not widely read during World War I, but succeeded within a few months in giving the poetry of anti-heroic protest as absolute an expression as the traditional heroic attitude had previously received in countless epics and dramas. Owen's poetry, with its emphasis on human suffering, is limited in range, but reflects a basic change in human sensibility: the realization that traditional concepts of honour and heroism had ceased to be viable. Of his poetry, Owen (1964, p. 31) declared that 'My subject is War, and the pity of War'. He deals with the slaughter, apparently endless, of young men, providing a realistic depiction of the details of death and mutilation and a despair that the war might drag on for an indefinite number of years. 'Dulce et Decorum Est' vividly evokes men dying of agony in a gas attack and implies that the horror of the means used in modern warfare discredits the end; 'Exposure' conveys the physical and moral desperation of the troops' condition; 'Futility' portrays the tragedy of individual death on the plane of cosmic significance (or, perhaps, cosmic futility); and 'Anthem for Doomed Youth' deals with the sorrow of war by presenting it as a solemn ritual (Stallworthy, 1984, pp. 188–93). Owen's poems, some of which were subsequently set to music in Benjamin Britten's *War Requiem* [1962], may have done more than any other work in English to form a sensibility that can understand the nature of modern technological warfare.

World War I also brought to public consciousness the connection between modern warfare and the devastation of the environment. The landscapes of the Western Front were a shattering experience, to which artists responded with pain and anger. The former romantic identification of landscape with tranquillity or mystical unity with the world was denied by shattered stumps of trees and fields full of craters. Paul Nash, an official war artist sanctioned by the British government, shocked the public in London by such paintings as his Cubist landscape of *Hill 60* (an area which had changed hands several times in the course of the fighting), in which the undulations of the ground were caused not by nature, but by military mining. Similarly, Otto Dix's *Flanders* indicts the inhumanities of war through its expressionist vision of a landscape scarred by human conflict in which all the natural elements—men, trees and barbed-wire-like bushes—are slowly being engulfed in devastation. The destructive potential of the new technology of warfare, especially aeroplanes, began to receive graphic expression in anti-war pictures such as Will Dyson's 1916 cartoon of a monkey hanging from an aeroplane dangling a bomb over a city.

The years after World War I saw a proliferation of two different types of book. On the one hand, there were popular war novels such as the 'Biggles' books of William E. Johns which turned war into a schoolboyish adventure illustrating the clash between two-dimensional good and bad individuals. On the other hand, remarkable memoirs and novels were produced which continued to express an ironic attitude to war. There were different responses in different countries. In general, works by European writers, such as Robert Graves's (1957) *Goodbye to All That*, comprehended war and accepted it as an integral part of life. In Germany, Erich Maria Remarque's (1929) *All Quiet on the Western Front*, which was subsequently made into a powerful film, suggested that the tradition of regimentation compelled even sensitive Europeans to move steadily into the slaughter. Remarque questions the system, but he does not make the gesture of individual protest and personal outrage at the indignities of war typical of such US novels as John Dos Passos's (1921) *Three Soldiers*, e. e. cummings's (1922) *The Enormous Room,* William Faulkner's (1926) *Soldiers' Pay* and Ernest Hemingway's (1929) *A Farewell to Arms*, in which the authors venture beyond realism, interpreting war as a metaphor for the ills besetting their generation (Aichinger, 1975).

The notion that war is too high a price to pay for any political aim or ideology was articulated in many different art forms during the 1920s and 1930s. Kurt Jooss's ballet *The Green Table* (first produced in Paris in 1932), in which a diplomatic conference turns into a dance of death, emphasized the profound stupidity and self-deception of people involved in war (Clarke & Crisp, 1981, pp. 146–47). Many science-fiction stories, such as John Gloag's (1932) black comedy *Tomorrow's Yesterday* [1931], presented war as the ultimate irrationality (Rabkin *et al.*, 1983). Similarly, Sidney Howard's play *Paths of Glory*, which opened in New York City in 1935 and was turned into a famous anti-war film, was intended to issue a warning against war in a year when Europe was rearming for the next one. However, as the 1930s proceeded, the element of black comedy was eliminated; and the rise of fascism undermined the view that no price would be too high to pay for the avoidance of war. The Spanish Civil War of 1936–39 and the German occupation of the Sudetenland in 1938 reopened the question of whether there were some circumstances in which war could be justified even at the cost of enormous human suffering.

Perhaps the most striking example of the influence of a work of art on public affairs is Pablo Picasso's *Guernica*, the most celebrated anti-war painting in the world, which was produced for the Republic of Spain's pavilion at the Paris world's fair in 1937 (Bruckner *et al.*, 1984, pp. 88–89; Keegan & Darracott, 1981, pp. 200–201; Silva *et al.*, 1963, pp. 63–64). It commemorates the bombing of the Basque town of Guernica by Franco's Nationalist Air Force on 25 April 1937, which caused extensive civilian casualties and international outrage, since it represented the first deliberate bombing of a civilian target in warfare. Although it is a matter of some controversy whether Picasso had completed the painting before the raid, it was nevertheless received both as a work of anti-nationalist propaganda and as a powerful condemnation of the brutality of war in general. Picasso's decision to consign the painting to the Museum of Modern Art in New York City until democracy was restored in Spain meant that it became perhaps the only piece of anti-war art ever to form the subject of international negotiations and to be used as a political weapon against a repressive government.

On the part of the Allies, World War II was 'that very rare thing—a just war' (Taylor, 1975, p. 21), a war that in its early years provoked very little anti-war protest either in literature or in art. In the longer term, World War II has had varied and contradictory effects on Western culture. One unfortunate consequence of the Allies' victory over fascism was that violence and militarism have come to play an important role in popular Western culture, reflecting the dominant militaristic values in society. Since 1945, the Western public has been assailed by a daily diet of pulp fiction reducing war to a stereotyped backdrop for shallow characters and implausible situations (Smith, 1980), western films from the USA featuring such 'macho' heroes as John Wayne and Clint Eastwood, violent television programmes and militaristic cartoon strips aimed at both children and adults. On a higher level, one major difference between fiction engendered by World War II and that which had been engendered by World War I is that in the case of World War II many writers regarded war and the society which produces it as intimately connected; and characters caught up in war not as alienated beings, but as products of their society who receive various types of gratification from it (Muste, 1984). Two of the greatest works resulting from World War II are *Les Chemins de la Liberté* [3 volumes, 1945–

49] by Jean-Paul Sartre and *La Peste* by Albert Camus (1947), which painfully assimilate the experience of capitulation (Craig & Egan, 1979). US novels, such as *The Naked and the Dead* by Norman Mailer (1948) and *From Here to Eternity* by James Jones (1951), see the brutalities of war as an expression of an irrepressible human instinct. In the United Kingdom, such novelists as Evelyn Waugh and Anthony Powell emphasize the absurd fate of the individual caught up in the great war machine.

Some Western writers experienced great difficulty in writing about World War II in the post-war world (Vonnegut, 1969, pp. 2–3). One reason for this may have been that the war was such a universal, overwhelming catastrophe that it did not provide the sort of experience out of which the artist could create. Many writers felt that war was too painful a subject to confront directly. Others considered it unnecessary to remind civilians, many of whom had suffered more than many soldiers, of something they already knew only too well. In Europe since 1945 many writers have preferred to turn their backs on war and suffering, and there has been a general taboo on anything reminding people of death and mourning (Ariès, 1976). Another reason for the difficulty experienced by novelists in dramatizing World War II perhaps derived from the effect that World War I had exerted on popular concepts of duty and heroism. As Fiedler (1964, p. 30) argues, 'The notions of glory, honor, and courage lose all meaning when in the West men, still nominally Christian, come to believe that the worst thing of all is to die—when, for the first time in a thousand years, it is possible to admit that no cause is worth dying for'. However, another important reason is that the atmosphere of the cold war was so threatening that the war seemed to continue in spirit, acting as a curb to the imagination and never settling into a past from which it could be seen in perspective (Newby, 1951). William Faulkner's (1965, pp. 119–20) 1950 Nobel Prize lecture conveyed the effect of the cold war on writers: 'Our tragedy today is a general and universal physical fear so long sustained by now that we can even bear it'. He argued that 'the question: When will I be blown up?' had so sapped the initiative of writers that they no longer dealt with the classic and enduring themes of 'love and honor and pity and pride and compassion and sacrifice'.

Since the development of nuclear weapons the menace of world annihilation has hung over the life of every human being more constantly than at any time in the past; and at the same time war has lost the moral and political justification that past generations could ascribe to it. Therefore, since 1945 it appears that no Western artist or writer has been able to depict war in terms other than of horror and indictment. By the time that artists had conceived of images of the bomb that were immediately recognizable and could convey a strong appeal, there was already a significant body of opinion ready to respond to that appeal, including the atomic scientists at Los Alamos as well as the general public, which was already quite well informed about the effects of the first bombs used and about the possible impact of larger bombs in future wars.

The mushroom cloud was the aspect of the atomic bomb which had the greatest impact on the artistic imagination. Within a few years numerous artistic representations of the nuclear explosion had appeared. Among the most memorable are Robert Osborn's drawing *Atom Bomb* [1946], which depicts the nuclear cloud as a death's head (Bruckner *et al.*, 1984, p. 96); Shigeo Fukuda's *No More*, which portrays a skull composed entirely of missiles (Bruckner *et al.*, 1984, p. 105); and Hans Erni's poster for the Swiss Peace Movement of 1952 which turns the earth itself into a skull with an atomic plume rising from its broken forehead (Bruckner *et al.*, 1984, p. 97). However, A. Paul Weber is the anti-war artist who has most consistently kept the possibility of war before the public in a series of devastating and relentless images (Bruckner *et al.*, 1984, pp. 80–81,104).

The development of nuclear weapons evoked a ready response in both anti-war art and music. However, with the exception of John Hersey's (1946) *Hiroshima* (based on the testimony of six people who were in Hiroshima when the bomb dropped), which created a sensation when it was published, writers were slower to respond (Brians, 1984). Indeed, the poet Aaron Kramer (1983) has spoken of his own 37-year failure to respond to Hiroshima, attributing his silence partly to his initial relief that the use of nuclear weapons had brought the war to a successful conclusion; and partly to the natural human desire to avoid confronting a frightening subject. Nuclear war is an intrinsically difficult subject for writers to handle. Most war fiction is based on memory. However, for a large-scale nuclear war writers must be able to find ways of anticipating the horrors of war on a hitherto unprecedented scale. This has proved difficult for the human imagination to encompass, as so many human words and traditions have been rendered outdated and useless in the nuclear age.

Even before 1953, when after the advent of the hydrogen bomb the US Secretary of Defense announced that both the USA and USSR had the ability to exterminate the human race, a few writers treated the theme of the nuclear holocaust, invoking the ancient image of the apocalypse (Rabkin *et al.*, 1983). The universal loss of faith in the stability of what used to be called 'the natural order', and the terrible knowledge that humankind itself had acquired the power of destroying the world, inspired such tales of atomic armageddon as Aldous Huxley's (1948) *Ape and Essence*, Judith Merril's (1950) *Shadow on the Hearth*, Nevil Shute's (1957) *On the Beach* and Walter Miller's (1959) *A Canticle for Leibowitz*. With the exception of a few works, including Shute's *On the Beach* and Masuji Ibuse's (1971) *Black Rain* (a work widely read in Japan that evokes the devastation caused to humans and nature by the bombing of Hiroshima), fiction depicting nuclear war has not achieved large sales, because such a tragic subject is not likely to have a wide popular appeal. However, fiction does have some advantages over non-fiction in conveying the horror of nuclear war—an exciting plot and characters with which the reader can identify—and thus reaches an audience that would probably not read a non-fiction book on the subject.

One significant work on the theme of nuclear war was Peter Watkins's (1966) film *The War Game* which provides a clear picture, rendered in concrete images, of the outbreak of nuclear war in the United Kingdom. The British Broadcasting Corporation banned the film, claiming that it was too realistic, and hence that it might cause mass panic and suicide. A secondary reason for censoring the film (or possibly even the more important one) was that it was critical of the British Home Office for failing to prepare the subjects of the United Kingdom adequately for a nuclear attack, and thus was potentially an embarrassment to the government (Welsh, 1983).

One way of dealing with the terror and apathy inspired by the contemplation of modern warfare was the use of black comedy. Joseph Heller's (1961) *Catch-22* and Kurt Vonnegut's (1969) *Slaughterhouse-Five,* which present war as an absurdity, were not only classics of war literature, but also proved to be great commercial and popular successes. Their portrayal of an anti-hero, apparently selfish and unpatriotic, but in reality optimistic and humane, provided a useful corrective to the hawkish sentiments currently prevalent in the USA. The anti-hero of *Catch-22* is a bomber pilot who has flown gallantly on a number of missions, but who has now had enough of the war. His principal opponent is not the Germans, but his commanding officer, who for reasons of personal glory is constantly increasing the number of missions his men must undertake before being sent home. The pilot affirms the absolute value of survival: his aim is to win the war and stay alive, since 'It doesn't make a damned bit of difference *who* wins the war to someone who's dead' (Heller, 1961, p. 136). Heller evokes the cynical exploitation of war through a lieutenant who is involved in elaborate commercial enterprises and is even prepared to bomb his own airfield in exchange for a promise of substantial profit from the Germans.

Another influential black comedy was Peter George's *Dr. Strangelove* [1963], made into a film by Stanley Kubrick (1964), which suggests the terrifying absurdity of the modern world, in which the best laid human plans can go dreadfully wrong, leading to the annihilation of the planet. Kubrick's film, like Miller's (1959) *A Canticle for Leibowitz,* implies that if the world were destroyed, it would be no more than just deserts for the human race. Thomas Pynchon's (1973) *Gravity's Rainbow,* which has been called the climactic war novel of this century (Muste, 1984, p. 9), also uses black humour to convey the extent to which war is part of everyone's life, a mere extension of the violent society in which all people live. The conclusion of the novel, in which a missile is about to strike the earth, affirms the value of the work of art that celebrates human triumph over the universal violence which seeks to engulf the world.

Music, traditionally a powerful popular medium for bringing people together in expressions of opinion, has, especially since the 1960s, been used by the US peace movement to communicate its message (Philbin, 1983). People committed to pacifism and radical social change were able to reach a wider audience through the mass media; peace music recorded by popular musicians was accepted as 'pop' music, sometimes even before the peace message itself was understood. Many of the singers in the peace movement suffered for voicing opinions unpopular with their governments. Pete Seeger and the

Weavers were blacklisted in the 1950s for the 'un-American' content of their music; Vern Partlow's song 'Old Man Atom' [1945] was attacked by the McCarthyites (Partlow, 1983); and Paul Robeson, a prominent anti-fascist, was blacklisted and prevented from performing in the USA following a speech at the Paris Peace Conference of 1949 in which he had urged Black people to ignore the hysteria of the cold war and to fight racism at home (Barrett *et al.*, 1983).

In the 1950s and early 1960s, with the coming of the folk-music revival, a number of anti-war songs were popularized, such as Ed McCurdy's famous song 'Strangest Dream' [1950], inspired by the Korean War of 1950–53 (Denisoff, 1983, p. 92):

Last night I had the strangest dream,
I'd never dreamed before;
I dreamed the world had all agreed to put an end to war.

Traditional pieces like 'Study War No More' were reintroduced; the anthem of the civil rights movement, 'We Shall Overcome', was developed by Pete Seeger and Guy Carawan from an old Baptist hymn; and new songs of protest were composed. The singing of protest songs was a powerful means of making the individual feel part of the group or movement. Perhaps the best known new song of the peace movement was John Lennon's 'Give Peace a Chance' [1969], a call to put aside all political differences and factionalism within the anti-war movement at the time of the Second Indochina War of 1961–75 (Wiener, 1983). The song was composed during John Lennon and Yoko Ono's 'bed-in' in Amsterdam, which had been inspired by a letter from Peter Watkins, director of *The War Game*, asking Lennon what he was doing to further the cause of peace (Lennon & Ono, 1983).

Many singers have a strong sense of social responsibility and feel that their songs have some impact, although they find it difficult to be specific about the influence that music exerts. Tom Paxton claimed that 'All music is effective. . . . John Lennon's "Give Peace a Chance" . . . certainly played its role in the struggle against the war' (Philbin, 1983, p. 57). Mary Travers said of the song 'Blowin' in the Wind'—which contains the lines: 'How many deaths will it take 'til he knows that too many people have died?'—that: 'When I sing the song I'm asking people to examine their responsibilities. Folk music does not present answers. It only articulates the questions. I believe one person can make a difference. Collective individual consciences are powerful' (Philbin, 1983, pp. 57–58).

The Second Indochina War is the most striking example in history of the way in which public opinion influenced a government to end a war which could not be won, either militarily or politically. That war gave rise to an extraordinary outpouring of art against war, an art that questioned the aims, rationality and morality of war (Beidler, 1982; Walsh, 1982). It was the first war the USA fought in which there were far more artistic statements against the war than in support of the government. All the arts—poetry, prose, music, drama, painting and film—were harnessed in order to demonstrate to the US public the limits of US power, the ambivalent moral implications of advanced technology and the horror of modern warfare in general. Undoubtedly the most powerful artistic medium for conveying the reality of the war was photography, either in the form of television or of still photography. Television film of the war—published immediately and uncensored—along with reportage of the events it depicted, exerted a vivid, terrifying impact on the human imagination. The Second Indochina War was the world's first experience of a 'television war', in which the visible brutality of war reached a mass audience every night in the privacy of its own homes. There is much truth in the view that the USA lost the war not on the battlefield, but on the television screens of the USA (Hooper, 1982, pp. 109–22).

Still photography continues to perform a valuable function even in the television age because it has a quality of permanence, capturing the essence of a single moment that can be looked at again and again. The Second Indochina War brought a new status to war photography. The war was protracted, and some photographers were permanently based in Viet Nam over a number of years, with considerable freedom of movement to explore the war in depth. Larry Burrows, Philip Jones Griffiths and Don McCullin produced haunting, unforgettable pictures of the ravages the war inflicted on the civilian population of Viet Nam (Lewinski, 1978). Such photographs as Nick Ut's picture in 1972 of a little girl running naked in terror from a napalm bomb (Lewinski, 1978, p. 231) had an immediate impact, engendering a sense of outrage at US policy and challenging the inevitability of war.

Much popular art and writing against the Second Indochina War was passionate, transitory art expressing moral outrage which has simply disappeared with the war itself, but some Viet Nam literature possesses a more lasting value: for example, Denise Levertov's poignant question-and-answer poem 'What Were They Like?' [1966] (Stallworthy, 1984, p. 323) and Adrian Mitchell's 'To Whom It May Concern' [1964] (Stallworthy, 1984, pp. 327–28):

I was run over by the truth one day.
Ever since the accident I've walked this way
So stick my legs in plaster
Tell me lies about Vietnam.

For many years after the end of the war the US public turned away from serious interpretations of the war, but in the 1970s and 1980s analysis of Viet Nam and its aftermath again became possible. Such novels as Robert Stone's (1974) *Dog Soldiers*, Tim O'Brien's (1978) *Going After Cacciato* and John Del Vecchio's (1982) *The 13th Valley*, and films like Michael Cimino's *The Deer Hunter* and Francis Ford Coppola's *Apocalypse Now* attempted to make sense of the experience.

Among non-fictional works, two of the most enduring books to have emerged from the Second Indochina War are Philip Caputo's (1977) *A Rumor of War* and Michael Herr's (1977) *Dispatches,* both prose accounts based on personal experience that emphasize the epic significance of the war, raising such events as the Khe Sanh siege of February 1968 and the My Lai massacre on 16 March 1968 to the level of legendary events embodying military vulnerability and national shame. Herr uses a rich colloquial language to subvert the incongruous military jargon by which 'a discreet burst' means a grandfather and two children ripped to pieces. Such works demonstrate how the Second Indochina War has come to be widely regarded as representative of modern warfare in general (Walsh, 1982, p. 199). This has recently been attested to by Oliver Stone's film *Platoon* [1987], which not only provides a realistic picture of warfare in Viet Nam, but also aims to issue a warning against further US involvement in Central America.

The environment

In the 1960s and 1970s, the prospect of atomic war faded from the immediate human consciousness into the background of the imagination. It was temporarily overshadowed by the discovery of other possible catastrophes which might ensue as a result of human alienation from nature: the population explosion; the pollution of the environment by industrial waste; the rapid consumption of non-renewable resources; and the built-in obsolescence of the way of life in the 'developed' countries. Humankind's psychic estrangement from nature was not a new condition which suddenly emerged in the late twentieth century, but a gradual development since the industrial revolution, deplored by romantic critics since William Blake. In the nineteenth century, as English society became more urbanized, much of English literature expressed nostalgia for a vanishing rural way of life (Wiener, 1981). Some English novelists, such as Thomas Hardy and D. H. Lawrence, advocated a new morality based on the individual's relationship with the natural world (Alcorn, 1977). In the USA, the philosopher Henry Thoreau, novelists such as James Fenimore Cooper and landscape artists such as George Catlin and Albert Bierstadt had, by emphasizing human links with nature, helped to form the climate of opinion that culminated in the establishment of Yellowstone National Park in 1872, the first in the world (Brooks, 1980; Tunnard, 1978).

Nonetheless, throughout the twentieth century, which has been described as an age of 'nature-hating' (Shepard, 1967, p. 214), the dominant setting of Western literature has been urban, reflecting the actual environment in which most Western people live. The characteristic setting of twentieth-century European literature is the Dublin of James Joyce's (1922) *Ulysses*, with its streets, bars and offices, and the 'stony rubbish' of T. S. Eliot's *The Waste Land* [1922] where the 'dead tree gives no shelter, the cricket no relief, and the dry stone no sound of water' (Eliot, 1963, p. 63). The process of banishing nature from literature culminated in Samuel Beckett's *Endgame* [1957], in which one character complains that 'Nature has forgotten us'; and another responds with 'There's no more nature' (Beckett, 1963, p. 16).

By the late twentieth century, human exploitation and destruction of nature had grown at such an alarming rate that it became necessary to awaken public consciousness to this danger. Ecological issues were brought to public prominence by Rachel Carson's (1962) *Silent Spring*, which warned of the danger that chlorinated hydrocarbons used as insecticides, such as DDT, were gradually being redistributed within the biosphere, threatening fish, birds and mammals; metal pollution, especially by lead and mercury, also gave cause for anxiety. Writers of science fiction reflected this new awareness: some of the most striking stories on the theme of ecological disaster were James Blish's (1969) 'We All Die Naked', John Brunner's (1972) *The Sheep Look Up,* Philip Wylie's (1972) *The End of the Dream* and Kit Pedler and Gerry Davis's (1974) *Brainrack*. In recent years the fear of pollution has been replaced by a more general anxiety about the future: Alvin Toffler (1970) coined the term 'future shock' to evoke the gathering anxiety about humankind's psychological and neurological fitness to cope with the rapid pace of change. John Brunner's (1975) novel *The Shockwave Rider* reflects this change of emphasis, depicting a complex chain-reaction disaster precipitated by a combination of terrible circumstances.

In the 1960s and 1970s science fiction became the principal medium by which a pessimistic image of the future was disseminated. Indeed, 'non-fictional' speculation and science fiction began to overlap when those involved in 'futures research' or 'futurology' began to invent scenarios like those of Kahn & Wiener (1967) and of Toffler (1970) or in computer simulations of the future like that produced for the Club of Rome in *The Limits to Growth* (Meadows *et al.*, 1972). Some science-fiction anthologies have been produced with an overtly didactic purpose: for example, *The Ruins of Earth* (Disch, 1971) and *Saving Worlds* (Elwood & Kidd, 1973). There is some dispute as to whether science fiction is an effective means of education, since banishing real contemporary social problems to the realms of imaginative fiction could be seen as a means of defusing anxieties rather than of confronting them (Rabkin *et al.*, 1983). However, the growth of concern about environmental problems in the real world would seem to suggest that images of ecocatastrophe in science fiction have had a positive, rather than negative, effect on human consciousness. Moreover, most contemporary science fiction is not selective in its choice of victims and does not seek scapegoats, but rather emphasizes that humankind as a whole is responsible for its own destiny. The nightmare visions in even the most despairing works of science fiction have the positive aim of not merely predicting the future, but of preventing it.

The 1980s

In the 1980s, fear of nuclear war has again been fuelled by the rhetoric of 'limited' nuclear war and of 'surviving' a nuclear war, as well as by the new cold-war atmosphere created since 1976 by numerous factors, including the failure of arms-control talks, Soviet–US rivalry in the Third World, and the Soviet entry into Afghanistan in 1979. This changing climate has had contradictory effects on Western culture. On the one hand, the 1980s have seen a resurgence of films extolling cold-war values, such as *Rambo* and *Rocky IV*. On the other hand, the topic of nuclear war has come not merely to suffuse such popular genres as the thriller, science fiction and men's combat fiction, but increasingly to inspire notable works by mainstream authors, such as Tim O'Brien's (1985) *The Nuclear Age* and Kurt Vonnegut's (1985) *Galápagos*. Humankind's growing 'eschatological anxiety' (Kermode, 1967, p. 95) found striking expression in Russell Hoban's (1980) *Riddley Walker* that presents a post-holocaust world in which a primitive race tries to make sense of the traces of its former civilization.

The 1980s have also seen a renaissance of rock music dealing with social concerns, including songs conveying the threat and reality of war and fears for the future (Hemmert, 1983). However, there has been a change of tone from the simple purity of John Lennon's 'Give Peace a Chance' [1969] to the black humour of 'The Dead Kennedys's' 'Holiday in Cambodia', or the apocalyptic visions of Peter Townsend's 'I've Known No War' and the 'Pink Floyd' album *The Final Cut*.

Peter Watkins's (1966) *The War Game* was finally shown on British television in the 1980s; and in the USA there has been a revival of atomic films containing documentary footage of US government propaganda films of the 1950s, but with the new aim of inspiring anti-war sentiments. However, in contrast to the 1950s, these films reach a much smaller audience, usually only those who are already committed to the anti-war cause (Titus, 1983). Comparatively few plays or commercial films have been concerned with nuclear war, although such films as *The China Syndrome* and *Silkwood* have popularized the dangers of radiation from nuclear power stations. Raymond Briggs's (1983) play *When The Wind Blows*, based on characters in a strip cartoon (Briggs, 1982), depicts the comic plight of an elderly husband and wife who, after the nuclear holocaust, attempt to follow the totally inadequate instructions in the British government pamphlet *Protect and Survive* (United Kingdom, 1976). The play (which was released as a film in 1987) uses gentle humour to reiterate the same message about the lack of information that the public has regarding nuclear war first conveyed 16 years earlier by Peter Watkins in *The War Game*. Some fictional works of the 1980s have already had a limited political effect: Briggs's work shamed the British government into withdrawing the offending pamphlet; and the US television film *The Day After*, which depicted the aftermath of a nuclear attack on a city in Kansas, USA, inspired that state to declare itself a nuclear-free zone.

IV. War and the environment in Soviet literature since World War II

In the Western world since World War II attitudes towards war and the environment expressed in art and literature have reflected the personal views of individuals, often of individuals who occupy a relatively isolated position in the societies they inhabit. However, in the USSR literature has consistently manifested much greater concern with topical social questions, partly because of the Soviet government's stringent control of literature, which places it directly at the service of its economic and political policies, and partly because of the long-standing Russian tradition of using fiction for the discussion of social and political issues. A number of Soviet writers came from a scientific background or were closely associated with the scientific intelligentsia, and thus had a particular interest in such topics as nuclear policy or the environment, as well as more general questions about the social and moral implications of the 'scientific and technological revolution' (Marsh, 1986b).

War and peace

Since World War II a vast amount of material has appeared in the press and literature about the Soviet victory over fascism; and 'war prose' has continued to account for a large proportion of the programmes of Soviet publishing houses. This is not only a result of the Soviet government's persistent demand for works on this subject, but also undoubtedly reflects the interests and concerns of Soviet writers themselves. Many writers prefer to choose a subject involving real conflicts and genuine heroism rather than the more artificial heroism required in works on the theme of industrial or agricultural production. Moreover, the persistence of the theme of war in Soviet fiction is a reflection of the terrible trauma war caused in the USSR (the country having lost approximately 10 million military personnel and perhaps again as many civilians) and the desire that it should never be repeated. For example, implicit in the war novels of Yuri Bondarev and Vasil Bykov is a warning against future wars and a concern about the moral questions of peace.

Nevertheless, the Soviet government also undoubtedly makes use of 'war prose' in order to inspire the Soviet people with patriotism and a sense of unity, and to encourage the population to support its policies. For example, in the years 1945–53 war literature became an instrument of Soviet government propaganda and a retrospective extension of the cold war; in the post-Stalin period 1953–64 it became an integral part of the literature of protest which followed Nikita Khrushchev's dethronement of Stalin at the twentieth Congress of the Communist Party in 1956 (Piper, 1984); and in the 1970s and 1980s it has been expected to support the military and foreign policies of the Soviet government, thus contributing to Soviet propaganda for peace and disarmament both at home and abroad. The duality inherent in Soviet war literature is illustrated by Evgeni Yevtushenko's poem 'Do the Russians Want War?' [1961], which was made into a popular song. Although this poem undoubtedly corresponds both to the poet's own feelings and to the deepest preoccupations of the Soviet people, who are fully conscious of the devastation that war can cause, it has become a useful ally of Soviet government policy and is much quoted to foreigners.

It is not surprising that Soviet writers treating the theme of nuclear research and nuclear policy adhere very closely to the Soviet government line, since a particularly stringent censorship has applied to the discussion of such a politically sensitive subject. A notable feature of post-Stalin literature is that, despite occasional changes of rhetoric, it has continued to express a remarkably consistent view on war, disarmament and nuclear policy (Marsh, 1986a). In the successive eras of Khrushchev's 'peaceful co-existence' (1953–64), the reaction caused by the Second Indochina War and by the invasion of Czechoslovakia in 1968, the period of détente under Leonid Brezhnev (1964–82) and the tension of the 1980s, fiction has faithfully reflected the ambiguous Soviet position, which can be defined as the combination of an avowedly defensive policy with an offensive posture. However, within this broad framework of conformity, different views held by 'liberal' and 'dogmatist' writers, can be distinguished. Such liberal writers as Yevtushenko, Bondarev and Chingiz Aitmatov lay more emphasis on peace; such dogmatist writers as Vsevolod Kochetov and Alexander Chakovsky on confrontation. This difference of emphasis perhaps reflects the continuing debate in the USSR between adherents of a 'scientific' view that nuclear war would mean total catastrophe, and the dogmatists who believe that victory is possible.

Certain Soviet writers, such as Bykov, Grigory Baklanov and Bulat Okudzhava, have been subjected to criticism for expressing sentiments of pure pacifism, sentiments that fail to distinguish between just and unjust wars. Okudzhava's (1961) 'Good-bye, Schoolboy!' which presents war in a starkly realistic way, was accused of Remarquism—that is, of portraying war in such dark colours that it implied that war itself was wrong. In 1964 the Soviet Ministry of Defence called a special conference at which the Minister (Marshal Rodion Malinovsky) upbraided writers, artists and film makers for composing unheroic, pacifist works. However, Okudzhava continued to express anti-war sentiments in some of his songs, which circulated unofficially on tape and enjoyed wide popularity. He said of one of his most famous songs on this subject, 'Paper Soldier', that 'I began singing about what was troubling me: about the fact that war is not a holiday and not a parade, but a terrible, absurd inevitability . . . that unfortunately the Paper Soldier can't always make the world happy' (Okudzhava, 1980, p. 16). The suspicion that Soviet peace propaganda is for foreign consumption only was again fuelled in 1983 when the military newspaper *Red Star* attacked *Teachers' Gazette* for its publication of the pacifist poem 'We Shall Play War No More' by the Daghestan poet Medzhid Medzhidov (Deane & Kass, 1983–84).

Throughout the post-Stalin era the Soviet government has considered it very important for Soviet writers to discuss the problems of nuclear war and disarmament, thus contributing to the Soviet 'peace campaign'. The significance that the authorities attach to writers' grasp of correct Soviet government policy on foreign and defence matters is illustrated by the periodic meetings held in the Union of Writers at which prominent military men outline current Soviet government thinking, and by frequent speeches by the Communist Party leaders and articles by literary functionaries exhorting writers to treat this subject. Many Soviet writers have treated this theme, combining propaganda for world peace with a justification for the arms race and a desire for the overthrow of capitalism. In Daniil Granin's (1954) 'The Seekers' the hero, leafing through US journals concerned with the development of the hydrogen bomb, reflects that 'these personages would long ago have put their bombs to use, were it not that we had similar bombs. And therefore, we shall have the same as they have, and even more, so that the whole world might live and work in tranquillity' (Granin, 1954, p. 356).

By the early 1960s some writers began to discuss general moral questions connected with the development of nuclear weapons, omitting any explicit anti-capitalist bias. Andrei Voznesensky, in his long poem 'Oza' [1964], which is set in the nuclear research station at Dubna, expresses an ambivalent attitude towards scientific progress: on the one hand he praises Dubna, where his scientist friends, 'the flower of the nation', are engaged in research designed to protect him; on the other hand, he warns that science and technology are powerful weapons that can be misused if evil, inhuman people control them; and he declares that 'All progress is retrogression/If the process breaks man down' (Voznesensky, 1967, p. 239). In the Brezhnev period, the strengthening of the censorship and the renewal of repression against Soviet writers meant that the issue of the harmful effects of Soviet nuclear research could not be directly confronted in mainstream literature. The subject was, however, obliquely treated in science fiction, particularly by Arkady and Boris Strugatsky (1977), who in *Roadside Picnic* (the basis of Andrei Tarkovsky's film *Stalker*) and several other works, raise the question of the desirability of scientific and technological development, and whether it should be limited (Marsh, 1986b, pp. 228–31).

In the USSR a clear distinction has always been drawn between the value of nuclear research for peaceful purposes and the destructive potential of nuclear weapons, so the possible harmful consequences of nuclear research is not a theme favoured by the Soviet authorities. However, in his poem 'Products of the Disintegration of Uranium', the poet Tafgat Dovletshin, writing under the pseudonym 'M. Lvov', expresses concern that nuclear waste may endanger humankind, and argues that 'it is not too soon' to think about its safe disposal (Lvov, 1960). Dovletshin's anxiety may have been aroused, not by the 'monstrous dreams' mentioned in the poem, but by a real event—the nuclear disaster in the Urals in the winter of 1957–58, which distributed radioactive products over a large area, perhaps over more than 2500 square kilometres, causing the death of several hundred people from radiation sickness. Voznesensky, in his 'Beatnik's Monologue' [1962], inspired by a journey to the USA in 1961, uses the Aesopian technique of referring to the USA in order to evoke the terrifying effects of nuclear fall-out: 'Women will give birth to Rolls-Royces throughout the nation—radiation' (Voznesensky, 1967, p. 159). Voznesensky was the first Soviet writer to respond publicly to the Chernobyl nuclear power plant disaster of April 1986. His poem 'Thoughts about Chernobyl' poses the question: 'Was it the fault of science or humankind?', warns of the danger of nuclear war and praises the courage of the man who went back into the reactor and 'saved Kiev and Odessa' (Voznesensky, 1986). Voznesensky's humanitarian poem was published in *Pravda* as a contribution to the Soviet authorities' campaign to present the accident to the Soviet population without causing widespread panic.

Two novels of the 1980s demonstrate that, within limits, Soviet writers have been able to treat the theme of nuclear war in very different ways. *Victory* [1980–82] by the influential editor of *Literary Gazette,* Alexander Chakovsky, reflects the main elements of Soviet foreign policy in the early 1980s and represents a dogmatist's response to a bleak international situation. Chakovsky blames the West for the failure of détente, expresses the view that Soviet weapons are based on a defensive and deterrent strategy, and presents the USSR as the main champion of peace in a troubled world. A softer approach was adopted by the liberal Kirghiz writer Chingiz Aitmatov (1983), who introduced into his novel *The Day Lasts More Than a Hundred Years* a science-fiction sub-plot that aroused some criticism because it suggested that distrust and war are still endemic on the earth and that the USSR and USA are equally responsible for poor international relations. Aitmatov depicts a Soviet cosmonaut and a US astronaut working together on a space station which has been set up to work on an energy programme designed to help the whole of humankind. (The name of the space station, 'Parity', suggests that international scientific and political co-operation can only occur when the USA and USSR maintain strategic parity.) The two cosmonauts unexpectedly receive a communication from extraterrestrial beings and journey to another planet, where they meet an advanced civilization that wishes to make contact with Earth. The people are friendly, do not believe in war or weapons, and want to help solve Earth's problems, such as the energy crisis. However, when the cosmonauts wire back to base asking if the planet can make contact with Earth, both the Soviet and US authorities refuse; Earth is so unprepared for a meeting with a harmonious extraterrestrial civilization that it avoids the challenge.

Aitmatov's genuine commitment to peace and international co-operation was also demonstrated in his speech at the seventh Congress of Soviet Writers in 1981, which made no ideological points, but argued only that 'the end of the world', 'the suicide of the human race' was unthinkable, and expressed the hope that humankind would 'avoid technological savagery and will not dare to press that atomic button to which all lives are connected' (Aitmatov, 1981). Aitmatov's liberal views would seem to correspond to the policy of the present Soviet leadership, since in October 1986 he was permitted to convene an international conference on problems of peace at his home near Lake Issyk-Kul (Aitmatov, 1986). The current Soviet government has encouraged writers and artists to play a part in influencing international public opinion. For example, many well known Soviet writers and artists, including Aitmatov, were enlisted to support the Soviet government in its peace and conservation initiatives at a major international forum convened by the USSR in Moscow in February 1987. And in June 1987 a Soviet 'Greenpeace' was established under the direction of the writer Sergei Zalygin as a commission of the Soviet Peace Committee (Rich, 1987).

Although the majority of Soviet writers have used the margin of freedom permitted to them after Stalin's death to demonstrate their obedience to the dictates of the Soviet government, others have exploited it effectively to express their own ideas, sometimes through Aesopian devices. However, it is only dissident Soviet writers who directly challenge the Soviet government's military and foreign policies. In his major revision of *The First Circle*, Alexander Solzhenitsyn (1978) claims that Stalin unwisely rejected the 1946 Bernard Baruch Plan to ban further research on nuclear weapons and place the US bomb under the control of an independent United Nations Atomic Energy Committee. He implies that the Soviet bomb is not merely a deterrent to capitalist aggression, but also a powerful means of internal control in the hands of the Soviet régime. Solzhenitsyn also takes a sceptical view of peace propaganda by both the USSR and the USA. In his play *Candle in the Wind* [1960], which is set in an imaginary country containing elements of both capitalism and socialism, a journalist preparing for a conference admits that: 'the idea is that every country should have the right to have nuclear weapons, but we have to serve it up as part of the struggle for peace. It's a very subtle business!' (Solzhenitsyn, 1973, p. 116).

The environment

The conservation of nature has figured quite prominently in post-Stalin Soviet fiction (Marsh, 1986b). The issue was brought to public attention soon after World War II by the writer Leonid Leonov (1947), whose article 'In Defence of a Friend' initiated a correspondence on forest conservation. Subsequently, in his novel *The Russian Forest* [1953], Leonov (1966) implied some criticism of forestry policy under Stalin, and advocated the planned, careful use of forests with continuous reforestation to conserve resources, in order to prevent their ruthless exploitation with no regard for the needs of future generations. Although the sensitive subject of environmental conservation is touched upon only obliquely in literature of the 1950s and 1960s, when it is mentioned it has a greater impact than the familiar complaints of environmentalists in the West.

Environmental problems were probably still not as severe in the USSR as in the USA or Western Europe, but in the twentieth century the encroachment of technology on nature and human life has been more rapid in the USSR than in the West, partly because Western countries were already more industrially developed than the USSR at the beginning of the century, and partly because in the democracies people have not been compelled to change their way of life, as there has been a gradual spread and acceptance of urban life and attitudes. However, in the USSR the pace of industrialization has been forced, especially in Stalin's five-year plans, thereby dragging people roughly into the modern world. A sense of impending doom created by rapid industrialization led in the 1960s to the emergence of a new literary genre, 'village prose', which laments the passing of the old rural way of life and the moral and spiritual stability associated with it.

In the post-Stalin era some scientists, writers and journalists formed a pressure group whose aim was to arouse public opinion about ecological problems and to try to change Soviet government policy; their campaign bore fruit in 1969 when, after a prolonged protest against the pollution of Lake Baikal by a cellulose plant, a government decree was issued affording special protection to the Baikal basin. In the 1970s environmental issues rose to political respectability, because the Soviet government sponsored a heavily funded environmental programme, aimed chiefly at preserving clean water. The official view was reflected in Alexander Kron's novel *Insomnia* [1978], which depicts a scientist who acknowledges that scientists of all countries want to conserve life on earth and prevent the disastrous cost of scientific and technological progress, but argues that the USSR has a greater opportunity for improving the ecological situation than the West, which is shackled by commercial interests.

Although conservation has been a generally acceptable subject for Soviet fiction since the 1970s, some writers have provoked criticism because they treat the issue in a way different from that sanctioned by the Soviet authorities. The Soviet environmental programme is not designed primarily to preserve wilderness or to protect natural beauty, but rather to improve public health and to promote economic growth. 'Boris Komarov' (1978; 1980), the pseudonym of Zeev Wolfson, a former Soviet television producer, in his work *The Destruction of Nature,* which has been published only in the West, raises serious doubts as to whether the USSR can really manage balanced growth after two generations of nearly exclusive emphasis on heavy industry, and whether conservation has ever been allowed to interfere with important economic targets. Some Soviet writers have touched upon these delicate topics, emphasizing the moral basis of the need for conservation, and expressing a more pessimistic view about the effects of scientific and technological advance in the countryside than is admitted in official propaganda.

The most famous work on the subject of the environment is Valentin Rasputin's (1979) lyrical story *Farewell to Matyora*, which depicts the gradual decline and death of a whole community, the island village of Matyora on the Angara River in Siberia, which is due to be flooded by the completion of a hydro-electric power scheme. Rasputin poses the question of whether industrial and technological progress, advancing into regions as yet untouched by humans, allegedly with the sole purpose of bettering the lives of the inhabitants, should be carried out against the wishes of the people concerned. How much of the past should be sacrificed for the sake of some problematic future gain? Another interesting work on this theme is Victor Astafiev's (1982) *Queen Fish*, which voices a passionate protest against the age-old tradition of predatory human behaviour in the Siberian taiga that leads to the extermination of mammals, birds and fish and to the despoliation of forests. In Astafiev's view, people themselves become savage if they fail to respect life. Both

Astafiev and Rasputin question the value of the rapid intrusion of progress into remote areas of Siberia, and feel that the pretensions of humans to control nature are ultimately absurd.

Some Soviet writers, both conformists and dissidents, have linked the issues of nuclear policy and environmental conservation. Victor Stepanov's (1983) novel *The Thunderers* condemns the US practice of training dolphins for anti-submarine warfare and presents the USSR as the protector not only of the human race, but of the entire planet. A very different view has been expressed in Solzhenitsyn's (1974) *Letter to the Soviet Leaders,* which criticizes Soviet leaders' predilection for excessive military expenditure and follows the Club of Rome in attacking unlimited economic growth and in advocating conservation and small-scale economic development.

It remains a matter of dispute whether Soviet public opinion actually influences government policy on conservation, or merely whether government policy occasionally corresponds to the wishes of the Soviet intelligentsia. The economist Academician Abel Aganbegyan (now the Soviet government's chief economic adviser) argued in 1972 that public opinion did eventually influence the Soviet government to change its policy on Lake Baikal, although he admitted that the problem had by no means been solved. However, Zeev Wolfson claimed that public opinion achieved nothing but the introduction of cosmetic, palliative measures, and that in the fictional works of Rasputin and of Astafiev there is 'more of the tragic truth about the destruction of nature than in strictly scientific works' (Komarov, 1978, p. 208). The Soviet government's plan for diverting Siberian rivers was declared ecologically unsound at the Eighth Congress of Soviet Writers in July 1986 by such prominent writers as Rasputin, Vasily Belov and Sergei Zalygin; and the project was, indeed, abandoned in August 1986. However, the protests of the artistic intelligentsia may have played only a minor part in this decision. Although Soviet writers still try to influence party policy on conservation, it is difficult to disagree with Wolfson's conclusion that neither artistic images nor scientific statistics have the power to change the Soviet government's industrial plans.

V. Conclusion

Throughout history, the arts have played an ambivalent role in relation to war. Art which protests against war has existed since the earliest times, but until the twentieth century anti-heroic works were occasional and exceptional, brooking no comparison with the quantity of literature and art celebrating war. However, World War I totally changed the climate of opinion. In the twentieth century the predominant view expressed in the arts has been ironic and hostile to war and the despoliation of the environment. World War I, the development of nuclear weapons and the Second Indochina War had a particularly striking and varied impact on art and literature, since they totally shattered pre-existing values and culture, providing in each case an unprecedented experience that prompted a search for new aesthetic forms to render it adequately. Nevertheless, modern writers, for all their originality, still draw upon age-old artistic images and traditions, such as the Garden of Eden and the apocalypse, in order to express the predicament of contemporary humankind.

Since World War II contradictory elements have co-existed in Western culture. On the one hand, popular culture has generally upheld the militaristic sentiments prevalent in society as a whole; yet on the other hand, some artists and writers have attempted to respond seriously to the threats of nuclear war and environmental devastation. It is difficult to assess whether popular culture is merely a mirror of a violent society, or whether it is itself part of the problem. The precise contribution made by the representation of violence in the arts and the media towards the inculcation of bellicose attitudes in society is probably impossible to calculate. However, the fact that popular culture—particularly the visual medium of television (with its propensity to emphasize the sensational and violent)—has some negative effects has been attested to by the numerous individual instances in which the reporting of terrorist acts has engendered similar acts. And violent films such as *A Clockwork Orange* have led to imitative acts of violence (Schmid & Graaf, 1982).

As has been seen, the higher arts have great power to convey the reality of war and to comment on commonly-held beliefs. However, it remains debatable whether they have the power to change cultural attitudes; and, more significantly, the policies of governments. Long ago Percy Shelley (1821, p. 1055) claimed that 'Poets are the unacknowledged legislators of the world'. This seems to hold true in so far as writers and artists are outstanding individuals who frequently act as the conscience of their nations, expressing views that may be in conflict with the ideas of their age or the policies of their governments. However, the arts have a complex effect on human beings, and their precise influence on the formation of cultural norms towards war or the environment seems impossible to assess.

Artists in the USSR are probably more convinced than their Western counterparts that their work will exert a moral or political influence, since in Russia and the USSR art has always been held in great esteem and considered to possess socio-political significance. For example, Tolstoy argued in *What is Art?* [1896] that the artist can 'infect' the reader with good feelings; and for Solzhenitsyn (1968, p. 361) a great writer is like 'another government'. However, the Western artist must frequently doubt whether art can inspire any emotion other than the aesthetic. For example, Kurt Vonnegut has expressed agreement with the sceptical film director Harrison Starr, who, when told by Vonnegut that he was writing an anti-war book, asked: 'Why don't you write an anti-*glacier* book instead?', implying thereby that 'there would always be wars, that they were as easy to stop as glaciers' (Vonnegut, 1969, p. 3). The voice of the anti-war artist has been called 'a feeble, ironic sound' in the teeth of the military machine (Bates, 1969, p. xx).

Successive generations of war artists have failed in their purpose of preventing another war. The warnings of Daumier, von Suttner, Owen, Remarque, Heller and Vonnegut have all been ignored. Their work has undoubtedly exerted a powerful influence on the consciousness of individuals, but it is difficult to avoid the suspicion that they are merely preaching to the converted. If the destruction of the world is to be avoided, it is more urgent than ever before that the warnings of the post-nuclear, post-Viet Nam generations of artists and writers be heeded. Unfortunately, there are certain factors that prevent the arts from having a wider influence in society. One limitation of war art and literature is that they merely present war as a nightmare of senseless killing, and rarely demonstrate understanding of the psychological and economic forces that lead to war, forces the arts themselves are powerless to control. Another disadvantage is that anti-war books, with their vivid descriptions of violence and destruction, may inflame the very emotions they seek to condemn. If there exists in humankind a love of vicarious suffering and violence, books about war may inadvertently fuel this hidden lust for destruction (Read, 1945). Another, more prosaic, reason for the powerlessness of the arts to influence the policies of governments is the philistinism of political leaders.

Nevertheless, in the twentieth century some works of art have undoubtedly exerted a great influence on public opinion and, occasionally, on government policy. The anti-war poetry of World War I totally reversed the former heroic ideal of war; Pablo Picasso's *Guernica* made the world aware of fascist atrocities in Spain; Rachel Carson's (1962) *Silent Spring* brought the whole issue of environmental pollution and conservation to public attention; and the arts contributed to the climate of opinion that persuaded the US government to disengage from the Second Indochina War. Moreover, anti-war art has evidently been regarded as a threat by political leaders, since it has frequently been subject to censorship, both in the Western world and in the USSR. Many writers and artists believe that they may be able to change cultural attitudes; and this belief, surely, is sufficient justification for their work.

The predicament of the contemporary artist has been aptly expressed by Robert Stone, author of novels about Viet Nam, who voices the hope that his work may have an influence on national consciousness. While admitting that 'the Secretary of State isn't going to read it and say, "okay I'm not going to do whatever nasty thing I was going to do"', Stone nevertheless believes that somebody has to 'keep the levels of consciousness sharp. . . . It's a small thing, but we're small people in a big world. So I'm writing a piece of fiction that a couple thousand people read; it's no big thing, but it's worth doing' (Schroeder, 1984, p. 164). The singer Joan Baez has expressed a similar opinion: 'We're really a flop. . . . Only violence is a bigger flop' (Rodnitzky, 1983, p. 84). It is to be hoped that the arts, by inspiring hatred of war and a sense of human kinship with nature, can play their part in influencing public opinion in a constructive manner.

In both the USSR and the West critics continue to emphasize the potential value of literature in shaping public opinion on war and on the environment, but complain that writers could be more effective in bringing these issues to public attention. In the USA there has been a demand for a new genre of 'nuclear criticism' (Diacritics, 1984); and in the USSR one commentator has urged writers to create a 'super-literature' (Adamovich, 1984). Yet it is governments that ultimately have to take the vital decisions about the future of the world. The role of the artist today is the same as it was in Wilfred Owen's time, during World War I (Owen, 1964, p. 31): 'All a poet can do today is warn'.

References

Adamovich, A. 1984. [Create super-literature!] (in Russian). *Oktyabr*, Moscow, 1984(11):188–194.

Aichinger, P. 1975. *American soldier in fiction, 1880–1963: a history of attitudes toward warfare and the military establishment.* Ames: Iowa State University Press, 143 pp.

Aitmatov, C. 1981. [Speeches by the participants of the congress: Chingiz Aitmatov (Kirghizia)] (in Russian). *Literaturnaya Gazeta*, Moscow, 1981(8 Jul):8.

Aitmatov, C. 1983. *The day lasts more than a hundred years* [translated from the Russian by J. French]. Bloomington: Indiana University Press, 352 pp.

Aitmatov, C. 1986. [The time requires new thinking] (in Russian). *Literaturnaya Gazeta*, Moscow, 1986(5 Nov):1–2.

Alcorn, J. 1977. *Nature novel from Hardy to Lawrence.* New York: Columbia University Press, 139 pp.

Ariès, P. 1976. *Western attitudes toward death: from the Middle Ages to the present* [translated from the French by P. M. Ranum]. London: Marion Boyars, 111 pp.

Astafiev, V. 1982. *Queen fish: a story in two parts and twelve episodes* [translated from the Russian by K. Cook *et al.*]. Moscow: Progress Publishers, 444 pp.

Barrett, R., Cochrane, K. & Wolff, M. A. 1983. On being involved. In: Philbin, M. (ed.). *Give peace a chance: music and the struggle for peace.* Chicago: Chicago Review Press, 122 pp. + 8 pl.: pp. 45–53.

Bates, S. (ed.). 1969. *Poems of war resistance from 2300 B.C. to the present.* New York: Grossman Publishers, 216 pp.

Beckett, S. 1963. *Endgame: a play in one act; followed by Act without Words, a mime for one player* [translated from the French by the author]. London: Faber & Faber, 60 pp.

Beidler, P. D. 1982. *American literature and the experience of Vietnam.* Athens: University of Georgia Press, 220 pp.

Bergonzi, B. 1965. *Heroes' twilight: a study of the literature of the great war.* London: Constable, 235 pp.

Blish, J. 1969. We all die naked. In: Silverberg, R., Zelazny, R. & Blish, J. *Three for tomorrow: three original novellas of science fiction.* New York: Meredith Press, 204 pp.: pp. 153–204.

Brians, P. 1984. Nuclear war in science fiction, 1945–59. *Science-Fiction Studies,* Montreal, 11(3):253–263.

Briggs, R. 1982. *When the wind blows.* London: Hamish Hamilton, 40 pp.

Briggs, R. 1983. *When the wind blows.* London: Samuel French, 46 pp.

Brock-Utne, B. 1985. *Educating for peace: a feminist perspective.* New York: Pergamon Press, 175 pp.

Brooks, P. 1980. *Speaking for nature: how literary naturalists from Henry Thoreau to Rachel Carson have shaped America.* Boston: Houghton Mifflin, 304 pp.

Bruckner, D. J. R., Chwast, S. & Heller, S. 1984. *Art against war: 400 years of protest in art.* New York: Abbeville Press, 128 pp.
Brunner, J. 1972. *The sheep look up.* New York: Harper & Row, 461 pp.
Brunner, J. 1975. *Shockwave rider.* New York: Harper & Row, 288 pp.
Camus, A. 1947. *La peste [The plague]* (in French). Paris: Gallimard, 332 pp.
Caputo, P. 1977. *A rumor of war.* New York: Holt, Rinehart & Winston, 346 pp.
Carson, R. 1962. *Silent spring.* Boston: Houghton Mifflin, 304 pp.
Clark, K. 1976. *Landscape into art.* 2nd edn. New York: Harper & Row, 248 pp.
Clark, K. 1977. *Animals and men: their relationship as reflected in Western art from prehistory to the present day.* London: Thames & Hudson, 240 pp.
Clarke, M. & Crisp, C. 1981. *Ballet goer's guide.* New York: Alfred A. Knopf, 368 pp.
Craig, D. & Egan, M. 1979. *Extreme situations: literature and crisis from the great war to the atom bomb.* London: Macmillan, 309 pp.
cummings, e. e. 1922. *The enormous room.* New York: Modern Library, 322 pp., 1934.
Deane, M. J. & Kass, I. 1983–84. Groupthink: a pacifist poem and the Soviet press. *Air University Review,* Maxwell Air Force Base, Alabama, 35(2):62–67.
Del Vecchio, J. M. 1982. *The 13th valley.* New York: Bantam Books, 609 pp.
Denisoff, R. S. 1983. Origins and inspirations of the protest song. In: Philbin, M. (ed.). *Give peace a chance: music and the struggle for peace.* Chicago: Chicago Review Press, 122 pp. + 8 pl.: pp. 87–92.
Diacritics. 1984. Nuclear criticism. *Diacritics,* Ithaca, NY, 14(2):2–3.
Disch, T. M. (ed.). 1971. *Ruins of earth: an anthology of stories of the immediate future.* New York: G. P. Putnam's Sons, 318 pp.
Dos Passos, J. 1921. *Three soldiers.* New York: George H. Doran, 433 pp.
Eliot, T. S. 1963. *Collected poems, 1909–1962.* London: Faber & Faber, 240 pp.
Elwood, R. & Kidd, V. (eds). 1973. *Saving worlds: a collection of original science fiction stories.* Garden City, NY: Doubleday, 237 pp.
Faulkner, W. 1926. *Soldiers' pay.* New York: Boni & Liveright, 319 pp.
Faulkner, W. 1965. *Essays, speeches and public letters* [ed. by J. B. Meriwether]. New York: Random House, 233 pp.
Ferguson, J. (ed.). 1972. *War and the creative arts: an anthology.* London: Macmillan, 380 pp. + 57 pl.
Fiedler, L. 1964. *Waiting for the end.* New York: Stein & Day, 256 pp.
Fussell, P. 1975. *The great war and modern memory.* New York: Oxford University Press, 363 pp.
Gloag, J. 1932. *Tomorrow's yesterday.* London: Allen & Unwin, 184 pp.
Goya, F. 1863. *Disasters of war.* New York: Dover Publications, 12 pp. + 83 pl., 1967.
Granin, D. 1954. [Seekers]. In: Granin, D. 1978. [*Collected works.* I] (in Russian). Leningrad: Khudozhestvennaya Literatura, 645 pp.: pp. 215–644.
Graves, R. 1957. *Goodbye to all that.* rev. edn. London: Cassell, 306 pp.
Heller, J. 1961. *Catch-22.* New York: Simon & Schuster, 443 pp.
Hemingway, E. 1929. *A farewell to arms.* New York: Charles Scribner's Sons, 355 pp.
Hemmert, T. 1983. *This ain't no foolin' around*: giving peace a chance in the '80s. In: Philbin, M. (ed.). *Give peace a chance: music and the struggle for peace.* Chicago: Chicago Review Press, 122 pp. + 8 pl.: pp. 35–44.
Herr, M. 1977. *Dispatches.* New York: Alfred A. Knopf, 260 pp.
Hersey, J. 1946. *Hiroshima.* New York: Alfred A. Knopf, 117 pp.
Hoban, R. 1980. *Riddley Walker.* New York: Summit Books, 220 pp.
Hooper, A. 1982. *Military and the media.* Aldershot, UK: Gower, 247 pp.

Huxley, A. 1948. *Ape and essence.* New York: Harper & Brothers, 205 pp.

Ibuse, M. 1971. *Black rain* [translated from the Japanese by J. Bester]. London: Secker & Warburg, 300 pp.

Jones, D. L. (ed.). 1968. *War poetry: an anthology*. Oxford: Pergamon Press, 142 pp.

Jones, J. 1951. *From here to eternity*. New York: Charles Scribner's Sons, 861 pp.

Joyce, J. 1922. *Ulysses*. Paris: Shakespeare, 732 pp.

Kahn, H. & Wiener, A. J. 1967. *Year 2000: a framework for speculation on the next thirty-three years.* New York: Macmillan, 431 pp.

Keegan, J. & Darracott, J. 1981. *Nature of war*. New York: Holt, Rinehart & Winston, 276 pp.

Kermode, F. 1967. *Sense of an ending: studies in the theory of fiction.* New York: Oxford University Press, 187 pp.

Komarov, B. 1978. [*Destruction of nature: the intensification of the ecological crisis in the USSR*] (in Russian). Frankfurt: Possev-Verlag, 209 pp.

Komarov, B. 1980. *Destruction of nature in the Soviet Union* [translated from the Russian by M. Vale & J. Hollander]. London: Pluto Press, 150 pp.

Kramer, A. 1983. Hiroshima: a 37-year failure to respond. *New England Review & Bread Loaf Quarterly,* Hanover, New Hampshire, 5(4):534–548.

Kubrick, S. 1964. *Dr. Strangelove: or, how I learned to stop worrying and love the bomb.* Hollywood, Calif.: Columbia, 35 mm B&W film, 93 min.

Lennon, J. & Ono, Y. 1983. Press conference: John Lennon and Yoko Ono talk about peace. In: Philbin, M. (ed.). *Give peace a chance: music and the struggle for peace.* Chicago: Chicago Review Press, 122 pp. + 8 pl.: pp. 19–25.

Leonov, L. 1947. [In defence of a friend] (in Russian). *Izvestia,* Moscow, 1947(28 Dec):2–3.

Leonov, L. 1966. *Russian forest* [translated from the Russian by B. Isaacs]. Moscow: Progress Publishers, 718 pp.

Lewinski, J. 1978. *Camera at war: a history of war photography from 1848 to the present day.* New York: Simon & Schuster, 240 pp.

Lvov, M. 1960. [Products of the disintegration of uranium] (in Russian). *Literaturnaya Gazeta,* Moscow, 1960(5 Nov):2.

Mailer, N. 1948. *The naked and the dead.* New York: Henry Holt, 744 pp.

Marsh, R. J. 1986a. Soviet fiction and the nuclear debate. *Soviet Studies,* Glasgow, 38:248–270.

Marsh, R. J. 1986b. *Soviet fiction since Stalin: science, politics and literature.* London: Croom Helm, 338 pp.

Meadows, D. H., Meadows, D. L., Randers, J. & Behrens, W. W., III. 1972. *Limits to growth: a report for the Club of Rome's project on the predicament of mankind.* New York: Universe Books, 205 pp.

Merril, J. 1950. *Shadow on the hearth.* Garden City, NY: Doubleday, 277 pp.

Miller, W. M., Jr. 1959. *A canticle for Leibowitz.* Philadelphia: J. B. Lippincott, 320 pp.

Muste, J. M. 1984. Singing back the silence: 'Gravity's Rainbow' and the war novel. *Modern Fiction Studies,* W. Lafayette, Indiana, 30(1):5–23.

Newby, P. H. 1951. *The novel, 1945–1950.* London: Longmans, Green, 58 pp.

O'Brien, T. 1978. *Going after Cacciato.* New York: Delacorte Press, 338 pp.

O'Brien, T. 1985. *Nuclear age.* New York: Alfred A. Knopf, 312 pp.

Okudzhava, B. 1961. Good-bye, schoolboy! [translated from the Russian by R. Szulkin]. In: Pomorska, K. (ed.). 1971. *Fifty years of Russian prose: from Pasternak to Solzhenitsyn.* II. Cambridge, Mass.: MIT Press, 354 pp.: pp. 171–227.

Okudzhava, B. 1980. *65 pesen: 65 songs* [musical arrangements, selection & editing by V. Frumkin; translated from the Russian by E. Shapiro]. Ann Arbor, Michigan: Ardis, 174 pp.

Olson, K. E., 1981. *Music and musket: bands and bandsmen of the American Civil War*. Westport, Connecticut: Greenwood Press, 299 pp.

Owen, W. 1964. *Collected poems* [ed. by C. Day Lewis]. London: Chatto & Windus, 191 pp.

Partlow, V. 1983. Just a song at twilight: *Old man atom* vs. the cold war. In: Philbin, M. (ed.). *Give peace a chance: music and the struggle for peace*. Chicago: Chicago Review Press, 122 pp. + 8 pl.: pp. 93–96.

Pedler, K. & Davis, G. 1974. *Brainrack*. London: Souvenir Press, 285 pp.

Philbin, M. (ed.). 1983. *Give peace a chance: music and the struggle for peace*. Chicago: Chicago Review Press, 122 pp. + 8 pl.

Piper, D. 1984. Soviet Union. In: Klein, H. *et al.* (eds). *Second World War in fiction*. London: Macmillan, 249 pp.: pp. 131–172.

Pope, A. 1867. *Iliad of Homer*. London: Bell & Daldy, 458 pp.

Pynchon, T. 1973. *Gravity's rainbow*. New York: Viking Press, 760 pp.

Rabkin, E. S., Greenberg, M. H. & Olander, J. D. (eds). 1983. *End of the world*. Carbondale: Southern Illinois University Press, 204 pp.

Rasputin, V. 1979. *Farewell to Matyora* [translated from the Russian by A. W. Bouis]. New York: Macmillan, 227 pp.

Read, H. 1945. Failure of the war books. In: Read, H. *Coat of many colours: occasional essays*. London: George Routledge, 352 pp.: pp. 72–76.

Remarque, E. M. 1929. *All quiet on the western front* [translated from the German by A. W. Wheen]. Boston: Little, Brown, 291 pp. (Translation of *Im Westen nichts neues*, 1928.)

Rich, V. 1987. Soviet writers protest successfully about environment science. *Nature*, London, 327:455.

Rodnitzky, J. 1983. They all sang songs of peace: pacificism and folk music in the 1960s. In: Philbin, M. (ed.). *Give peace a chance: music and the struggle for peace*. Chicago: Chicago Review Press, 122 pp. + 8 pl.: pp. 77–84.

Sassoon, S. 1918. *Counter-attack, and other poems*. London: William Heinemann, 64 pp.

Schmid, A. P. & Graaf, J. de. 1982. *Violence as communication: insurgent terrorism and the Western media*. London: Sage Publications, 283 pp.

Schroeder, E. J. 1984. Two interviews: talks with Tim O'Brien and Robert Stone. *Modern Fiction Studies*, W. Lafayette, Indiana, 30(1):135–164.

Shelley, P. B. 1821. Defence of poetry. In: Glover, A. S. B. (ed.). 1951. *Selected poetry, prose and letters*. London: Nonesuch Press, 1142 pp.: pp. 1023–1055.

Shepard, P. 1967. *Man in the landscape: a historic view of the esthetics of nature*. New York: Alfred A. Knopf, 290 pp.

Shute, N. 1957. *On the beach*. New York: William Morrow, 312 pp.

Silva, A. de, Simson, O. v. & Hinks, R. 1963. *Man through his art. I. War and peace*. London: Educational Productions, 64 pp. + 20 pl.

Smith, M. J., Jr. 1980. *War story guide: an annotated bibliography of military fiction*. Metuchen, New Jersey: Scarecrow Press, 437 pp.

Solzhenitsyn, A. 1968. *The first circle* [translated from the Russian by M. Guybon]. London: Collins & Harvill, 581 pp.

Solzhenitsyn, A. 1973. *Candle in the wind* [translated from the Russian by K. Armes]. Minneapolis: University of Minnesota Press, 141 pp.

Solzhenitsyn, A. 1974. *Letter to the Soviet leaders* [translated from the Russian by H. Sternberg]. New York: Harper & Row, 59 pp.

Solzhenitsyn, A. 1978. [*Collected works: In the first circle*]. rev. edn (in Russian). Paris: YMCA Press, vols I–II (420+406 pp.).

Stallworthy, J. (ed.). 1984. *Oxford book of war poetry*. Oxford: Oxford University Press, 358 pp.

Stepanov, V. 1983. [Thunderers] (in Russian). *Nash Sovremennik*, Moscow, 1983(8):3–101;(9):16–126.

Stone, R. 1974. *Dog soldiers*. Boston: Houghton Mifflin, 342 pp.

Strugatsky, A. & Strugatsky, B. 1977. *Roadside picnic: tale of the troika* [translated from the Russian by A. W. Bouis]. New York: Macmillan, 245 pp.

Suttner, B. v. 1889. *Die Waffen nieder!: eine Lebensgeschichte [Down with weapons!: a biography]*. Dresden: E. Pierson's Verlag, 2 vols (309+324 pp.). English-language edn: *Lay down your arms: the autobiography of Martha von Tilling* [translated from the German by T. Holmes & rev. by the authoress]. London: Longmans, Green, 435 pp., 1892.

Taylor, A. J. P. 1975. *Second World War: an illustrated history*. London: Hamish Hamilton, 234 pp.

Titus, A. C. 1983. Back to ground zero: old footage through new lenses. *Journal of Popular Film & Television,* Washington, 11(1):3–11.

Toffler, A. 1970. *Future shock*. New York: Random House, 505 pp.

Tunnard, C. 1978. *World with a view: an inquiry into the nature of scenic values*. New Haven: Yale University Press, 196 pp.

United Kingdom Central Office of Information. 1976. *Protect and survive*. London: UK Home Office, 31 pp.

Vonnegut, K. 1969. *Slaughterhouse-five, or the children's crusade: a duty-dance with death*. New York: Delacorte Press, 186 pp.

Vonnegut, K. 1985. *Galápagos*. New York: Delacorte Press, 295 pp.

Voznesensky, A. 1967. *Antiworlds, and the fifth ace: poetry* [translated from the Russian by W. H. Auden *et al.*; ed. by P. Blake & M. Hayward]. Garden City, NY: Anchor Books, 296 pp.

Voznesensky, A. 1986. [Thoughts about Chernobyl] (in Russian). *Pravda,* Moscow, 1986(3 Jun):6.

Walsh, J. 1982. *American war literature, 1914 to Vietnam*. New York: St Martin's Press, 218 pp.

Watkins, P. 1966. *The war game*. London: British Broadcasting Corporation, 16 mm B&W film, 47 min.

Welsh, J. 1983. Modern apocalypse: the War Game. *Journal of Popular Film & Television,* Washington, 11(1):25–41.

Wiener, J. 1983. *Give peace a chance*: an anthem for the anti-war movement. In: Philbin, M. (ed.). *Give peace a chance: music and the struggle for peace*. Chicago: Chicago Review Press, 122 pp. + 8 pl.: pp. 11–17.

Wiener, M. 1981. *English culture and the decline of the industrial spirit, 1850–1980*. Cambridge, UK: Cambridge University Press, 217 pp.

Wylie, P. 1972. *The end of the dream*. Garden City, NY: Doubleday, 264 pp.

10. Towards non-violent conflict resolution and environmental protection: a synthesis

ARTHUR H. WESTING
Stockholm International Peace Research Institute

I. Introduction

Some 300 millennia of population growth and technological development by the human species have finally led to an inability of the life-support systems of the earth to provide adequate resources on the one hand, and to adequately dispose of its pollutant discharges on the other. Indeed, considering the ever more drastic inroads being made into the habitats of the other living species on earth, this transgression of the global carrying capacity for humans has now attained huge proportions. Nonetheless, human numbers, as well as human aspirations, continue to increase at exponential rates, thereby intensifying the problem day by day.

At the same time, at least nine millennia of advances in military technology by the human species have finally led to an inability of civilization to withstand the holocaust that can now be achieved. Moreover, the arms race that nourishes the military sector of society exacerbates the global environmental problems; concurrently, these environmental problems contribute to the rationale for maintaining armed forces.

The norms of human behaviour that have permitted civilization to arrive at the brink of collapse, whether via environmental or military folly, have operated for millennia. The occasional challenges directed towards these norms through the ages—as erudite and eloquent as some of them have been—are consistently derided, shrugged off, ignored or (at best) accepted in principle but disregarded in practice. Responsible for this tragic dilemma is some combination of (*a*) innate (inherited) human characteristics, and (*b*) environmentally imposed (culturally determined) factors. Thus, at least the latter, social component of the underlying causes remains potentially amenable to revision.

Prior chapters have served to establish the nature of the environmental and military problems faced by humankind which have just been summarized here, and have also indicated their dimensions. Further identified in prior chapters have been those existing cultural norms that serve to constrain damage to the human environment, with special attention having been devoted to such damage from military sources. Not only was the existence of relevant norms established—as modest and incomplete as these were found to be—but also that these norms are by no means immutable. Their malleability was evidenced, for example, by their evolution through history and by their differences from one civilization or society to another.

Detailed attention was paid in prior chapters to the shaping (moulding) of cultural norms by such societal institutions or forces as the law, formal education, the mass media and the arts; and more cursory attention to governments, international organizations, religion, citizen groups and individuals. It was concluded that the various components of society examined mirrored the prevailing cultural norms more strongly than they influenced them. The norms were nonetheless seen as potential forces of change for the better.

Having established that much, it now remains to at least suggest in the present chapter some approaches to preventing the world from ending (to lean upon T. S. Eliot [1925]) with either a 'whimper' or a 'bang'. Outlined first are the actions necessary for the safeguarding of society through population controls, pollution abatement and habitat protection. The need is stressed for nations finally to submit to compulsory arbitration as a means of settling their disputes without resort to violence. The chapter concludes with the suggestion that the cultural norms necessary to ensure the survival of humankind in a socially and environmentally acceptable fashion either exist or can be developed.

II. Safeguarding civilization

A four-pronged approach is required to initiate an attack on the problem of safeguarding civilization from environmental collapse (Westing, 1988b): one that deals with population; another that deals with pollution; a third that deals with habitat protection; and a fourth that deals with conflict resolution. Adjustments in population will most often directly affect developing nations; adjustments in pollution, developed nations; and adjustments in habitat protection and conflict resolution, both developing and developed nations. At least the indirect ramifications of adjustments in any of these four areas will have to be internationalized to the extent possible. It is obvious that the necessary internationalization will require the establishment of amicable relations among the nations of the world.

Population control

Regarding population, growth must be arrested in whatever nation it occurs as an immediate first step towards achieving the global carrying capacity for humans. Each nation, without exception, must forthwith institute an effective programme that will maintain or reduce its birth rate to a level that, in any event, does not exceed its death rate. One sensible system that any nation could elaborate upon might involve the introduction of child-right chits (Boulding, 1964, pp. 135–36; Heer, 1975; Russett, 1970). In this initial step, every person who reaches his or her majority would receive from the government no more than one child-right chit, entitling the holder to have a child (with multiple births treated as a single child; and with the chit being replaced if the child fails to reach the age of one year). Such chits would be transferable (negotiable) commodities within a nation.

The right just suggested of no more than one child per person, on the average, would arrest continued population growth and would even lead to a modestly negative growth rate. However, more stringent measures would be necessary in many nations. Thus, the denomination of the child-right chit in grossly overpopulated nations might well be set at 0.5 (i.e., one child permitted, on the average, for every two adults). The indicators to consider are suggested to be staple-food production per capita, gross national product per capita, rate of infant mortality, life expectancy and literacy rate. The values of these indicators in relation to those of the aggregate of the developed nations of the world would provide one measure of over-population. However, worsening trends in these values within a nation would provide the most compelling demonstration of its over-population (as has been pointed out a number of times [by, e.g., Ehrlich *et al.*, 1977, p. 716; Hardin, 1985, p. 472; Singer, 1973]).

Finally, in conjunction with this programme of world-wide population attrition there would have to be established a world-wide old-age pension plan, to be financed by all nations through a progressive scheme of taxation based on the wealth of a nation. Moreover, to more nearly equalize other immediate burdens that population controls might impose upon a developing nation, a more general international fund should be established, again based upon progressive taxation, to provide further measures of relief. These could be paid out in the form of loans that would subsequently be forgiven to the extent that the necessary population goals were being achieved.

Pollution abatement

Regarding pollution, its global increase must also be arrested, as the second immediate step towards achieving the global carrying capacity for humans. Here industrial growth must be regulated especially in the developed nations in some appropriate fashion so as to prevent any future increases in air pollution (see, e.g., Broecker, 1987). This action would be carried out initially in terms of national emission levels of carbon dioxide and sulphur, and perhaps also of oxides of nitrogen or other contaminants. Such a step would have to be a prelude to international co-operation in achieving, over a limited period of years, a world-wide reduction in air pollution to global levels that can be safely absorbed by the environment. Preventing further increases in the concentration of atmospheric carbon dioxide will be difficult owing to their association with the consumption of fossil fuels, but is nevertheless feasible (Lovins *et al.*, 1981).

To achieve safe levels of pollution discharge into the atmosphere might well require as much as, say, a reduction by one-half in the global emission rate of today—that is, perhaps a reduction to the levels of about the year 1965.

Permitted emissions—whatever they might turn out to be—would have to be distributed to each nation on a unit-area basis. Each nation would be awarded the number of one-square-kilometre chits that corresponds to the size of its national territory (not including claimed ocean areas), such chits being negotiable commodities among nations, at least to the extent that they could be leased.

The necessary reductions in emissions would be achieved by a nation through the closure of industries, through restrictions on transportation and so forth, to the extent that improvements in emission control or other means were not able to cope with the problem.

Habitat protection

Regarding habitat protection, of highest priority on the agenda is, of course, the avoidance of nuclear war. At a more mundane level, world-wide action must be taken to expand the extent of protected areas (nature reserves) as the third immediate step towards achieving the global carrying capacity for humans. Today only about 3 per cent of the land area of the world is reported to have a protected status (Mathews *et al.*, 1986, tbl. 7.1). In only about a dozen nations is at least 10 per cent of the land area claimed to be protected today; and in only about 40 nations, 5 per cent or more. Indeed, many nations have no protected area at all. Thus as an immediate step, each nation should have to set aside as a nature reserve at least 5 per cent of its land area (covering a range of habitat types), with the longer term goal being at least 10 per cent (see also Harrison *et al.*, 1984; Miller, 1984; Myers, 1979, pp. 219–31). Here again, a world-wide fund should be established to facilitate this programme, with all countries contributing on the basis of a progressive scheme of taxation. Indeed, some small moves have recently occurred in the direction of internationalizing the financial burden resulting from habitat protection (Goodland, 1987; Page, 1987; Walsh, 1987). Finally, every effort should be made to have the nature reserves protected against both civil and military depredations.

Conflict resolution

The human species persists in functioning and interacting in the form of some 170 discrete states, the sovereignty of which is considered, above all else, as being sacrosanct. However, as the foregoing presentation would appear to have made unequivocally clear, continued resort to violence in the settlement of international conflicts serves only to hasten the day of civilizational collapse from environmental causes, and might even precipitate such civilizational collapse more directly from military causes.

Thus, there exists an urgent necessity for the community of nations to embrace the concept of international law both in theory and practice (Ferencz, 1985; Schachter, 1977). Indeed, it has become imperative that as an immediate step towards the abolition of international conflict—now necessary for the first time in human history—the nations of the world must finally submit to the compulsory adjudication or arbitration of their inevitably numerous disputes. Such an abolition will at the same time be a step towards world government.

At least two important structures are already in place that would serve well as vehicles for the necessary compulsory arbitration among nations: (*a*) the Permanent Court of Arbitration, established at the Hague in 1899; and (*b*) the International Court of Justice (the so-called World Court), established at the Hague in 1920 as the Permanent Court of International Justice, and in its present form, within the United Nations system, in 1945. The Permanent Court of Arbitration has associated with it commendable provisions for an investigatory mechanism. The International Court of Justice has recently emphasized its suitability and willingness to deal with disputes related to environmental protection (Singh, 1986, p. 8).

A number of states have from the inception of the International Court of Justice supported the concept of submitting to its compulsory arbitration; by contrast, both the USA and the USSR opposed such a notion at that time (Padelford, 1945, pp. 473–74) and since. It is therefore most heartening to note that the USSR has very recently come out in favour of mandatory jurisdiction by the International Court (Gorbachev, 1987, p. 6).[1]

Dimensions of the task

The twin goals of conserving the environment and of achieving non-violent conflict resolution, would seem to be formidable tasks, indeed (Westing, 1988a). But as Lao Tzu is said to have recognized some two and one half millennia ago, 'a journey of a thousand miles starts from beneath one's feet' (*Tao Te Ching* 2:64). Much needs to be done on many fronts (legal, political, educational and scholarly), in many locales (rich and poor, temperate and tropical, rainy and arid, territorial and extra-territorial) and at many levels (governmental, intergovernmental, non-governmental and individual).

The Third World countries require assistance in the fields of research, education, regulation and administration so that they can bring the production of basic foods and wood into balance with human population numbers on the one hand, and the needs of nature on the other. Responsible environmental involvement in the community of nations, as indicated *inter alia* by treaty participation, should be fostered by diplomatic means. Trans-frontier nature reserves could serve the dual purpose of conservation and of reducing border conflicts (Saussay, 1980; Thorsell, 1985). The same approach of earmarked aid and other incentives should be used regarding the preparation and adoption of a national conservation strategy in co-operation with the International Union for Conservation of Nature and Natural Resources (IUCN).

Various Third World countries devote a substantial level of human, material

[1] A compilation of the declarations by states regarding their level of submission to compulsory jurisdiction by the International Court of Justice is provided elsewhere (*International Court of Justice Yearbook*, The Hague, 40:60–92 [1985–86]).

and financial resources to the military sector. The question, of course, arises under what conditions, and to what extent, a nation's security would be enhanced by shifting a portion of its military expenditures into civil expenditures for population control, public health, agriculture, forestry, range management, fishery management, nature conservation and other social and environmental needs. A research effort is clearly in order to rigorously examine the several ramifications of this question. For example, how large (and what type of) a military sector is conscionable and desirable? How can the need for a military sector be reduced? In this regard, the importance should be pointed out of the widest possible participation in arms-control treaties as a means of reducing world tensions. To what extent does soil and other environmental degradation or over-exploitation of renewable resources lead to unrest, civil disturbance, civil war or even international armed conflict? To what extent do reversals of environmental degradation and the adoption of sustainable harvesting of renewable resources improve public health, foster social tranquillity and enhance economic well-being? To what extent would land reform facilitate reversals of environmental degradation and over-exploitation of renewable resources? What private and public advantages accrue from stable population numbers? Which types of foreign aid foster conservation and which types hinder it?

A number of related and somewhat broader questions of research interest also come to mind. Under what conditions do international environmental problems lead to co-operation rather than conflict? How can regional treaties be fostered that focus on the environmental problems of one ecosystem—for example, on a river system or watershed, a sea or gulf, an island or peninsula? To what extent do such treaties also contribute to a reduction in regional political tensions? To what extent does local or regional environmental degradation (e.g., in the Sahel) adversely influence other regions or even the world at large? To what extent are the often overwhelming environmental problems of the poor nations attributable to actions—past or present—of the rich nations? To what extent do the various environmental problems of the day *require* for their alleviation foreign aid or international co-operation or even the collective action by the entire world community of nations, via, for example, the United Nations system (UNEP, UNESCO, etc.) (Caldwell, 1985)? To what extent *ought* they? Under what conditions does international interdependence lead to conflict rather than to co-operation (Gasiorowski, 1986)? And, most importantly, to what extent does the solving of these problems require peaceful conditions and to what extent does it foster peaceful conditions?

III. Conclusion

No doubt remains that the survival of humankind will require new ways of thinking about nature on the one hand (Ehrlich, 1986) and about nuclearism on the other (Holt, 1984; Somerville, 1986). The development of a heightened concern for the future would seem to be especially valuable in the necessary transformation (Boniecki, 1977).

Although the need for new ways of thinking is not in question, the task of transformation is a formidable one owing to entrenched militarism (Koenig, 1977; Riley, 1986; Smith, 1986; Vagts, 1959); perhaps even to a growing tendency for many to accept the 'unthinkable' (Peattie, 1984); and, at any rate, because the establishment of new concepts of any sort can take a long time (Barber, 1961; Deutsch *et al.*, 1971). Nonetheless, there are some important signs of hope: (*a*) the pathology of nuclearism is becoming ever more widely and firmly recognized (Frank, 1960; 1983; Hall, 1983; Lifton, 1985; Middleton, 1987); (*b*) there is increasing understanding in both the developed and developing worlds that the global environment is in serious danger (Frolov, 1982; Holdgate *et al.*, 1982); (*c*) military threats to the environment are being ever more widely recognized (Westing, 1980; 1986); and (*d*) the need for international trust and co-operation to solve the global problems in question is receiving growing appreciation (Kapitza, 1981; Krass, 1985; Müller & Rode, 1984). Perhaps not yet as widely accepted, but a further sign of hope is the slowly emerging recognition that the existing patriarchal and patricentric structure of society contributes to the military problems facing humankind (Brock-Utne, 1985; Woolf, 1938).

As noted at the outset of the study, the military norm that 'the right of belligerents to adopt means of injuring the enemy is not unlimited' is, in fact, slowly expanding to encompass 'means of warfare which are intended, or may be expected, to cause widespread, long-term and severe damage to the natural environment'. Such an expansion implies a growing realization that the human life-support systems have become seriously threatened. As such, this emerging concern for the environment represents the first small, but exceedingly welcome, step by humankind in its 'journey of a thousand miles' in the direction of ecological and social sanity.

References

Barber, B. 1961. Resistance by scientists to scientific discovery. *Science,* Washington, 134:596–602.

Boniecki, G. J. 1977. Is man interested in his future?: the psychological question of our times. *International Journal of Psychology,* Montreuil, France, 12:59–64.

Boulding, K. E. 1964. *Meaning of the twentieth century: the great transition.* New York: Harper & Row, 199 pp.

Brock-Utne, B. 1985. *Educating for peace: a feminist perspective.* New York: Pergamon Press, 175 pp.

Broecker, W. S. 1987. Unpleasant surprises in the greenhouse? *Nature,* London, 328:123–126.

Caldwell, L. K. 1985. Cooperation and conflict: international response to environmental issues. *Environment,* Washington, 27(1):6–11,38–39.

Deutsch, K. W., Platt, J. & Senghaas, D. 1971. Conditions favoring major advances in social science. *Science,* Washington, 171:450–459.

Ehrlich, P. R. 1986. *Machinery of nature.* New York: Simon & Schuster, 320 pp.

Ehrlich, P. R., Ehrlich, A. H. & Holdren, J. P. 1977. *Ecoscience: population, resources, environment.* San Francisco: W. H. Freeman, 1051 pp.

Eliot, T. S. 1925. The hollow men. In: Eliot, T. S. *Complete poems and plays, 1909–1950.* New York: Harcourt, Brace & World, 392 pp.: pp. 56–59, 1962.

Ferencz, B. B. 1985. *Common sense guide to world peace.* London: Oceana Publications, 112 pp.

Frank, J. D. 1960. Breaking the thought barrier: psychological challenges of the nuclear age. *Psychiatry,* Washington, 23:245–266.

Frank, J. D. 1983. Nuclear arms and prenuclear leaders: sociopsychological aspects of the nuclear arms race. *Political Psychology,* New York, 4:393–408.

Frolov, I. 1982. *Global problems and the future of mankind.* Moscow: Progress Publishers, 311 pp.

Gasiorowski, M. J. 1986. Economic interdependence and international conflict: some cross-national evidence. *International Studies Quarterly,* Guildford, UK, 30:23–38.

Goodland, R. J. A. 1987. World Bank's wildlands policy: a major new means of financing conservation. *Conservation Biology,* New Brunswick, New Jersey, 1:210–213.

Gorbachev, M. 1987. Reality and guarantees for a secure world. *New Times,* Moscow, 1987(39):3–6.

Hall, F. 1983. United States' search for security: a psychotherapist's viewpoint. *Journal of Peace Research,* Oslo, 20:299–309.

Hardin, G. 1985. Human ecology: the subversive, conservative science. *American Zoologist,* USA, 25:469–476.

Harrison, J., Miller, K. & McNeely, J. 1984. World coverage of protected areas: development goals and environmental needs. In: McNeely, J. A. & Miller, K. R. (eds). *National parks, conservation, and development: the role of protected areas in sustaining society*. Washington: Smithsonian Institution Press, 825 pp.: pp. 24–33.

Heer, D. M. 1975. Marketable licenses for babies: Boulding's proposal revisited. *Social Biology*, Madison, Wisconsin, 22:1–16.

Holdgate, M. W., Kassas, M. & White, G. F. (eds). 1982. *World environment 1972–1982: a report by the United Nations Environment Programme.* Dublin: Tycooly International, 637 pp.

Holt, R. R. 1984. Can psychology meet Einstein's challenge? *Political Psychology*, New York, 5:199–225.

Kapitza, P. 1981. Global problems, international solutions. *Bulletin of the Atomic Scientists,* Chicago, 37(1):40–43.

Koenig, M. E. D. 1977. Toy theory of Western history. *Bulletin of the Atomic Scientists,* Chicago, 33(8):16–18.

Krass, A. S. 1985. Verification and trust in arms control. *Journal of Peace Research*, Oslo, 22:285–288.

Lifton, R. J. 1985. Toward a nuclear-age ethos. *Bulletin of the Atomic Scientists,* Chicago, 41(7):168–172.

Lovins, A. B., Lovins, L. H., Krause, F. & Bach, W. 1981. *Least-cost energy: solving the CO_2 problem.* Andover, Mass.: Brick House, 184 pp.

Mathews, J. T. *et al.* 1986. *World resources 1986: a report by the World Resources*

Institute and the International Institute for Environment and Development. New York: Basic Books, 353 pp.

Middleton, H. 1987. Psychosocial view of the nuclear arms race. *Medicine & War,* London, 3:11–22.

Miller, K. R. 1984. Bali action plan: a framework for the future of protected areas. In: McNeely, J. A. & Miller, K. R. (eds). *National parks, conservation, and development: the role of protected areas in sustaining society.* Washington: Smithsonian Institution Press, 825 pp.: pp. 756–764.

Müller, H. & Rode, R. 1984. How to talk about interdependence and keep ignoring it: parochial world politics. *Bulletin of Peace Proposals,* Oslo, 15:79–91.

Myers, N. 1979. *Sinking ark: a new look at the problem of disappearing species.* Oxford: Pergamon Press, 307 pp.

Padelford, N. J. 1945. Fourth Commission: the judicial organization. *International Conciliation,* New York, 1945(413):469–479.

Page, D. 1987. Cutting the debt, saving the forest. *Environment*, Washington, 29(7):4–5.

Peattie, L. 1984. Normalizing the unthinkable. *Bulletin of the Atomic Scientists,* Chicago, 40(3):32–36.

Riley, R. T. 1986. Militarism in America. *Defense Monitor,* Washington, 15(3):1–8.

Russett, B. M. 1970. Licensing: for cars and babies. *Bulletin of the Atomic Scientists,* Chicago, 26(9):15–19.

Saussay, C. du. 1980. Transfrontier parks. *Unasylva,* Rome, 32(127):16–22.

Schachter, O. 1977. *Sharing the world's resources.* New York: Columbia University Press, 172 pp.

Singer, S. F. 1973. Possibilities and usefulness of defining optimum population levels. *International Journal of Health Services,* Farmingdale, NY, 3:617–622.

Singh, N. 1986. *Commemoration of the fortieth anniversary of the International Court of Justice.* Hague: UN International Court of Justice, Communiqué No. 86/5, 11 pp.

Smith, J. 1986. Reagan, star wars, and American culture. *Bulletin of the Atomic Scientists,* Chicago, 43(1):19–25.

Somerville, J. 1986. Einstein's legacy and nuclear omnicide. *Peace Research,* Brandon, Manitoba, 18(1):21–25,53–58.

Thorsell, J. 1985. Parks that promote peace. *WWF News,* Gland, Switzerland, 1985(38):2.

Vagts, A. 1959. *History of militarism: civilian and military.* rev. edn. New York: Meridian Books, 542 pp. + 8 pl.

Walsh, J. 1987. Bolivia swaps debt for conservation. *Science,* Washington, 237:596–597.

Westing, A. H. 1980. *Warfare in a fragile world: military impact on the human environment.* London: Taylor & Francis, 249 pp. [a SIPRI book]

Westing, A. H. (ed.). 1986. *Global resources and international conflict: environmental factors in strategic policy and action.* Oxford: Oxford University Press, 280 pp. [a SIPRI book]

Westing, A. H. 1988a. Military sector *vis-à-vis* the environment. Forthcoming.

Westing, A. H. 1988b. Our place in nature: reflections on the carrying capacity for humans. *International Conference on Environmental Future,* Edinburgh, 3: forthcoming.

Woolf, V. 1938. *Three guineas.* San Diego, Calif.: Harcourt Brace Jovanovich, 188 pp.

Appendix 1. Cultural norms in relation to war and the environment: select bibliography

Aichinger, P. 1975. *American soldier in fiction, 1880–1963: a history of attitudes toward warfare and the military establishment.* Ames: Iowa State University Press, 143 pp.

Beker, A. 1985. *Disarmament without order: the politics of disarmament at the United Nations.* Westport, Connecticut: Greenwood Press, 212 pp.

Best, G. 1980. *Humanity in warfare: the modern history of the international law of armed conflicts.* London: Weidenfeld & Nicolson, 400 pp.

Boyer, P. 1985. *By the bomb's early light: American thought and culture at the dawn of the atomic age.* New York: Pantheon Books, 441 pp.

Brians, P. 1987. *Nuclear holocausts: atomic war in fiction, 1895–1984.* Kent, Ohio: Kent State University Press, 398 pp.

Brock-Utne, B. 1985. *Educating for peace: a feminist perspective.* New York: Pergamon Press, 175 pp.

Caldwell, L. K. 1984. *International environmental policy: emergence and dimensions.* Durham, N. Carolina: Duke University Press, 368 pp.

Cohen, A. & Lee, S. (eds). 1986. *Nuclear weapons and the future of humanity.* Totowa, New Jersey: Rowman & Allanheld, 508 pp.

Dowling, D. 1987. *Fictions of nuclear disaster.* Iowa City: University of Iowa Press, 245 pp.

Easlea, B. 1983. *Fathering the unthinkable: masculinity, scientists and the nuclear arms race.* London: Pluto Press, 230 pp.

Falk, R. A. 1983. *End of world order: essays on normative international relations.* New York: Holmes & Meier, 358 pp.

Ferguson, J. (ed.). 1972. *War and the creative arts: an anthology.* London: Macmillan, 380 pp. + 57 pl.

Ferguson, J. 1977. *War and peace in the world's religions.* London: Sheldon Press, 166 pp.

Ferguson, R. B. (ed.). 1984. *Warfare, culture, and environment.* Orlando, Florida: Academic Press, 417 pp.

Frei, D. 1984. *Assumptions and perceptions in disarmament.* New York: UN Document No. UNIDIR/84/10, 321 pp.

Frolov, I. 1982. *Global problems and the future of mankind.* Moscow: Progress Publishers, 311 pp.

Glacken, C. J. 1967. *Traces on the Rhodian shore: nature and culture in Western thought from ancient times to the end of the eighteenth century.* Berkeley: University of California Press, 763 pp.

Harries, M. & Harries, S. 1983. *War artists: British official war art of the twentieth century.* London: Michael Joseph, 310 pp. + 32 pl.

Held, V. 1984. *Rights and goods: justifying social action.* New York: Free Press, 327 pp.

Held, V., Morgenbesser, S. & Nagel, T. (eds). 1974. *Philosophy, morality, and international affairs.* New York: Oxford University Press, 338 pp.

Keegan, J. & Darracott, J. 1981. *Nature of war.* New York: Holt, Rinehart & Winston, 276 pp.

Khozin, G. 1979. *The biosphere and politics.* Moscow: Progress Publishers, 229 pp.

Koistinen, P. A. C. 1980. *Military-industrial complex: a historical perspective.* New York: Praeger, 170 pp.

Lifton, R. J. & Falk, R. 1982. *Indefensible weapons: the political and psychological case against nuclearism.* New York: Basic Books, 301 pp.

Marsh, R. J. 1986. *Soviet fiction since Stalin: science, politics and literature.* London: Croom Helm, 338 pp.

McNeill, W. H. 1982. *Pursuit of power: technology, armed force, and society since A.D. 1000.* Chicago: University of Chicago Press, 405 pp.

Merchant, C. 1980. *Death of nature: women, ecology, and the scientific revolution.* San Francisco: Harper & Row, 348 pp.

Passmore, J. 1980. *Man's responsibility for nature: ecological problems and Western traditions.* 2nd edn. London: Duckworth, 227 pp.

Schachter, O. 1977. *Sharing the world's resources.* New York: Columbia University Press, 172 pp.

Smith, M. J., Jr. 1980. *War story guide: an annotated bibliography of military fiction.* Metuchen, New Jersey: Scarecrow Press, 437 pp.

Stallworthy, J. (ed.). 1984. *Oxford book of war poetry.* Oxford: Oxford University Press, 358 pp.

Stone, C. D. 1972. Should trees have standing?: toward legal rights for natural objects. *Southern California Law Review*, Los Angeles, 45:450–501. Also: Los Altos, Calif.: William Kaufmann, 103 pp., 1974.

Stone, C. D. 1985. *Should trees have standing?* revisited: how far will law and morals reach?: a pluralist perspective. *Southern California Law Review,* Los Angeles, 59:1–154.

Stone, C. D. 1987. *Earth and other ethics: the case for moral pluralism.* New York: Harper & Row, 320 pp.

Vagts, A. 1959. *History of militarism: civilian and military.* rev. edn. New York: Meridian Books, 542 pp. + 8 pl.

Westing, A. H. (ed.). 1986. *Global resources and international conflict: environmental factors in strategic policy and action.* Oxford: Oxford University Press, 280 pp. [a SIPRI book]

Wittner, L. S. 1984. *Rebels against war: the American peace movement, 1933–1983.* 2nd edn. Philadelphia: Temple University Press, 364 pp.

Zars, B., Wilson, B. & Phillips, A. (eds). 1985. *Education and the threat of nuclear war.* Cambridge, Mass.: Harvard Educational Review, 166 pp.

Appendix 2. Multilateral treaties constraining military disruption of the environment: excerpts[1]

I. Hague Convention II of 1899 with respect to the Laws and Customs of War on Land[2]

Depositary: The Netherlands. *Entry into force:* 1900. *Parties as of late 1987:* 47 or more states, including France, the United Kingdom, the USA and the USSR (and including 17 or more not a party to Hague Convention IV of 1907).

Annex Article XXII. The right of belligerents to adopt means of injuring the enemy is not unlimited.

Annex Article LV. The occupying State shall only be regarded as administrator and usufructuary of the public buildings, real property, forests and agricultural works belonging to the hostile State, and situated in the occupied country. It must protect the capital of these properties, and administer it according to the rules of usufruct.

II. Hague Convention IV of 1907 respecting the Laws and Customs of War on Land[2]

Depositary: The Netherlands. *Entry into force:* 1910. *Parties as of late 1987:* 35 or more states, including France, the United Kingdom, the USA and the USSR (and including 5 or more not a party to Hague Convention II of 1899).

Annex Article XXII. The right of belligerents to adopt means of injuring the enemy is not unlimited.

Annex Article LV. The occupying State shall be regarded only as administrator and usufructuary of public buildings, real estate, forests, and agricultural estates belonging to the hostile State, and situated in the occupied country. It must safeguard the capital of these properties, and administer them in accordance with the rules of usufruct.

III. Geneva Protocol of 1925 on Chemical and Bacteriological Warfare[3]

Depositary: France. *Entry into force:* 1928. *Parties as of late 1987:* 109 or more states, including China, France, the United Kingdom, the USA and the USSR.[4]

[1] The full texts of one or more of the quoted documents are available in various works (e.g., Goldblat, 1982; Kiss, 1982; Roberts & Guelff, 1982; Schindler & Toman, 1981), as are the parties to them, together with reservations, if any (e.g., Goldblat & Ferm, 1987; UNEP, 1985); or else are available from the respective depositaries.

[2] Hague Convention II of 1899 is replaced, as applicable, by Hague Convention IV of 1907 (see its Article IV) among the parties to the latter.

[3] The Geneva Protocol of 1925 was a protocol to the Geneva Convention of 1925 for the Supervision of the International Trade in Arms and Ammunition and in Implements of War, which did not itself enter into force.

[4] About 42 of the parties to the Geneva Protocol of 1925 (39 per cent) have reserved an option (a

[The parties accept a prohibition of] the use in war of asphyxiating, poisonous or other gases, and of all analogous liquids, materials or devices [and] agree to extend this prohibition to the use of bacteriological methods of warfare.

IV. Antarctic Treaty of 1959

Depositary: The USA. *Entry into force:* 1961. *Parties as of late 1987:* 37 or more states, of which 20—including China, France, the United Kingdom, the USA and the USSR—are full ('consultative') and 17 are limited ('non-consultative').

Article I.1. Antarctica shall be used for peaceful purposes only. There shall be prohibited, *inter alia*, any measures of a military nature, such as the establishment of military bases and fortifications, the carrying out of military maneuvers, as well as the testing of any type of weapons.

V. Partial Test Ban Treaty of 1963

Depositaries: The United Kingdom, the USA and the USSR. *Entry into force:* 1963. *Parties as of late 1987:* 114 or more states, including the United Kingdom, the USA and the USSR.

Article I.1. Each of the Parties to this Treaty undertakes to prohibit, to prevent, and not to carry out any nuclear weapon test explosion, or any other nuclear explosion,[5] at any place under its jurisdiction or control: (*a*) in the atmosphere; beyond its limits, including outer space; or under water, including territorial waters or high seas; or (*b*) in any other environment if such explosion causes radioactive debris to be present outside the territorial limits of the State under whose jurisdiction or control such explosion is conducted. . . .

VI. Outer Space Treaty of 1967

Depositaries: The United Kingdom, the USA and the USSR. Entry into force: 1967. *Parties as of late 1987:* 87 or more states, including China, France, the United Kingdom, the USA and the USSR.

Article I. The exploration and use of outer space, including the moon and other celestial bodies, shall be carried out for the benefit and in the interests of all countries, irrespective of their degree of economic or scientific development, and shall be the province of all mankind. . . .

Article IV. . . . The moon and other celestial bodies shall be used by all States Parties to the Treaty exclusively for peaceful purposes. The establishment of military bases, installations and fortifications, the testing of any type of weapons and the conduct of military manoeuvres on celestial bodies shall be forbidden. . . .

VII. Nuclear-weapon Non-proliferation Treaty of 1968

Depositaries: The United Kingdom, the USA and the USSR. *Entry into force:* 1970. *Non-nuclear-weapon parties as of late 1987:* 133 or more states.

Article II. Each non-nuclear-weapon State Party to the Treaty undertakes not to receive the transfer from any transferor whatsoever of nuclear weapons or other nuclear explosive

'right') to retaliate in kind to a chemical attack, including China, France, the United Kingdom, the USA and the USSR. An analysis of this protocol is available elsewhere (Westing, 1985b).

In an earlier treaty—Hague Declaration 2 of 1899 concerning Asphyxiating Gases—the parties 'agree to abstain from the use of projectiles the sole objective of which is the diffusion of asphyxiating or deleterious gases' (parties as of late 1987: 29 or more states, including France, the United Kingdom and the USSR).

[5] The phrase 'any other nuclear explosion' in article I.1 of the Partial Test Ban Treaty of 1963 is interpreted to mean 'any other *non-hostile* nuclear explosion' (see, e.g., Kennedy, 1963).

devices or of control over such weapons or explosive devices directly, or indirectly; not to manufacture or otherwise acquire nuclear weapons or other nuclear explosive devices; and not to seek or receive any assistance in the manufacture of nuclear weapons or other nuclear explosive devices.

VIII. Seabed Treaty of 1971

Depositaries: The United Kingdom, the USA and the USSR. *Entry into force:* 1972. *Parties as of late 1987:* 78 or more states, including the United Kingdom, the USA and the USSR.

Article I.1. The States Parties to this Treaty undertake not to emplant or emplace on the seabed and the ocean floor and in the subsoil thereof beyond the outer limit of a seabed zone [of 22 kilometres] any nuclear weapons or any other types of weapons of mass destruction as well as structures, launching installations or any other facilities specifically designed for storing, testing or using such weapons.

IX. Bacteriological and Toxin Weapon Convention of 1972

Depositaries: The United Kingdom, the USA and the USSR. *Entry into force:* 1975. *Parties as of late 1987:* 108 or more states, including China, France, the United Kingdom, the USA and the USSR.[6]

Article I. Each State Party to this Convention undertakes never in any circumstances to develop, produce, stockpile or otherwise acquire or retain: 1. Microbial or other biological agents, or toxins whatever their origin or method of production, of types and in quantities that have no justification for prophylactic, protective or other peaceful purposes; 2. Weapons, equipment or means of delivery designed to use such agents or toxins for hostile purposes or in armed conflict.

X. World Heritage Convention of 1972

Depositary: UNESCO. *Entry into force:* 1975. *Parties as of late 1987:* 95 or more states, including China, France, the United Kingdom and the USA.

Article VI.1. . . . The States Parties to this Convention recognize that [the natural] heritage[7] constitutes a world heritage for whose protection it is the duty of the international community as a whole to co-operate.

Article VI.3. Each State Party to this Convention undertakes not to take any deliberate measures which might damage directly or indirectly the . . . natural heritage . . . situated on the territory of other States Parties to this Convention.

XI. Environmental Modification Convention of 1977

Depositary: UN Secretary-General. *Entry into force:* 1978. *Parties as of late 1987:* 50 or more states, including the United Kingdom, the USA and the USSR.

[6] An analysis of the Bacteriological and Toxin Weapon Convention of 1972 is available elsewhere (Westing, 1985a).

[7] The World Heritage Convention of 1972 defines 'natural heritage' as: 'natural features consisting of physical and biological formations or groups of such formations, which are of outstanding universal value from the aesthetic or scientific point of view; geological and physiographical formations and precisely delineated areas which constitute the habitat of threatened species of animals and plants of outstanding universal value from the point of view of science or conservation; natural sites or precisely delineated natural areas of outstanding universal value from the point of view of science, conservation or natural beauty' (Article II).

It is for each State Party to this Convention to identify and delineate the different properties

Article I.1. Each State Party to this Convention undertakes not to engage in military or any other hostile use of environmental modification techniques[8] having widespread, long-lasting or severe effects as the means of destruction, damage or injury to any other State Party.

XII. Bern [Geneva] Protocol I of 1977 on the Protection of Victims of International Armed Conflicts[9]

Depositary: Switzerland. *Entry into force:* 1978. *Parties as of late 1987:* 67 or more states, including China.

Article XXXV.1. In any armed conflict, the right of the Parties to the conflict to choose methods or means of warfare is not unlimited.

Article XXXV.3. It is prohibited to employ methods or means of warfare which are intended, or may be expected, to cause widespread, long-term and severe damage to the natural environment. [See also article LV.1]

Article LIV.2. It is prohibited to attack, destroy, remove or render useless objects indispensable to the survival of the civilian population, such as foodstuffs, agricultural areas for the production of foodstuffs, crops, livestock, drinking water installations and supplies and irrigation works, for the specific purpose of denying them for their sustenance value to the civilian population or to the adverse Party, whatever the motive, whether in order to starve out civilians, to cause them to move away, or for any other motive.

Article LV.1. Care shall be taken in warfare to protect the natural environment against widespread, long-term and severe damage. This protection includes a prohibition of the use of methods or means of warfare which are intended or may be expected to cause such damage to the natural environment and thereby to prejudice the health or survival of the population. [See also article XXXV.3]

Article LVI.1. Works or installations containing dangerous forces, namely dams, dykes and nuclear electrical generating stations, shall not be made the object of attack, even where these objects are military objectives, if such attack may cause the release of dangerous forces and consequent severe losses among the civilian population. Other military objectives located at or in the vicinity of these works or installations shall not be made the object of attack if such attack may cause the release of dangerous forces from the works or installations and consequent severe losses among the civilian population.

XIII. Bern [Geneva] Protocol II of 1977 on the Protection of Victims of Non-international Armed Conflicts[10]

Depositary: Switzerland. *Entry into force:* 1978. *Parties as of late 1987:* 61 or more states, including China and France.

Article XIV. Starvation of civilians as a method of combat is prohibited. It is therefore prohibited to attack, destroy, remove or render

situated on its territory as a potential component of the world natural heritage (Article III). The States Parties select from among these the composition of the world natural heritage (Article XI.2).

[8] The Environmental Modification Convention of 1977 defines 'environmental modification technique' as: 'any technique for changing—through the deliberate manipulation of natural processes—the dynamics, composition or structure of the earth, including its biota, lithosphere, hydrosphere and atmosphere, or of outer space' (Article II). An analysis of this convention is available elsewhere (Westing, 1984).

[9] Both Bern Protocols I and II of 1977 are additional to the Geneva Conventions of 1949 relating to Protection of Victims of Armed Conflicts.

[10] Both Bern Protocols I and II of 1977 are additional to the Geneva Conventions of 1949 relating to Protection of Victims of Armed Conflicts.

useless, for that purpose, objects indispensable to the survival of the civilian population, such as foodstuffs, agricultural areas for the production of foodstuffs, crops, livestock, drinking water installations and supplies and irrigation works.

Article XV. Works or installations containing dangerous forces, namely dams, dykes and nuclear electrical generating stations, shall not be made the object of attack, even where these objects are military objectives, if such attack may cause the release of dangerous forces and consequent severe losses among the civilian population.

XIV. Moon Agreement of 1979

Depositary: UN Secretary-General. *Entry into force:* 1984. *Parties as of late 1987:* 7 or more states.

Article III.1. The moon shall be used by all States Parties exclusively for peaceful purposes.

Article XI.1. The moon and its natural resources are the common heritage of mankind. . . .

XV. Inhumane Weapon Convention of 1981

Depositary: UN Secretary-General. *Entry into force:* 1983. *Parties as of late 1987:* 26 or more states, including China and the USSR.

Protocol III, Article II.4. It is prohibited to make forests or other kinds of plant cover the object of attack by incendiary weapons except when such natural elements are used to cover, conceal or camouflage combatants or other military objectives, or are themselves military objectives.

References

Goldblat, J. 1982. *Agreements for arms control: a critical survey.* London: Taylor & Francis, 387 pp. [a SIPRI book]

Goldblat, J. & Ferm, R. 1987. Major multilateral arms control agreements. *SIPRI Yearbook,* Oxford, 1987:457–486.

Kennedy, J. F. 1963. *A step towards peace: report to the people on the Nuclear Test Ban Treaty.* Washington: US Arms Control & Disarmament Agency, Publication No. 16, 20 pp.

Kiss, A. C. (ed.). 1983. *Selected multilateral treaties in the field of the environment.* Nairobi: UN Environment Programme, Reference Series No. 3, 525 pp.

Roberts, A. & Guelff, R. (eds). 1982. *Documents on the laws of war.* Oxford: Clarendon Press, 498 pp.

Schindler, D. & Toman, J. (eds). 1981. *Laws of armed conflicts: a collection of conventions, resolutions and other documents.* 2nd edn. Alphen aan den Rijn, Netherlands: Sijthoff & Noordhoff, 933 pp.

UNEP (United Nations Environment Programme). 1985. *Register of international treaties and other agreements in the field of the environment.* Nairobi: UN Environment Programme, Document No. UNEP/GC/INFORMATION/11/REV.1, 209 pp.

Westing, A. H. (ed.). 1984. *Environmental warfare: a technical, legal and policy appraisal.* London: Taylor & Francis, 107 pp. [a SIPRI book]

Westing, A. H. 1985a. Threat of biological warfare. *BioScience,* Washington, 35:627–633.

Westing, A. H. 1985b. Towards eliminating the scourge of chemical war: reflections on the occasion of the sixtieth anniversary of the Geneva Protocol. *Bulletin of Peace Proposals,* Oslo, 16:117–120.

Appendix 3. International declarations constraining military disruption of the environment: excerpts

I. Declaration on the Human Environment of 1972

Promulgator: United Nations Conference on the Human Environment, Stockholm, 5–16 June 1972 (UNGA, 1973). *Support:* 113 states, including China, France, the United Kingdom and the USA.

Principle XXVI. Man and his environment must be spared the effects of nuclear weapons and all other means of mass destruction. States must strive to reach prompt agreement, in the relevant international organs, on the elimination and complete destruction of such weapons.

II. World Charter for Nature of 1982

Promulgator: United Nations General Assembly (UNGA, 1982). *Support:* 112 states in favour, including China, France, the United Kingdom and the USSR; 1 actively against, the USA.[1]

Article V. Nature shall be secured against degradation caused by warfare or other hostile activities.

Article XI.e. Areas degraded by human activities shall be rehabilitated for purposes in accord with their natural potential and compatible with the well-being of affected populations.

Article XII.b. Special precautions shall be taken to prevent discharge [into natural systems] of radioactive or toxic wastes.

Article XX. Military activities damaging to nature shall be avoided.

Article XXIV. Each person has a duty to act in accordance with the provisions of the present Charter; acting individually, in association with others or through participation in the political process, each person shall strive to ensure that the objectives and requirements of the present Charter are met.

References

Burhenne, W. E. & Irwin, W. A. 1986. *World Charter for Nature: legislative history; commentary.* 2nd edn. W. Berlin: Erich Schmidt Verlag, 194 pp.

UNGA (United Nations General Assembly). 1973. *Report of the United Nations Conference on the Human Environment, Stockholm, 5–16 June 1972.* New York: UN General Assembly Document No. A/CONF.48/14/Rev.1, 77 pp.

UNGA (United Nations General Assembly). 1982. *World charter for nature.* New York: UN General Assembly Resolution No. 37/7 of 28 Oct. 1982, 5 pp.

Wood, H. W., Jr. 1985. United Nations World Charter for Nature: the developing nations' initiative to establish protections for the environment. *Ecology Law Quarterly,* Berkeley, Calif., 12:977–996.

[1] Analyses of the World Charter for Nature of 1982 are available elsewhere (Burhenne & Irwin, 1986; Wood, 1985).

Appendix 4. Codes constraining military disruption of the environment: excerpts

I. Biblical law of *ca* 7th century BC

Promulgator: Ascribed to Moses (Deuteronomy 20:19–20). *Support:* Orthodox Jews and others.

When you besiege a city for a long time, making war against it in order to take it, you shall not destroy its trees by wielding an axe against them; for you may eat of them, but you shall not cut them down. Are the trees in the field men that they should be besieged by you? Only the trees which you know are not trees for food you may destroy and cut down. . . .

II. Soviet physicians' oath of 1983

Promulgator: Supreme Soviet of the USSR (Andropov & Menteshashvili, 1983). *Support:* Oath taken by all Soviet physicians upon graduation.[1]

Recognizing the danger which nuclear weaponry presents for humankind, to struggle tirelessly for peace, for the prevention of nuclear war [translation].

III. Code of ethics for scientists of 1984

Promulgator: Uppsala University Seminar on Ethics in the Sciences (Gustafsson *et al.*, 1984). *Support:* Intended for the individual scientist.

This code of ethics for scientists has been formulated as a response to a concern about the applications and consequences of scientific research. In particular it appears that the potential hazards deriving from modern technological warfare are so overwhelming that it is doubtful whether it is ethically defensible for scientists to lend any support to weapons development.

In this connection the following should particularly be considered: 1. Research shall be so directed that its applications and other consequences do not cause significant ecological damage. 2. Research shall be so directed that its consequences do not render it more difficult for present and future generations to lead a secure existence. . . .

IV. US scientists' and engineers' statement on star wars of 1985

Promulgator: Strategic Defense Initiative Organization (Kogut, 1987; Kogut & Weissman, 1986). *Support:* Approximately 7000 professional scientists and engineers in the USA (as of early 1987).[2]

We, the undersigned scientists and engineers, believe that the Strategic Defense Initiative (SDI) program (commonly known as Star Wars) is ill-conceived and dangerous. . . . The program is a step toward the type of weapons and strategy likely to trigger a nuclear holocaust. . . . Accordingly, as working scientists and engineers, we pledge neither to solicit nor accept SDI funds, and we encourage others to join us in this refusal. . . .

[1] An analysis of physicians' oaths regarding their relevance to nuclear war is available elsewhere (Cassel *et al.*, 1985).

[2] Similar statements have received considerable support in Japan and the United Kingdom (Johnstone, 1986; Kogut, 1987).

References

Andropov, Y. & Menteshashvili, T. 1983. [*On an addendum to the text of the oath of a physician of the Soviet Union.*] (in Russian). Moscow: USSR Presidium of the Supreme Soviet, ukase of 15 Nov 83, 1 p.

Cassel, C. K., Jameton, A. L., Sidel, V. W. & Storey, P. B. 1985. Physician's oath and the prevention of nuclear war. *Journal of the American Medical Association,* Chicago, 254:652–654.

Gustafsson, B., Rydén, L., Tibell, G. & Wallensteen, P. 1984. Uppsala code of ethics for scientists. *Journal of Peace Research*, Oslo, 21:311–316.

Johnstone, B. 1986. Strategic defense initiative: British echo US boycott of star wars research. *Nature,* London, 323:747.

Kogut, J. B. 1987. Scientists' campaign against the Strategic Defense Initiative. *Journal of the American Medical Association,* Chicago, 258:658–660.

Kogut, J. & Weissman, M. 1986. Taking the pledge against Star Wars. *Bulletin of the Atomic Scientists,* Chicago, 42(1):27–30.

Index